The Legal Rights of the Convicted

The Legal Rights of the Convicted

Barbara Belbot and Craig Hemmens

LFB Scholarly Publishing LLC
El Paso 2010

Library of Congress Cataloging-in-Publication Data

Belbot, Barbara.
  The legal rights of the convicted / Barbara Belbot & Craig Hemmens.
     p. cm.
  Includes bibliographical references and index.
  ISBN 978-1-59332-424-7 (hardcover : alk. paper)
  1. Prisoners--Legal status, laws, etc.--United States. I. Hemmens, Craig.
II. Title.
  KF9731.B45 2010
  344.7303'56--dc22
                                    2010014569

ISBN 978-1-59332-424-7 (paperback)

Printed on acid-free 250-year-life paper.
Manufactured in the United States of America.

Table of Contents

CHAPTER 1:
Introduction

State correctional departments are very large bureaucracies. In some states, the prison, probation and parole systems are operated by separate agencies, each with their own missions, leadership structures, and budgets. In other states, both institutional and community-based corrections are under a single umbrella agency led by an executive director with deputy directors in charge of managing the prison, probation, and parole components. Whatever the organizational structure, however, within each correctional agency you will find legal counsel, generally reporting to the highest level of administration. Depending on the size of the agency and state law, that office may house one attorney or dozens.

A quick visit to the Internet homepages of three state correctional agencies provides insight into the important role of legal counsel in corrections today. The Ohio Department of Rehabilitation and Correction has a Legal Services Division that, among other things, manages in-house legal issues for the department and develops litigation strategy with the Office of the Ohio Attorney General to help administrators avoid litigation. The Legal Division also drafts and reviews administrative rules and policies. The Texas Department of Criminal Justice has an Office of the General Counsel. Different sections within the Office have specific responsibilities. The Legal Affairs section provides advice to officials on corrections law, employment law, government law, transactions and the open records act. The Litigation Support section evaluates every lawsuit filed against the agency or its employees to determine liability and assists the Texas Attorney General in cases that go to trial. The Preventive Law section keeps up with emerging legal issues, identifies legal risks, and monitors events and trends in the prison units. The Governmental Affairs section liaisons with the legislature.

The Legal Affairs Division in the California Department of Corrections has a Correctional Law Unit that provides legal advice and training to management and staff. The Employment Law Unit represents the department in administrative proceedings and civil lawsuits filed by employees and former employees. The Governmental Law Unit counsels on legal issues related to the department's business operations, construction contracts, and disputes with vendors. The Liability Response Unit reviews all civil lawsuits filed against the department and its employees, assesses liability, and acts as a liaison with counsel. The Major Litigation Unit monitors, supervises, and assures that the department complies with court orders that result from class action lawsuits. Agency legal counsel try to prevent lawsuits by providing sound legal advice, participating in personnel training, helping to write policies and procedures that follow the requirements of the law, and monitoring the enforcement of those policies. Once a lawsuit is filed, in most states attorneys from the state Attorney General's Office who specialize in litigation defend the agency and its employees.

Clearly, much of the business of corrections involves law, making it essential that correctional administrators and legal counsel communicate regularly and effectively. While many legal issues that concern correctional officials are shared by all governmental agencies and even private enterprise, other issues are totally unique to the field of corrections. Issues about disciplining inmates who break prison rules or the right to search the homes of probationers without a warrant raise matters outside the scope of what most attorneys deal with on a regular basis. Corrections law has developed into its own area of expertise and requires an understanding of the special context in which the legal issues develop. It is also clear that the legal side of the corrections business has a high price tag, including salaries for staff - attorneys, legal assistants, legal secretaries, and administrative staff, the cost of furnishing and equipping office space, and building and maintaining law libraries and access to electronic legal databases. Not only do agency legal counsel incur these expenses, so do the litigating attorneys in the Offices of the State Attorney Generals who defend the lawsuits in court.

This book concentrates on the area of corrections law that specifically concerns the legal rights of convicted offenders, whether they are incarcerated in prisons or jails or serving time in a community corrections program on probation or parole. It does not address many other areas of law that also affect correctional officials, such as employment or business law. Chapter 1 presents important background material that introduces students to the source of law and the role that courts play in legal proceedings filed by prisoners. Chapter 2 discusses sentencing issues. Chapter 3 examines the First Amendment rights of access to the courts and outside world. Chapter 4 examines the First Amendment rights of freedom of religion and association. Students read about prisoners' Fourth Amendment protections in Chapter 5 and how the law governs the use of force in correctional settings in Chapter 6. Chapter 7 looks at prison disciplinary systems, followed by Chapter 8, which introduces the Eighth Amendment's cruel and unusual punishment clause and its impact on living conditions in correctional institutions. Chapter 9 moves the focus of the book away from offenders incarcerated in prison to jail detainees. Chapter 10 focuses on the rights of convicted offenders who are not incarcerated and have been released to the community on probation and parole. In Chapter 11, students learn more about the legal "mechanics" of a prisoner civil rights lawsuit and how defendants defend such a suit.

For students who are or aspiring to become criminal justice professionals, the study of prisoners' rights is especially interesting because it extends your understanding of legal issues beyond what happens up to the point of a criminal conviction. Most criminal justice courses that deal with legal issues spend little time examining the rights of convicted offenders during sentencing and even less time examining their rights while incarcerated or on community supervision. It is as if the story ends with conviction. In reality, for millions of offenders, the story is just beginning. What happens after conviction often includes a significant amount of time under correctional supervision, and for some that supervision is highly intrusive and controlling. It is important to understand the extent to which correctional supervision is governed by the laws and constitutions of both the state and federal governments. Correctional officials have an enormous amount of authority. Just as law enforcement officers and prosecutors must be held accountable for their exercise of authority and use of discretion during the investigation, arrest, and prosecution of a crime, so must correctional officials account for how they incarcerate or otherwise supervise an offender after conviction.

Abuse of authority can occur as easily, perhaps even more easily, in a correctional setting than anywhere else in the criminal justice system – and, arguably with even greater negative consequences for the offender and the system as a whole. Not only is the potential for abuse always present (24 hours a day in a jail or prison), it can occur in the dark shadows of a prison cellblock – far away from "outside" scrutiny. In Chapter 10 students will read about the poor prison conditions in this country as recently as the 1960s and 1970s, before officials were subject to more stringent oversight. Other factors contribute to the problem of abuse. Since offenders have not volunteered to live under government control and do not always willingly comply with even the most reasonable rules, their behavior can help create an environment that makes it difficult to respect their rights. Security and order concerns take precedence and inmate rights are relegated to the back seat. Prison administrators frequently have to perform a problematic balancing act between the two. Prisoners are not a popular cause for the average American who abides by the rules and sacrifices to maintain a home and care for a family. There is little public outcry calling for protecting the rights of prisoners. Prisons administration is a demanding job; and it is especially challenging to afford incarcerated offenders their constitutional and statutory rights in light of all the factors that complicate the challenge.

HISTORY OF THE PRISONERS' CIVIL RIGHTS MOVEMENT

For many years courts were extremely reluctant to consider cases filed by prisoners complaining about their living conditions or the conduct of prison officials. Unofficially labeled the "hands-off" doctrine, courts routinely dismissed prisoners' rights cases on several grounds: 1) judges are not experts in penology and are not equipped to evaluate prison policies and practices; 2) the separation of powers doctrine prohibited the judiciary from interfering in the executive branch's responsibility to build and operate prisons; and 3) concerns that judicial involvement would undermine the stability of correctional institutions. Federal judges who reviewed lawsuits filed by state prison inmates were particularly wary of intruding on the business of state governments. A Virginia Court of Appeals opinion dating back to 1871, *Ruffin v. Commonwealth of Virginia*, set the stage for the hands-off doctrine. In that case, the court described prisoners, "For the time being, during his term of service in the penitentiary, he is in a state of penal servitude to the State. He has, as a consequence of his crime, not only forfeited his liberty, but all his personal rights except those which the law in its humanity accords to him. He is for the time being the slave of the State…"

The dramatic shift in the judiciary's approach to prisoners' rights evolved over time, climaxing in 1964 in the U.S. Supreme Court's decision in *Cooper v. Pate*. To fully appreciate this evolution, it is important to understand that in a series of landmark opinions during the first half of the Twentieth Century, the

Supreme Court incorporated much of the federal Constitution's Bill of Rights to the Fourteenth Amendment's due process clause. (Incorporation will discussed in detail later in this chapter; for now, suffice to say it means the Supreme Court has interpreted "due process" to include many of the individual rights contained in the Bill of Rights). As this happened, state and local officials became obligated to observe the incorporated rights; in the same way that federal officials had always been obligated.

The Eighth Amendment's prohibition against cruel and unusual punishment was incorporated by the Supreme Court's decision in *Robinson v. California* (1962). As a consequence of incorporation, state and local laws, regulations, and official policies and practices could no longer violate the prohibition, and prisoners could now argue that prison and jail regulations and practices must not violate the Eighth Amendment. The Supreme Court's incorporation of the Eighth Amendment occurred during the Warren Court era (1953-1969), a sixteen-year period, during which the High Court incorporated several important constitutional amendments that significantly expanded the rights of persons suspected of committing crimes and those charged with crimes. It was during the Warren Court that the composition of the federal court dockets began to change. Until the 1950s and 1960s, issues involving business and commerce dominated the work conducted in federal courts. The Warren Court thrust the federal judiciary into deciding issues surrounding the constitutional rights of individuals, including the rights of criminals.

Events outside the nation's prisons also contributed to the shift in the judiciary's approach to prisoners' rights. The civil rights movement forced Americans to reevaluate their perspective on matters of individual rights and heightened the consciousness of African-Americans to racial oppression. It was not long before the movement influenced the attitudes of African-American prisoners. The influence came at a time when the composition of some of the larger state prison systems was in flux. America's prisons, 70% white in the 1950s, were almost 70% African-American and Latino by 2000. Until the 1970s, correctional officers and higher-ranking prison officials were almost all white males. Many state prisons segregated prisoners by race, if not by policy then by practice. Inmates of different races were housed separately. It was not unusual to restrict desirable prison work assignments to white inmates.

The changing prison population demographics and the prisoners' growing political consciousness translated into demands for prisoners' rights. The Nation of Islam played a particularly important role in developing a political consciousness among African-American inmates in the 1950s and 1960s. Muslim prisoners openly challenged prisons as racist and discriminatory. Muslims were organized, disciplined, and articulate. Officials were threatened by their rhetoric and labeled them as dangerous. They were not permitted to meet and worship together. They were not permitted to receive printed religious materials from the outside. Prison staff kept files on inmates belonging to the Nation, detailing their backgrounds and activities.

The first prisoner rights lawsuits to break through the "hands-off" doctrine were filed by members of the Nation of Islam demanding their right to worship under the First Amendment. Initially these lawsuits were dismissed on the basis of the "hands-off" doctrine. In 1962, Thomas Cooper filed a lawsuit alleging he had been confined to administrative segregation in Illinois's Stateville Prison as retribution for his religious beliefs. He claimed he was denied access to the Koran, Muslim literature, and Muslim clergy. While he initiated his suit *pro se*, the Nation of Islam eventually hired attorneys to assist him. In 1964, in flagrant disregard for the "hands-off" doctrine, the Supreme Court ruled that Cooper had the right to file a lawsuit that alleged prison officials had violated his constitutional rights under the First Amendment and to seek an injunction. The importance of the *Cooper* decision cannot be overstated and the Court's opinion is discussed further in Chapter 11. Argued over a specific set of facts involving an inmate who claimed his First Amendment rights had been violated, the case's significance lies in the legal precedent it established: prisoners are entitled to file lawsuits alleging violations of their federal constitutional or statutory rights.

Not to be underestimated is the role that lawyers played in opening up the federal courts to prisoners' rights cases. Lawyers dedicated to the civil rights movement sharpened their skills in tough courtroom battles and created new and challenging interpretations of the Constitution and federal law. The lawyers soon recognized that the same legal arguments they fashioned for issues involving African-Americans were also applicable to other oppressed groups who were in the process of developing a political consciousness. Some of these attorneys gravitated to representing inmates. Organizations like the American Civil Liberties Union (ACLU), the NAACP Legal Defense Fund (LDF), and the National Lawyers' Guild took on prisoners' rights issues. Although the majority of inmates still file their lawsuits *pro se* (meaning without the assistance of legal counsel) attorneys have represented inmates in some of the more high profile cases with important issues at stake.

The hands-off doctrine eroded as the Supreme Court and the entire federal judiciary became more sensitive to the rights of individuals, including the rights of alleged criminals. Add to that a politically savvy and assertive population of prisoners who were in tune with the civil rights movement and were eager to litigate. Include in that mix a group of attorneys who had gained experience in the civil rights movement and were willing to apply their expertise to help redefine the status of convicted offenders incarcerated in America's jails and prisons. Events coalesced, resulting in the *Cooper v. Pate* decision. The doors of the federal courthouses opened wide to a flood of prisoner civil rights litigation.

The National Prison Project

The American Civil Liberties Union (ACLU) founded the National Prison Project (NPP) in 1972. It is the only national litigation program on behalf of prisoners. The organization claims it has represented over 100,000 confined men, women, and children since 1972. The Project is primarily involved in class-action lawsuits. Those lawsuits have addressed a broad range of issues, such as improved care for inmates with tuberculosis, cancer, HIV/AIDS, and mental illness. Other lawsuits have attacked overcrowding and the failure to provide prisoners with a safe and secure living environment.

Examples of Recent Litigation Where the NPP Has Played a Role:

- The NPP filed a lawsuit in 2002 against Extraditions International, Inc., a private prisoner transportation company and several of its employees, alleging that a driver/correctional officer for the company sexually harassed, assaulted, and threatened a prisoner in his custody, and the company was deliberately indifferent to inmate safety concerns.

- In *Hart v. Arpaio*, filed in federal court in Arizona, the NPP entered the case at the request of local counsel when Sheriff Joe Arpaio filed a motion to terminate an existing consent decree that protects pretrial detainees in the Maricopa County Jail in Phoenix.

- The NPP represents the plaintiffs in a lawsuit against the El Paso County Jail in Colorado Springs, CO on the grounds that the jail provides inadequate mental health care to the inmates.

- The NPP reentered a lawsuit in the District of Columbia that challenged the conditions in juvenile facilities. In 1986, the District entered into a consent decree and agreed to make changes, but a hearing in 2000 revealed that the District was violating some of the provisions of the decree regarding population limits, diagnostic services, programming, and aftercare.

- In addition to providing attorneys for prisoners' lawsuits, the Project also advocates for prison reform and tries to educate the public about the ramifications of America's current incarceration policy. The NPP publishes a biannual newsletter that features articles, reports, legal analysis, and legislative news about prisoners' rights. It also publishes a number of other reports and bibliographies dealing with inmates' constitutional rights.

Before we proceed to an examination of the legal rights of prisoners, it is important that we provide some background on the history and development of the law in general and individual rights in particular. The next section provides an overview of the common law, sources of law, and the manner in which the U.S. Supreme Court interprets state actions that affect individual rights.

THE COMMON LAW

Understanding what is meant by "common law" is essential for understanding how law evolves, even today, in the United States. Our legal heritage comes from England where the common law was judge-made law. That is, it was law created by judges as they heard cases and settled disputes. Judges wrote down their decisions, and in doing so attempted to justify their decision by reference to custom, tradition, history, and prior judicial decisions. As judges in England began to rely on previous judgments, they developed the concepts of *stare decisis* (Latin for "let the decision stand") and precedent. Of course, for there to be precedent, there must be prior decisions. At first, judges made decisions without referring to other cases or courts. They simply heard the case and decided the appropriate outcome, based on their understanding of the law as they had learned it through the reading of legal treatises and encyclopedias. But as time went by, judges came to rely on prior decisions as a means of justifying their decision in a particular case. From this came the reliance on precedent and the concept of *stare decisis*. By the reign of the English King Henry II (1154-1189), a body of law had been developed, and was applied not just in local courts, but nationally. Decisions began to be written down, circulated, and summarized. The result was a more unified body of law, which came to be known as the common law, because it was in force throughout the country; it was literally the law in common throughout the country. The common law system was well developed in England by the thirteenth century.

PRECEDENT AND *STARE DECISIS*

Under the common law system, every final decision by a court creates a precedent. This precedent governs the court issuing the decision as well as any lower, or inferior, courts in the same jurisdiction. The common law system, developed in England, was brought to America by the early colonists. Many of the principles of the common law, including precedent and belief in *stare decisis*, remain in force today in American courts. Thus, all courts in a state are bound to follow the decisions of the highest court in the state, usually known as the state supreme court. All courts in the federal court system are bound to follow the decisions of the U.S. Supreme Court. This is the notion of precedent.

Precedent is binding only on those courts within the jurisdiction of the court issuing the opinion. Thus a decision of the Idaho Supreme Court is not binding on any court in Texas. Texas courts are not subject to the jurisdiction or control of Idaho courts, and thus are free to interpret the law differently from Idaho courts, if they see fit to do so. Decisions from courts in other jurisdictions, while not binding, may be persuasive, however. This simply means that another court may give consideration and weight to the opinion of other courts. Thus a Texas court may, if it chooses, consider the judgment of an Idaho court. Courts may do this when faced with an issue which they have not dealt with before, but which other courts have examined.

Under the principle of *stare decisis*, if there is a prior decision on a legal issue which applies to a current case, the court will be guided by that prior decision and apply the same legal principles in the current case. *Stare decisis,* then, is a means of establishing the value of prior decisions, or precedent. In other words, if an issue has been decided one way, it will continue to be decided that way in future cases. Through a reliance on precedent and the principle of *stare decisis*, common law courts were able to provide litigants with some degree of predictability regarding the courts' decisions.

Precedent is not necessarily unchangeable. Judge-made law may be set aside, or overruled, by an act of the legislature, if the constitution permits the legislature to do so. Additionally, the court that issued the precedent may overrule it, or a higher court may reverse the decision of a lower court. If an intermediate level appeals court decides an issue one way and the losing party appeals to a higher appeals court (such as the state supreme court), that higher court may reverse the decision of the lower court. Higher level appeals courts are not bound by the judgments of lower courts. They are bound only by the decisions of courts above them in the court structure. *Stare decisis*, then, involves a respect for and belief in the validity of precedent. Precedent is simply the influence of prior cases on current cases.

Courts are understandably reluctant to reverse decisions they made previously, as this is a tacit admission of error. Courts do so, however, when presented with a compelling justification for doing so. Thus, *stare decisis* is not an inflexible doctrine, but one that is merely the general rule—there are always exceptions, as with most areas of the law!

Alternatively, rather than expressly overrule a prior decision; a court may instead seek to distinguish the prior case from the present case, on the ground that the facts are slightly different. By doing so the court can avoid overruling a prior decisions while coming to what it considers the proper result in the present case. Until a decision is expressly overruled, it stands as an accurate statement of legal principles, or "good law."

SOURCES OF LAW

The law that students will study in this textbook about prisoners' rights, like all law, is grounded in several sources, including the U.S. Constitution, state constitutions, federal and state statutes, administrative regulations, and case law. Each of these is discussed, in turn, below.

The U.S. Constitution

The U.S. Constitution establishes the powers and limits of the government. It defines the relationship between the three branches of the federal government: the legislative branch, responsible for enacting laws, the executive branch, responsible for enforcing the law, and the judicial branch, responsible for interpreting the laws and applying them in formal legal proceedings. It establishes the basic structure of the three branches and outlines their power and authority within the national government. According to the Constitution's separation of powers doctrine, each branch of government is limited to performing its own functions, leaving each branch independent. The Constitution also provides a procedure for amendment. It is a difficult process because the framers of the Constitution believed it should be amended only for the most important reasons. The government cannot change the Constitution, only the people can amend it through their elected representatives. An amendment can be initiated by a two-thirds vote of both houses of Congress or by two-thirds majority of the state legislatures. It must then be approved by the state legislatures in three-fourths of the states or by constitutional conventions in three-fourths of the states.

In 1791, the first ten amendments to the U.S. Constitution, known as the Bill of Rights, were ratified. The Bill of Rights details the fundamental rights of individuals, such as freedom of religion and speech and freedom from unreasonable searches and seizures by the government. The Bill of Rights is of primary importance in the study of the rights of convicted offenders because courts have decided that several of the first ten amendments, specifically the First, Fourth, Fifth, Sixth, Eighth also provide constitutional protection for convicted offenders. This text's focus is on the court decisions that have interpreted those amendments, including the Fourteenth Amendment, ratified after the Civil War in 1868, as they apply to incarcerated offenders and offenders on probation and parole.

The First Amendment's protections for free speech, the right of association, and freedom of religious expression have been hotly contested in many court cases involving incarcerated offenders. Courts have addressed to what extent prisoners, probationers, and parolees are protected against unreasonable searches under the Fourth Amendment. Pursuant to the Eighth Amendment, courts have had to decide what constitutes cruel and unusual punishment. Students, however, may be a bit confused about how the Fifth and Fourteenth Amendments play a role in prisoners' rights. Section One of the Fourteenth Amendment is important for several reasons. First, based on the Fourteenth Amendment's due process clause the Supreme Court reasoned that most of the Bill of Rights, including the Eighth Amendment's cruel and unusual punishment clause, should be incorporated, applying constitutional protections not only to federal officials but to state and local government officials as well.

Second, that same due process clause is significant in cases where inmates argue that correctional officials must abide by specific regulations before they can take certain actions, such as changing a prisoner's security classification or housing assignment, and that failing to follow the regulations is a denial of due process. It is this second application that also makes the Fifth Amendment's due process clause important to the study of prisoner's rights. By its very language, the Fourteenth Amendment's due process clause only applies to actions taken by state and local governments. The Fifth Amendment's due process clause applies

Amendments to the U.S. Constitution
that Impact Convicted Offenders

First Amendment:

Congress shall make no law respecting an establishment of religion, or prohibiting the free exercise thereof; or abridging the freedom of speech, or of the press; or the right of people to peaceably assemble, and to petition the Government for redress of grievances.

Fourth Amendment:

The right of the people to be secure in their persons, houses, papers, and effects, against unreasonable searches and seizures, shall not be violated, and no Warrants shall issue, but upon probable cause, supported by Oath or affirmation, and particularly describing the place to be searched, and the persons or things to be seized.

Fifth Amendment:

No person shall be held to answer for a capital, or otherwise infamous crime, unless on a presentment or indictment of a Grand Jury, except in cases arising in the land or naval forces, or in the Militia, when in actual service in time of War or public danger; nor shall any person be subject for the same offence to be twice put in jeopardy of life or limb; nor shall be compelled in any criminal case to be a witness against himself, nor be deprived of life, liberty, or property, without due process of law; nor shall private property be taken for public use, without just compensation.

Sixth Amendment:

In all criminal prosecutions, the accused shall enjoy the right to a speedy and public trial, by an impartial jury of the State and district wherein the crime shall have been committed, which district shall have been previously ascertained by law, and to be informed of the nature and cause of the accusation; to be confronted with the witnesses against him; to have compulsory process for obtaining witnesses in his favor, and to have the Assistance of Counsel for his defence.

Eighth Amendment:

Excessive bail shall not be required, nor excessive fines imposed, no cruel and unusual punishments inflicted.

Fourteenth Amendment:

Section One: All persons born or naturalized in the United States, and subject to the jurisdiction thereof, are citizens of the United States and of the State wherein they reside. No State shall make or enforce any law which shall abridge the privileges or immunities of citizens of the United States; nor shall any State deprive any person of life, liberty, or property, without due process of law; nor deny to any person within its jurisdiction the equal protection of the laws.

only to actions taken by federal officials. Which due process clause applies in a corrections lawsuit depends on whether the prisoner is housed in a federal or state/local facility. In addition to the due process clause, Section One of the Fourteenth Amendment prohibits the government from denying any person equal protection under the law. Students will discover that this clause has also played an important role in prisoners' rights cases.

The Fifth and Fourteenth Amendments, along with the Sixth Amendment, are also important in connection with the rights of offenders after conviction, during the sentencing phase of their case. The due process protections found in the Fifth and Fourteenth Amendments apply to the taking of guilty pleas and to the type and scope of information a judge can consider in making a sentencing decision. The Sixth Amendment right to counsel and right to a jury trial are both triggered during sentencing. Chapter 2 examines the important issues that sentencing raises and how the Supreme Court has responded. Sentencing has become a very controversial topic with significant policy and legal implications.

According to the U. S. Constitution, it is the supreme law of the land and judges in all of the states are bound by it, notwithstanding what federal or state statutes or state constitutions may provide. The Constitution was written with a broad brush. Its language is ambiguous and requires interpretation. Under the principle of judicial review, established by Supreme Court in *Marbury v. Madison* (1803), interpreting the terms and provisions of the Constitution is the responsibility of the courts, and ultimately the Supreme Court. Neither Congress nor the President has the final word about the meaning of the Constitution. Under the doctrine of judicial review, courts are charged with determining if laws enacted by either the state legislatures or the U.S. Congress are in accord with the provisions of the U.S. Constitution. If they violate the Constitution, the courts' responsibility is to declare the laws null and void.

Standard of Review

Often in constitutional law, the outcome of a case is determined as much by the standard of review the court employs as by the facts of the case. Not all of the individual protections set forth in the Bill of Rights are accorded the same respect—rather; there is a hierarchy of rights. The court employs either strict scrutiny or rational basis review, depending on whether a fundamental right is implicated or a suspect classification is impacted.

Fundamental rights are those freedoms essential to the concept of ordered liberty, rights without which neither liberty nor justice would exist (*Palko v. Connecticut*, (1937)). Examples include virtually all of the various provisions of the Bill of Rights, as well as the Fourteenth Amendment guarantees of due process and equal protection. To date, the Supreme Court has held that only race and religion are suspect classifications in all circumstances, although gender, illegitimacy, and poverty have occasionally been treated as suspect classifications.

Under strict scrutiny review, the state may not enact legislation which abridges a fundamental right unless: (1) it has a compelling interest which justifies restricting a fundamental right; and (2) the legislation is "narrowly tailored" so that the fundamental right is not abridged any more than absolutely necessary to effectuate the state's compelling interest. An example of a compelling interest is the state's interest in the health and safety of its citizens. Additionally, the Supreme Court requires that for legislation to be narrowly tailored, there must exist a sufficient nexus between the legislative body's stated interest and either the classification drawn or the means chosen to advance the state's compelling interest.

This standard of review is referred to as the strict scrutiny test because the court looks closely at the purpose and effect of the legislation rather than merely accepting the claims of the legislature that the legislation is needed or accepting the legislation as presumptively valid. The reason for employing a higher standard of review when legislation impacts on a fundamental right or suspect classification is that closer analysis is required when individual liberties are threatened.

If neither a fundamental right nor a suspect classification is implicated, a state may enact legislation abridging that right or impacting that class so long as there is a rational basis for the legislation. This standard of review is generally referred to as the rational basis test, since under it the court will not strike down legislation that appears to have some rational basis. The court does not look closely at the effects of the legislation, unlike the strict scrutiny test. Under this standard of review, state actions are presumptively valid. This standard of review is obviously a much easier one to pass. The legislature need not choose the best possible means; it must merely appear that it has chosen means that are not wholly unrelated to achievement of the legislative purpose.

Incorporation of the Bill of Rights in the Fourteenth Amendment

Originally the Bill of Rights applied only to the federal government. State and local governments were not bound by the various provisions of the Bill of Rights. This was because there was at the time of the adoption of the Constitution a fear of a strong centralized government. State governments were viewed much more favorably, and many state constitutions contained protections of individual rights similar to those in the Bill of Rights. In 1833 the Supreme Court, in *Barron v. Baltimore*, expressly held that the Bill of Rights applied only to the federal government.

After the Civil War and the failed attempt by the Southern states to secede from the Union, federal legislators felt it was necessary to amend the Constitution to provide greater protections for individuals from the actions of state governments. There was in particular a fear that the Southern states would attempt to limit the ability of the recently freed slaves to become equal citizens. The result was the passage in 1868 of the Fourteenth Amendment.

The Fourteenth Amendment contains three clauses: the privileges and immunities clause, the due process clause, and the equal protection clause. The essence of each of these clauses is that they bar states, not the federal government, from infringing on individual rights. The amendment was expressly intended to control state action, but it was unclear exactly how far the amendment went. The original spur for it was a desire to protect the rights of the freed slaves, but the language of the amendment was broad, and not specifically limited to state actions infringing on the rights of blacks.

During the later part of the Nineteenth Century, the Supreme Court began to use the due process clause of the Fourteenth Amendment to strike down state action involving economic regulation. Under a theory known as substantive due process the Court repeatedly held that states could not impose regulations such as minimum wage laws and child labor laws on private businesses because doing so violated due process. The violation of due process consisted of the regulation taking of a right, such as the right to work, or to enter into a contract.

During the 1930s the use of the due process clause to protect economic interest fell into disfavor, in part because the Supreme Court used it to strike down much of President Roosevelt's New Deal legislation, which was intended to ease the burden of the Great Depression. At the same time, however, the Supreme Court began to use the due process clause of the Fourteenth Amendment to protect individual rights from state action. Beginning in the late 1930s the Supreme Court incorporated most of the provisions of the Bill of Rights into the Fourteenth Amendment's due process clause and applied them to the states. Many of the criminal law provisions were applied to the states during the 1960s by the Supreme Court under the leadership of Chief Justice Earl Warren.

By incorporation is simply meant the Justices interpreted the due process clause of the Fourteenth Amendment, which says no state shall deprive a person of life, liberty, or property without "due process of law," as prohibiting states from abridging certain individual rights. Many of these rights are included in the Bill of Rights (which originally applied only to the federal government); hence these rights were included (or incorporated) in the definition of "due process." There are several different approaches to incorporation that have been advocated by various Supreme Court justices during the Twentieth Century.

Under the total incorporation approach, the due process clause of the Fourteenth Amendment made the entire Bill of Rights applicable to the states. In essence, the phrase "due process of law" was interpreted to mean "all of the provisions of the Bill of Rights." This approach has never commanded a majority of justices on the Court. A prominent supporter of this approach was Justice Hugo Black.

As the name implies, under the total incorporation plus approach, the due process clause of the Fourteenth Amendment includes the Bill of Rights and, in addition, other, unspecified rights. A principal advocate of this approach was

Justice William Douglas, who argued that the various provisions of the Bill of Rights created a "penumbra" (*Griswold v. Connecticut*, 1965) in which the whole was greater than the sum of the parts—that the individual rights contained in the Bill of Rights, when examined together, created other rights. Thus, he argued the various provisions limiting the ability of the government to intrude into a person's private life (such as the Fourth Amendment prohibition on unreasonable searches and the Third Amendment prohibition on quartering troops in private residences) created a general right to privacy.

In *Twining v. New Jersey* (1908) the Supreme Court suggested that some of the individual rights in the Bill of Rights might also be protected from state action, not because the Bill of Rights applied to the States, but because these rights "are of such a nature that they are included in the conception of due process of law." This became known as the "fundamental rights" or "ordered liberty" approach. Under this approach, there is no necessary relationship between the due process clause of the Fourteenth Amendment and the Bill of Rights. The due process clause has an independent meaning, which prohibits state action that violates rights "implicit in the concept of ordered liberty" or those rights which are "fundamental" (*Palko v. Connecticut*, 1937). Exactly what constitutes a fundamental right is left to the judges, considering the history and tradition of the law and the "totality of the circumstances" of each case in determining whether a right is fundamental. This approach provides justices with greater discretion, and they may interpret it either narrowly or broadly. This approach enjoyed strong support on the Court until the late 1960s. A principal advocate of this approach was Justice Felix Frankfurter.

The selective incorporation approach combines elements of the fundamental rights and total incorporation approaches, in modified form. Selective incorporation rejects the notion that all of the rights in the Bill of Rights are automatically incorporated in the due process clause of the Fourteenth Amendment, but does look to the Bill of Rights as a guide for which rights are incorporated. Selective incorporation rejects the "totality of the circumstances" component of the fundamental rights approach, and instead incorporates rights deemed fundamental to the same extent and in the same manner as applied to the federal government.

As an example, under the total incorporation approach, the Fourth Amendment prohibition on unreasonable searches and the exclusionary rule, which states evidence seized in violation of the Forth Amendment cannot be used at trial, apply to the federal government and the states. Under the fundamental rights approach, the Fourth Amendment was deemed fundamental and applied to the states, but the exclusionary rule was deemed non-fundamental and not applied to the states. Consequently, state law enforcement were told by the Court they must obey the Fourth Amendment, but failure to do so would not result in the exclusion of the evidence they sought to obtain through a violation of the Fourth Amendment. Under selective incorporation, the Court held both the right (freedom form unreasonable searches) and the means of enforcing the right (the exclusionary rule) to be part of the due process clause of the Fourteenth Amendment.

Selective incorporation became popular in the 1960s with the Warren Court. A principal advocate was Justice William Brennan. While selective incorporation accepted the idea that the due process clause protects only "fundamental rights" and that not every right in the Bill of Rights is necessarily fundamental, over time it has led to the incorporation of virtually everything in the Bill of Rights. The criminal protections not yet included are the right to an indictment by a grand jury and the prohibition on excessive bail.

Judicial Review

Given the varied sources of law, and the ambiguous language of many statutes and constitutional provisions, it is inevitable that laws will come into conflict or interpretations of statutes will differ. When this happens, who decides which law is paramount? In the United States, the answer to that question is the courts, through the power of judicial review.

Judicial review simply means the power of the court, specifically judges, to examine a law and determine whether the law is constitutional. If the judge determines the law is constitutional, he or she upholds the law. If the judge determines the law is not constitutional, he or she declares it unconstitutional and therefore void. In order to make this determination, judges must examine the law, and compare it with the constitution. This requires them to interpret the language of both the statue and the constitution.

For example, the Fourth Amendment prohibits "unreasonable" searches. Suppose a state legislature passes a law allowing police officers to search anyone they encounter on a public street. Is this law constitutional? Or does it violate the prohibition on unreasonable searches? To answer this question, judges must examine the history and meaning of "unreasonable" as contained in the Fourth Amendment. They do this by examining precedent.

Judicial review is not specifically provided for in the Constitution. Rather, judicial review is judge-made law. *Marbury v. Madison* (1803) established the authority of the United States Supreme Court to engage in judicial review of the acts of the other branches of government. The Supreme Court stated in *Marbury* that it was the duty of the judiciary to interpret the Constitution, and to apply it to particular fact situations. The Court also said that it was the job of the courts to decide when other laws (acts of Congress or state laws) were in violation of the Constitution, and to declare these laws null and void. This is the doctrine of judicial review.

State Constitutions

Each state also has a constitution that creates the basic structure of the state government. A state constitution also guarantees rights to the residents of that state generally in terms very similar to the rights guaranteed by the federal Constitution and the Bill of Rights. Some state constitutions, however, guarantee rights that are not mentioned in the U.S. Constitution. In those cases, the U.S. Constitution is said to set the minimum standard, with the state free to raise the minimum and provide greater protections and rights through the state constitution. State Supreme Courts are the final interpreters of the meaning of state constitutional provisions.

Termed the "new judicial federalism," during the last couple decades there has been a trend in several state supreme courts to look more frequently to the state constitution for guidance about the rights of their state residents. For instance, in *Sterling v. Cupp*, 625 P.2d 123 (Oregon 1981), the Oregon Supreme Court interpreted the Oregon State Constitution's Bill of Rights to hold that except in emergencies, female correctional officers cannot engage in searches of male prisoners if the search involves touching a prisoner's genital or anal areas. The Oregon court relied on article I, section 13 of the state constitution that provides "No person arrested, or confined in jail, shall be treated with unnecessary rigor." There is currently no equivalent protection to prisoners under the U.S. Constitution.

In *Brandon v. State Department of Corrections,* 938 P.2d 1029 (Alaska 1997), the Alaska Supreme Court interpreted the Alaska Constitution to guarantee prisoners in Alaska the right to have a court review an administrative classification decision to transfer a prisoner to a facility outside the state. In reaching that decision, the court recognized that the state constitution creates a fundamental right to rehabilitation and that any violation of a fundamental state constitutional right must be afforded judicial review.

Compare the *Brandon* decision to a case decided by the U.S. Supreme Court, *Olim v. Wakinekona* (1983). In that case, the Court ruled that because prisoners have no justifiable expectation that they will be incarcerated in a particular state, they have no due process rights as a result of an interstate transfer. The Alaska Constitution, as interpreted by the state supreme court, provides greater protections to inmates transferred out of the state of Alaska than are provided by the due process clause of the U.S. Constitution. It is important to remember that state supreme courts do not always interpret state constitutions to provide more rights than those provided by the federal Constitution. Indeed, it is far more likely that a state court will conclude that the protections afforded in the state constitution parallel those of the U.S. Constitution. Nonetheless, there are instances, including in the area of prisoners' rights, where a state supreme court has broadened the reach of individual rights by relying on state constitutional provisions.

Statutes

The details and specifics of the law are found in statutes. The U.S. Congress is responsible for drafting and enacting the federal statutes, which are published in the United States Code. The various state legislatures draft and enact state statutes. No federal or state statute may conflict with the provisions of the U.S. Constitution. Statutes enacted by a state legislature may not conflict with the state constitution.

Statutory law is more detailed than constitutions, however, as detailed as it can sometimes be, there are often ambiguities and room for debate about how a statute should be interpreted. It is impossible to predict human behavior, and statutory law simply cannot account for every possible circumstance than will arise. Some statutes are passed by legislatures after intense debate and controversy. Statutory provisions are sometimes left intentionally vague in order to reach a compromise that will allow the legislation to be enacted. Other statutes are written to include the flexibility needed to address changing circumstances.

It is the courts' job to interpret the meaning of vague statutory terms. The federal judiciary interprets federal legislation, and state courts interpret the meaning of state legislation. Statutes are easily and frequently amended. Legislatures meet regularly and often vote to change statutory provisions to meet specific and timely demands. Local levels of government also enact statutory law generally referred to as municipal ordinances.

Pennsylvania Department of Corrections v. Yeskey (1998), profiled in this chapter below, is an example of the Supreme Court interpreting various provisions of a federal statute, in that case the Americans With Disabilities Act, in order to determine if the Act applied to prisoners. In Chapter 11, students will study the Prison Litigation Reform Act (PLRA), enacted by the U.S. Congress in 1996, which was enacted to help reduce the number of lawsuits that prisoners file and has successfully withstood challenges to its constitutionality. In Chapter 4, students will learn about the Religious Land Use and Institutionalized Persons Act (RLUIPA) as it affects prisoners' right to the free exercise of their religious beliefs. Not all the important legislation in this area comes from the federal Congress. State legislatures also pass statutes that affect the prisoners incarcerated in their state institutions.

Administrative Regulations

Federal and state statutes have created administrative agencies to oversee important governmental duties. A few examples of such agencies on the federal level include the Social Security Administration, the Internal Revenue Service, the Environmental Protection Agency, the Occupational Safety and Health Administration, the Federal Aviation Administration, and the Food and Drug Administration. In the box following this paragraph are examples of a handful of the administrative regulations that govern the Federal Bureau of Prisons, which are published in a large collection called the Federal Code of Regulations.

The Americans With Disabilities Act

Congress enacted the Americans with Disabilities Act (ADA) in 1990 to protect the rights of disabled individuals. There are several important provisions in the Act. Section II prohibits a "public entity" from discriminating against a "qualified individual with a disability" because of the individual's disability.

In 1998, the U.S. Supreme Court decided the case *Pennsylvania Department of Corrections v. Yeskey*, which involved a convicted offender who had been sentenced to serve 18 to 36 months in the state prison. The sentencing court, however, recommended that instead of being sent to prison, he be assigned to the state boot camp for first-time offenders. Inmates who successfully completed the boot camp could be paroled in as little as six months. Correctional officials refused to admit Yeskey into the boot camp program because he had a medical history of hypertension. He filed a lawsuit alleging that his exclusion violated the ADA.

The Supreme Court had to interpret the provisions of the ADA to decide whether state prisoners were protected by the Act. In reaching its' ruling, the Court compared the ADA's provisions to other similar federal statutes that address illegal discrimination and how those laws have been interpreted in previously decided cases.

The *Yeskey* case is a good example of how a statute, in this case the ADA, is a source of law for correctional officials. Not only must they abide by the U.S. Constitution and applicable state constitution, statutory law, here a federal statute, imposes important legal obligations. Additionally, *Yeskey* is a good example of the Supreme Court interpreting the terms of a statute as opposed to interpreting the meaning of the Constitution. The legal issue in *Yeskey* was not whether the ADA violated the Constitution; rather the issue was did Congress intend for the ADA to apply to state prisons and prisoners.

The Supreme Court relied on the history surrounding the passage of the law and concluded that the plain meaning of the ADA unambiguously includes state prison inmates. The Court wrote, "State prisons fall squarely within the statutory definition of "public entity," which includes "any department, agency, special purpose district, or other instrumentality of a State or States or local government." In addition, it decided that the term "qualified individual with a disability" includes prisoners with disabilities.

The regulations featured below relate to the inmate disciplinary process which is discussed in detail in Chapter 7, but there are dozens of federal regulations that address a wide range of matters involving prisoners sentenced to the federal prison system. State legislatures create similar agencies on the state level. Some state agencies perform similar functions as federal agencies, while others have duties more specific to the state's needs. Legislatures give these agencies the authority to adopt rules and regulations that are consistent with the statutes that created the agencies. Administrative rules and regulations are even more specific and detailed than statutory law. They address a myriad of circumstances with as much precision as possible. Today, administrative regulations constitute an extensive body of law that governs many aspects of our lives. As is true with statutory law, when necessary, judges have the authority to interpret the meaning of administrative rules and regulations and decide if they conflict with the U.S. Constitution. State judges have the authority to decide if state administrative regulations violate a state constitution.

Case Law

The American colonists brought with them the common law tradition from England. Today, law in the Unites States is primarily found in statutes enacted by popularly elected legislatures or administrative law adopted by agencies created by legislatures. Nonetheless, the common law tradition continues to shape the law making process in this country.

Judges are called upon in lawsuits to interpret the meaning of various provisions of constitutions, statutes, and administrative regulations. Sometimes their task is to decide if there is a constitutional violation. Sometimes their job is to decide what the legislature intended when it enacted a statutory provision that is ambiguous. Sometimes they must interpret the meaning of an administrative rule as it relates to the statute that created the agency and defined its responsibilities.

Judges do not reinvent the wheel every time they are called upon to engage in judicial review. They treat previously decided cases as case precedent and apply the interpretations used by judges who decided a same or similar matter in previous cases. Over the last two centuries, courts have created an extensive body of case law. "Case law" is the term used to describe written court opinions in which judges explain their decisions and provide, often in long and excruciating detail, the reasons why they decided as they did. In their opinions, judges outline that previously decided cases provided legal precedent for their decision. They review the facts of the case they must decide and compare those facts to previously decided cases to determine which cases provide "good" legal precedent (precedent that is applicable to the case before them) and which do not. Although judges are reluctant to break with precedent, the doctrine of stare decisis is not totally inflexible. If a court decides that legal precedent should not be followed, its opinion explains the reasons for refusing to follow precedent and why a new rule is appropriate and more beneficial. Court opinions are often quite long. That is because it is important that judges clearly explain the reasons for their decisions.

The opinions discuss the various cases that attorneys for the litigants have argued should be considered legal precedent and, therefore, should guide the court's decision. Judges take the time to analyze the cases that could potentially be precedent for a decision in the case before them. They explain why one case,

---

The Code of Federal Regulations and Corrections

Many of the regulations that govern the operations of the Federal Bureau of Prisons, which is under the jurisdiction of the Department of Justice, are found in the Code of Federal Regulations (CFR). The CFR is the codification of the rules of the executive departments and agencies of the federal government. It is divided into 50 titles that represent the areas subject to federal regulation. An example of an agency regulation that is a source of law to correctional officials in the Federal Bureau of Prisons can be found in 28 C.F.R. section 541.16: Establishment and Functioning of the Discipline Hearing Officer. Notice how detailed the regulation is.

(a) Each Bureau of Prison institution shall have an independent hearing officer (DHO) assigned to conduct administrative fact-finding hearings covering alleged acts of misconduct and violations of prohibited acts, including those acts which could result in criminal charges. In the event a serious disturbance or other emergency, or if an inmate commits an offense in the presence of the DHO, an alternate Discipline Hearing Officer will be appointed to conduct hearings with approval of the appropriate Regional Director. If the institution's DHO is not able to conduct hearings, the Warden shall arrange for another DHO to conduct the hearings. This person must be trained and certified as a DHO, and meet the other requirements for DHO.

(b) In order to assure impartiality, the DHO may not be the reporting officer, investigating officer, or UDC [Unit Discipline Committee] member, or a witness to the incident or play any significant part in having the charge(s) referred to the DHO.

(c) The Discipline Hearing Officer shall conduct hearings, make findings, and impose appropriate sanctions for incidents of inmate misconduct referred for disposition following the hearing required by Sec. 541.15 before the UDC. The DHO may not hear any case or impose any sanctions in a case not heard and referred by the UDC. Only the Discipline Hearing Officer shall have authority to impose or suspend sanctions A through F.

(d) The Warden at each institution shall designate a staff member, hereinafter called the Segregation Review Official (SRO), to conduct reviews of inmates placed in disciplinary segregation and administrative detention in accordance with the requirements of Sec. 547.20 and Sec. 541.22.

---

even though it might look like good precedent, is not applicable, while another, different case is the appropriate precedent under the circumstances. In order to understand the meaning of a constitutional, statutory, or administrative provision it is critical to review any case law that has interpreted that provision. In fact, this textbook is a study of the case law that interprets the First, Fourth, Fifth, Sixth, Eighth, and Fourteenth Amendments of the U.S. Constitution and federal statutes as they relate to the rights of convicted offenders. A good example of how courts determine the correct legal precedent(s) can be found in the Supreme Court's opinion in Block v. Rutherford (1984), featured in the box below and also discussed in Chapter 9.

Block v. Rutherford (1984)

The case involved a regulation imposed by the Los Angeles County Central Jail that prohibited contact visits for all inmates, including pretrial detainees. Remember pretrial detainees have not yet been convicted of a crime. The pretrial detainee inmates filed a lawsuit alleging that the restriction violated the due process clause of the Fourteenth Amendment because they were still presumed innocent and because there was evidence that contact visiting has penological value. The Federal District Court agreed ruled that contact visits for detainees could only prohibited for inmates with high security classifications or those who had histories of escape attempts or substance abuse.

The Los Angeles County officials appealed to the Ninth Circuit Court of Appeals who remanded (returned) the case back to the District Court to reconsider because after the District Court had issued its decision, the U.S. Supreme Court decided the case *Bell v. Wolfish* (1979). *Bell v. Wolfish* involved pretrial detainees in a Washington, D. C. jail who also complained about policies they claimed violated their constitutional rights to due process based on their presumption of innocence. In that case, the Supreme Court outlined the principles to be applied in evaluating the constitutionality of conditions of pretrial detention. Courts must consider whether the regulation or practice was imposed for the purpose of punishing the detainees. Policies that are nonpunitive do not violate the due process clause. To determine whether a policy is punitive requires investigating whether the regulation is reasonably related to a legitimate penological purpose, or if "it appears excessive in relation to the alternative purpose assigned to it." The Court emphasized that ordinarily judges should defer to the expertise of correctional officials in the absence of substantial evidence that their response was exaggerated.

The District Court reconsidered the detainees' constitutional claims – this time, as instructed - in light of the Supreme Court's decision in *Bell v. Wolfish*, and it reaffirmed its prior decision. The District Court decided that nothing in *Bell v. Wolfish* challenged their initial ruling. The court found the jail policy was excessive in relation to the security objectives it was intended to promote. Los Angeles appealed a second time, and for a second time the Ninth Circuit Court of Appeals upheld the District Court's decision.

The Supreme Court granted *certiorari* because the issue was important and there was a conflict among the federal appeals courts. The Second, Fifth, and Ninth Circuits had held that pretrial detainees have a constitutional right to contact visits, but five other circuit courts had decided otherwise.

The Supreme Court began its analysis by observing that, "The principles articulated in *Wolfish* govern resolution of this case." The Court applied those principles to the issue of whether the prohibition on contact visits was reasonably related to the jail's security. Obviously, contact visits raise security issues, primarily the introduction of drugs, weapons, and other contraband. Although the District Court and Ninth Circuit found the restriction went too far in response to these concerns, the Supreme Court found otherwise.

> **Block v. Rutherford (1984) (cont.)**
>
> Wrote the Court, "We conclude that petitioner's blanket prohibition is an entirely reasonable, nonpunitive response to the legitimate security concerns identified, consistent with the Fourteenth Amendment." If routine body cavity searches following contact visits do not violate the Constitution (as the Court concluded in *Bell v. Wolfish*) then a total ban on contact visits is not excessive. The Court emphasized again that it was unwilling to substitute its judgment on difficult matters of institutional administration for that of the experts who actually operate the facilities.
>
> The Supreme Court chastised the District and Circuit Courts for not properly applying the legal precedent set forth in *Bell v. Wolfish*. Instead, the judges in both courts interpreted *Bell v. Wolfish* to allow them to balance the detainees' rights to contact visits with the institution's security concerns. According to the Supreme Court in *Block v. Rutherford*, that was an incorrect application of the principles first established in *Bell v. Wolfish*.

SUMMARY

The study of the rights of convicted offenders is important because there are more than two million people incarcerated in America's prisons and jails and almost five million on community supervision. The story of their legal rights does not end with their convictions. Correctional administrators are subject to constitutional and statutory restraints in the same way that law enforcement officers, judges, and prosecutors are. The corrections industry must invest significant resources in making certain they abide by the ever-expanding body of law that governs their activities. Corrections law involves controversial and politically sensitive issues, forcing us to examine our most fundamental social values. It also forces us to ask questions about the nature of punishment, and its goals and objectives.

This textbook examines the rights of convicted offenders from sentencing, through incarceration, and into community supervision. It follows the historical development of the law in this area, brings the student up to present time, and speculates about the future. This chapter focuses on the sources of prisoners' rights law and explains the role played by federal and state constitutions, statutes, administrative regulations, and case law.

The chapter provides specific examples of how each of those sources shapes prisoners' rights. Chapter One builds the foundation for the rest of the text. Students are encouraged to re-read parts of this chapter if they get confused while moving through the rest of the book. Sometimes, it is easy to get lost in the detail of individual court decisions and forget the foundation – the sources of law.

DISCUSSION QUESTIONS

1. Explain why federal judges adopted a "hands-off" approach to prisoners' civil rights lawsuits and describe the case that led to the Supreme Court's abrogation of that approach.

2. Which provisions of the Bill of Rights are applicable in inmate rights cases? How does due process play a role in these cases and where in the Constitution are due process protections afforded?

3. Explain how state constitutions can provide prisoners with greater legal protections than are afforded to them in the U.S. Constitution.

4. What is "case law" and why is it important in understanding law?

5. Discuss why it is important that the Constitution apply to people who have been convicted of crimes and are still serving their sentences – incarcerated in jail or prison, on probation or parole.

SUGGESTED READINGS AND REFERENCES

Conrad, J.P. (1989), "From barbarism toward decency: Alabama's long road to prison reform," Journal of Research in Crime and Delinquency 26(4), 307-328.

Crouch, B., & Marquart, J. (1989). *An appeal to justice: litigated reform of Texas prisons*. Austin: University of Texas Press.

Glaze, L. & Palla S. (2004). Bureau of Justice Statistics bulletin: Probation and Parole in the United States, 2003. Washington, D.C.: Department of Justice.

Oshinsky, D.M (1996). *Worse than slavery: Parchman Farm and the ordeal of Jim Crow justice*. New York: The Free Press.

Sampson, R & Lauritsen, J. (1997). Racial and ethnic disparities in crime and criminal justice in the U.S. In M. Tonry (Ed.), *Ethnicity, crime and immigration: Comparative and cross-national perspectives* (pp. 311-374). Chicago: University of Chicago Press.

Smith, C. (2000). Boundary changes in criminal justice organizations: The governance of corrections: Implications of the changing interface of courts and corrections. Washington, DC: National Institute of Justice.

Yackle, L.W. (1989). *Reform and regret: The story of federal judicial involvement in the American penal system.* New York and Oxford: Oxford University Press.

CHAPTER 2:
Sentencing

INTRODUCTION

Before conviction, defendants have a full array of Constitutional rights that protect the presumption of their innocence. After conviction, the presumption of innocence no longer applies. Sentencing statutes throughout the United States have become very complex over the last 25 years, and new issues continue to be raised. The process by which defendants are sentenced has also become more complex, and the rights of defendants during sentencing have expanded. Even with these changes, however, a defendant's constitutional protections are significantly reduced after a guilty plea or verdict. This chapter begins with a discussion about sentencing reform. Next, it highlights some of the most important rights that defendants have during the actual sentencing process. Finally, it examines several constitutional issues that relate specifically to defendants who plead guilty. The sentencing process is the beginning of a defendant's life as a convicted offender. From this point on, he or she will not be able to rely on the extensive constitutional rights they enjoyed before conviction. Beginning with the limited rights they have during the sentencing phase in the courtroom and continuing throughout the term of their sentence, the legal status of defendants undergoes a radical transformation.

THE EVOLUTION OF SENTENCING STATUTES IN THE UNITED STATES

History

Until the 1970s, all state and federal sentencing statutes were based on the indeterminate sentencing model, in which the law provides a broad range of years for the sentence. Nevertheless, there were some differences among the states. In some states, judges specified only the maximum sentence length within the range provided by statute. In others states, judges specified both the maximum and minimum length within the statutory sentence range. Most importantly, however, was that judges had significant discretion to decide the length of a sentence, and an administrative agency, the parole board, had the discretion to decide when to release an offender. The board's responsibility was to evaluate the offender's progress toward rehabilitation and decide whether he or she should be released into the community under parole conditions before the complete sentence was served in prison. Parole statutes guided the board's decision and outlined at what point during a sentence an offender would be eligible for parole consideration. The indeterminate model was considered an enlightened approach toward sentencing because, ideally, the length of an offender's incarceration matched the length of time he or she needed to be rehabilitated. As part of the ideal, correctional personnel, clinicians, social workers, and educators developed rehabilitation programs to suit the particular needs of individual offenders. The first indeterminate sentencing laws were enacted on a very limited scale in Michigan in 1869. States gradually adopted the indeterminate model across all of the United States.

The debate about sentencing reform started in the 1970s. Critics of indeterminate sentencing alleged it was unfair because it resulted in serious sentencing disparity. Not only did indeterminate sentencing laws give judges wide discretion when making sentencing decisions, parole boards had wide discretion to decide which prisoners were sufficiently rehabilitated and ready for early release. They charged that individualized sentencing resulted in arbitrary sentencing practices that more severely impacted minority offenders. Indeterminate sentencing was under attack from both liberals and conservatives. Some prisoners emphasized the cruel uncertainty of serving an indeterminate sentence and the lack of consistency in both judicial and administrative use of discretion. Other critics suggested that indeterminate sentencing allowed judges to be soft on criminals. They pointed to the rising crime rate and Supreme Court cases that expanded the rights of the accused. In response to these growing concerns, the National Research Council appointed a panel of social scientists headed by Albert Blumstein to study sentencing in the United States. It concluded that for these reasons and more, many professionals in the criminal justice system believed that indeterminate sentencing systems needed serious reform. (Blumstein 1983). Very quickly, sentencing philosophy began to shift from the rehabilitative ideal to the just deserts principle.

Call for Reform

In response to the growing criticism, many state legislatures reexamined their sentencing laws. Today, there is no standard approach to sentencing. Michael Tonry (1999) reported that some states still have parole; others have abolished it. Although most states still grant good time credits to incarcerated offenders, the amount of good time has been reduced significantly. Eight or nine jurisdictions have presumptive sentencing guidelines; eight to ten have voluntary guidelines. Five states have some form of determinate sentencing, but thirty states still have some form of indeterminate sentencing. Tonry described sentencing in the United States as fractured. It is difficult to report the numbers of jurisdictions that have adopted reforms because there are so many variations of reform. What is clear is the decline of indeterminate sentencing and that within that trend there are wide and important variations. With "pure" determinate sentencing, the sentence of incarceration is a fixed term that can be reduced by good time or earned time. An offender's release date is set with no parole board review; although in some jurisdictions there is some form of post-release supervision for certain offenders.

Sentencing Guidelines and Mandatory Minimums

In several jurisdictions, the move to determinate sentencing has included creating sentencing guidelines to reduce judicial discretion. Legislatures create commissions charged with devising detailed sentencing laws that severely limit judicial decision-making. Judges use the commission's sentencing guidelines during the sentencing process. No longer does a judge have discretion to sentence within a wide minimum and maximum range set by the legislature. The commission recommends the sentence within a much tighter range. In some jurisdictions, the guidelines are voluntary, meaning they are advisory and not required by law. In other jurisdictions, the guidelines are presumptive, and judges must follow them. Under presumptive guidelines, judges are required by law to explain the reasons for deviating (departing) from the sentence provided by the guidelines. Both the prosecution and the defense can appeal a departure.

To improve on predictability and consistency, sentencing guidelines are based on the seriousness of the offense and the offender's prior criminal history. There is little opportunity for judges to consider an offender's individual circumstances, such as educational and employment background, marital history, and medical and mental health issues. Minnesota took the lead in adopting structured sentencing in 1980. The Sentencing Reform Act of 1984 created the United States Sentencing Commission and abolished federal parole, creating a structured and determinate sentencing system for offenders convicted of federal crimes. In 1989, the U.S. Supreme Court ruled in *Mistretta v. United States* that the U.S. Sentencing Guidelines are constitutional and do not violate the separation of powers doctrine.

Another approach to reducing judicial discretion in sentencing and getting "tough on crime" involves mandatory minimum sentencing laws, which all 50 states and the federal government have enacted to some degree. These laws specify a minimum sentence that must be applied for all convictions for a certain offense, such as a specific minimum prison sentence for possession of cocaine, or an offense committed under special circumstances, such as selling drugs to a minor within 1000 feet of a school.

Although in some jurisdictions the mandatory minimum laws focus almost exclusively on crimes committed by firearms, driving while under the influence and those related to drugs, in other jurisdictions they are more comprehensive. In Oregon, for example, voters passed Measure 11 in 1994, which imposes mandatory minimum prison terms for 21 designated violent and sex-related crimes and prohibits offenders convicted of those crimes from earning good time during their prison term. Judges sentencing offenders convicted of a crime that has a mandatory minimum sentence are not permitted to impose a sentence below the required minimum, regardless of the offender's prior criminal history or special circumstances.

Mandatory minimum sentencing statutes are not new to the "get tough" on crime era of the last 30 years. Massachusetts enacted the Bartley-Fox Amendment in the 1970s, which required a one-year prison term for individuals convicted of carrying an unlicensed firearm. The Michigan Felony Firearms Statute of 1977 imposed a two-year prison term for possession of a firearm during the commission of a felony. The 1973 the Rockefeller Drug Laws in New York imposed severe mandatory penalties for drug offenses. In the 1990s, however, many new mandatory minimum sentencing laws were enacted addressing many different types of offenses.

Three-Strike Laws and Truth-in-Sentencing

Three-strike and two-strike sentencing laws are another variation of mandatory minimum sentencing that specifically target repeat offenders. The highly publicized California three strikes law requires that offenders who are convicted of a third felony (any felony) and have two prior felony convictions for serious or violent crimes, as defined by the statute, must serve a 25-years to life sentence with no release before serving 80% of the sentence. The law also doubles the prison term for offenders convicted of a second felony if their first offense involved a serious or violent crime. Habitual offender statutes that enhance punishment for repeat criminals have been a part of sentencing in the United States for a long time; however, typically prosecutors have had the discretion to seek sentencing under habitual offender laws and judges the discretion to do so. California's three strikes law is mandatory. Twenty-three states have implemented a version of "three strikes and you're out" sentencing laws. Only in California, however, can any felony offense trigger a three-strikes 25-years to life sentence. In the other 22 states with three strikes legislation, the third felony must be a violent offense (Schiraldi, Colburn, & Lotke 2004). Despite its harshness, challenges to the California three strikes law were struck down by the U.S. Supreme Court in *Lockyer v. Andrade* (2003) and *Ewing v. California* (2003).

The U.S. Congress imposed an 85% prison term requirement on federal offenders as part of the Sentencing Reform Act of 1984 that also abolished federal parole. In 1994, Congress passed the Violent Crime Control and Law Enforcement Act, which provides federal grant money to states to expand prison capacity if they increase the incarceration of violent offenders convicted in their states. To receive funding under the Violent Offender Incarceration program, states must assure the federal government they will implement policies to insure that violent criminals will serve a substantial amount of their sentence and that their punishment is severe. Under what has been termed the Truth-in-Sentencing (TIS) program, to receive federal funds states must implement laws that require violent offenders to serve at least 85% of their sentence or have laws that require serious repeat violent offenders and drug offenders to serve 85% of their sentence. Truth-in-sentencing laws limit, and in some jurisdictions, eliminate the discretion of parole boards. They are another type of mandatory minimum sentencing and reflect the trend toward a more determinate approach. A 2002 report prepared by researchers for the Urban Institute's Justice Policy Center noted that thirty states made no changes in their truth-in-sentencing structure after the federal TIS grant program was enacted, but 12 states increased the severity of their sentencing laws and the remainder states made comparatively large changes by introducing new truth-in-sentencing laws. An example of TIS at work is New Jersey's No Early Release Act, enacted in 1997. The New Jersey law requires offenders who have committed violent crimes to serve a minimum of 85% of their prison terms before becoming eligible for parole consideration.

Does the Punishment Fit the Crime?

The Eighth Amendment prohibits punishments that are "cruel and unusual." What constitutes a cruel and unusual sentence? The Supreme Court has struggled with this question for many years.

In *Trop v. Dulles* (1958), the Supreme Court held that the Eighth Amendment prohibits taking away a defendant's citizenship as punishment for a crime. The Court acknowledged that the meaning of the "cruel and unusual punishment" clause is ambiguous and that its' meaning will never be precise. Wrote the Court, "The Amendment must draw its meaning from the evolving standards of decency that mark the progress of a maturing society."

In *Rummel v. Estelle* (1980), the Supreme Court considered whether a life sentence was grossly disproportionate to the severity of the crime and, therefore, in violation of the Eighth Amendment. Rummel was sentenced to a mandatory term of life in the Texas prison system for the felony of obtaining $120.75 by false pretenses. Prosecutors were able to charge him as a habitual offender because he had two prior felony theft convictions, one involving $80 (for which he was sentenced to three years' confinement) and the other involving $28.36 (for which he was sentenced to four years' confinement).

The *Rummel* Court decided that the state has a valid interest in establishing harsh punishments for repeat offenders. The appropriate length of a sentence is a matter for the legislature to decide. According to the Court even corrections experts cannot agree on the proper severity of a sentence. It should remain within the discretion of the state to decide the amount of time a recidivist offender should be incarcerated.

The next opportunity for the Supreme Court to consider the proportionality question came in *Solem v. Helm* (1983). Helm had been convicted of six nonviolent felony offenses, prior to pleading guilty to passing a "no account" check for $100. Instead of being sentenced to up to five years imprisonment, the maximum penalty for that crime, he was sentenced to life without parole because he was a repeat offender. The *Solem* Court held that the Eighth Amendment's cruel and unusual punishment clause requires that a criminal sentence, including a felony prison sentence, must be proportionate to the crime for which the defendant was convicted. Appellate courts must defer to the authority of the legislatures to devise types and terms of punishments, but no punishment is automatically constitutional because it was enacted by the legislature. In deciding whether a particular sentence is proportionate, a court should consider three factors: the severity of the offense and the punishment, sentences imposed on other criminals in the same jurisdiction, and sentences imposed for the same crime in other jurisdictions.

The Court concluded that Helms' sentence was much harsher than the sentence considered in *Rummel v. Estelle*, because, unlike Rummel who would eventually be eligible for parole, Helms would never be released and would spend the rest of his life incarcerated. After reviewing how South Dakota sentences offenders for other crimes and how other states sentence offenders with criminal histories similar to Helms, the Court ruled that his life without parole sentence was disproportionate to his offense and violated the Constitution.

Does the Punishment Fit the Crime? (cont.)

As if the law about proportionate sentencing was not complicated after the *Rummel and Helm* cases, along came the Supreme Court 5-4 decision in *Harmelin v. Michigan* (1991). Harmelin was convicted of possessing 672 grams of cocaine and sentenced to a mandatory term of life in prison without parole. He had no prior criminal history. Harmelin challenged his sentence as disproportionate to his crime and because the judge was required by Michigan law to impose the sentence and was prohibited from taking into account the particular circumstances of the crime and of him.

After examining the historical background of the Constitution, this time the Supreme Court ruled that the Eighth Amendment's cruel and unusual punishment clause was never meant to forbid disproportionate punishments. The *Harmelin* Court decided that each of the three *Solem* factors were problematic. Who is decide the severity of an offense? The legislature, decided the Court. Who is to decide whether one offense is more or less severe than another? Also, the job of the legislature. Finally, under our federal system of government each state is entitled to enact its own sentencing laws. The Court noted that the Constitution prohibits cruel *and* unusual punishments and that while severe mandatory sentences may be severe, they are not unusual. The Supreme Court ruled that Harmelin's sentence was constitutional.

Interestingly, in 1992, the Michigan Supreme Court held in *People v. Bullock*, 485 N.W.2d 866 (Michigan 1992) that the statute under which Harmelin was sentenced violated the Michigan Constitution and ordered the no-parole provision be stricken, making Harmelin eligible for parole after serving ten years of his sentence. The state court recognized the difference between the federal and Michigan Constitutions. The U.S. Constitution forbids cruel *and* unusual punishments, while the Michigan Constitution forbids cruel *or* unusual punishments.

The most recent Supreme Court cases to address the proportionality principle were decided on the same day in 2003. In both cases, the Court was faced with challenges to California's three strikes law. It provides that when a defendant is convicted of a felony and he or she has been previously con-victed of one or more prior serious or violent felonies, the defendant must be sentenced under the three strikes law. With one serious or violent prior felony, he or she must be sentenced to twice the term provided for the current conviction. With two or more prior serious or violent felony convictions, the judge must sentence the defendant to an indeterminate life sentence, essen-tially 25 years to life. Ewing was convicted of stealing three golf clubs priced at $399 apiece, a felony theft. He had a list of prior felony convictions for theft, battery, possession of drug paraphernalia and a firearm, burglaries and a robbery and was sentenced to 25 years to life under the three strikes law.

Does the Punishment Fit the Crime? (cont.)

The five-member majority in *Ewing v. California* (2003) discussed the *Rummel*, *Solem*, and *Harmelin* decisions and decided that the constitutional issue is whether the punishment is grossly disproportionate to the crime. Unfortunately for Gary Ewing, the Supreme Court ruled that his sentence was not grossly disproportionate. The Court pointed to the need to address recidivist offenders, the state's interest in deterring crime, and its policy of deferring to the legislature's judgment in matters of sentencing.

In the companion case to *Ewing*, Andrade was convicted of two counts of petty theft after stealing videotapes from two different stores amounting to $150. He had three prior serious felony convictions and was sentenced to consecutive terms of 25 years to life. Under California law, the prosecutor had the discretion to prosecute the two thefts as felonies because of Andrade's prior criminal record. In *Lockyer v. Andrade* (2003), the Supreme Court ruled that Andrade's sentence was not so extraordinary that it could be considered grossly disproportionate to his crimes.

The Court has ruled that if a sentence is grossly disproportionate to the offense, it violates the cruel and unusual punishment clause. It appears, however, that the three factors announced by the Court in *Solem v Helm*, while not overruled, no longer apply. The Supreme Court did not rely on them when it decided *Ewing v. California* and *Lockyer v. Andrade*.

The most recent Supreme Court cases to address the proportionality principle were decided on the same day in 2003. In both cases, the Court was faced with challenges to California's three strikes law. It provides that when a defendant is convicted of a felony and he or she has been previously convicted of one or more prior serious or violent felonies, the defendant must be sentenced under the three strikes law. With one serious or violent prior felony, he or she must be sentenced to twice the term provided for the current conviction. With two or more prior serious or violent felony convictions, the judge must sentence the defendant to an indeterminate life sentence, essentially 25 years to life. Ewing was convicted of stealing three golf clubs priced at $399 apiece, a felony theft. He had a list of prior felony convictions for theft, battery, possession of drug paraphernalia and a firearm, burglaries and a robbery and was sentenced to 25 years to life under the three strikes law.

The five-member majority in *Ewing v. California* (2003) discussed the *Rummel*, *Solem*, and *Harmelin* decisions and decided that the constitutional issue is whether the punishment is grossly disproportionate to the crime. Unfortunately for Gary Ewing, the Supreme Court ruled that his sentence was not grossly disproportionate. The Court pointed to the need to address recidivist offenders, the state's interest in deterring crime, and its policy of deferring to the legislature's judgment in matters of sentencing.

In the companion case to *Ewing*, Andrade was convicted of two counts of petty theft after stealing videotapes from two different stores amounting to $150.

He had three prior serious felony convictions and was sentenced to consecutive terms of 25 years to life. Under California law, the prosecutor had the discretion to prosecute the two thefts as felonies because of Andrade's prior criminal record. In *Lockyer v. Andrade* (2003), the Supreme Court ruled that Andrade's sentence was not so extraordinary that it could be considered grossly disproportionate to his crimes.

The Court has ruled that if a sentence is grossly disproportionate to the offense, it violates the cruel and unusual punishment clause. It appears, however, that the three factors announced by the Court in *Solem v Helm*, while not overruled, no longer apply. The Supreme Court did not rely on them when it decided *Ewing v. California* and *Lockyer v. Andrade*.

IMPACT OF REFORM

There has been a great deal of research on the efficacy of the sentencing reforms enacted since the 1970s. To what degree have the reforms contributed to the skyrocketing incarceration rates in this country? Did the reforms contribute to the decrease in crime rates during the 1990s? How have prosecutors and defense attorneys adapted to the new sentencing statutes? How frequently do judges depart from the sentences provided in sentencing guidelines and under what circumstances? Have the reforms reduced disparity in sentencing? The results are mixed, and the research is ongoing. In states with sentencing guidelines, commissions are required to revisit the guidelines periodically and adjust sentence lengths based on studies that address these very questions. Sentencing reform has become a significant political and social issue during the last several decades. All the states and the federal government have implemented some version of sentencing reform. With these reforms there is generally a requirement or expectation from the legislature that follow-up research will be conducted to evaluate their impact.

OFFENDER'S RIGHTS AT SENTENCING

Right to Counsel

The Supreme Court has recognized that one of the most important rights a criminal defendant has is the Sixth Amendment right to counsel. The Supreme Court has also recognized the importance of counsel during sentencing. In *Townsend v. Burke* (1948), the Court held that Townsend's constitutional rights were violated when he was denied counsel during a guilty plea because the Fourteenth Amendment's due process clause requires counsel be available to ensure a defendant's sentence is not based on inaccurate information. In *Mempa v. Rhay* (1967), the Court concluded that the Sixth Amendment guarantees counsel during sentencing because an attorney can help the client assemble facts and introduce mitigating evidence relevant to sentencing.

The Court has also addressed the assistance of counsel during interviews intended to gather information from the defendant for use during the sentencing hearing. In *Estelle v. Smith* (1981), the defendant, charged with murder, was interviewed by a psychiatrist to determine if he was competent to stand trial. He was found competent and convicted of capital murder. During his sentencing hearing, the same psychiatrist testified that treatment would not help the defendant because he was a sociopath. The psychiatrist's testimony was introduced to help show the defendant's future dangerousness, which was part of the State's argument for why he should be sentenced to death. The Supreme Court decided that the defendant's Sixth Amendment right was violated because he was not provided prior notification that the psychiatrist's interview would include issues involved in a sentencing decision. He did not have the opportunity to refuse to participate in the interview. The Court did not hold the defendant's attorney had the right to be present during a psychiatric evaluation, only that the attorney should have had notice.

Most convicted defendants are interviewed by a probation officer who is responsible for preparing a presentence investigation report (PSI) for the judge to use in making sentencing decisions. Lower courts, however, have ruled that the reasoning of the *Estelle v. Smith* case does not apply to those interviews. They determined that a probation officer is an extension of the court and is a neutral party gathering information to assist a judge. Unlike the psychiatrist in Estelle whose testimony about future dangerousness was legally required proof before a death sentence could be imposed, probation officers are not gathering information that will be used as evidence toward an element of the prosecution's case.

The Supreme Court has interpreted the Sixth Amendment right to counsel during a criminal trial to mean the right to effective assistance. The *Strickland v. Washington* (1984) decision involved a capital murder case that challenged how effectively Strickland's attorney presented his client's against the death penalty during sentencing. In this watershed case, the Supreme Court established a two prong test: did the attorney act reasonably, according the professional standards in the community at that time and, if not, was the defendant prejudiced by the attorney's performance. Under this test, appellate courts must look at the totality of the circumstances and start with the presumption that the defense counsel was reasonably competent. To establish prejudice the defendant must show there is a reasonable probability that the death penalty would not have been imposed if counsel had performed competently. The *Strickland* test is not limited to the punishment phase of capital murder cases. It provides the standard for courts to use in evaluating the effectiveness of legal representation in all criminal cases, during both the trial on guilt or innocence and the sentencing hearing.

Evidence a Judge Can Use in Sentencing

In *Williams v. New York* (1949), the Supreme Court ruled that when judges make sentencing decisions they are not restricted to evidence introduced at the trial on guilt or innocence. In *Williams*, the trial judge imposed the death sentence on a convicted murderer even though the jury recommended life. The judge stated he relied not only on evidence that led to the defendant's conviction but also on information laid out in a presentence investigation report, which stated the defendant had been implicated in over thirty burglaries. Even though he had not been convicted of those crimes, the defendant had confessed to some and been identified as the offender in others. He had not challenged the accuracy of the report. The Supreme Court held that not all of the strict evidentiary standards that apply to issues of guilt or innocence apply during a sentencing hearing. A judge engaged in sentencing is not confined to the narrow issue of guilt and requires the fullest possible information in order for him or her to assess punishment. The Constitution does not prohibit a judge from considering information that was not received in open court. The judge is free to conduct a broader inquiry because the punishment should fit the offender and not just the offense.

In a number of important cases, the Court has continued to uphold the right of judges to conduct a broad inquiry when making sentencing decisions. Grayson escaped from a federal prison. During his trial on the escape charge, he testified he fled prison because another inmate threatened him in order to collect a gambling debt. The alleged assailant testified there was no such debt. The government introduced other evidence that contradicted Grayson's testimony about the escape, and he was convicted. The judge explained that the sentence he imposed was influenced by Grayson's false testimony. On appeal, Grayson argued that by considering his false statements, the trial judge was punishing him for perjury, for which he had not been indicted, much less convicted. He also argued the judge's actions chilled his right under the Constitution to testify on his own behalf. In *United States v. Grayson* (1978), the Supreme Court decided it was not unconstitutional for a judge to consider a defendant's false testimony when assessing a sentence. The Court concluded that judges are not limited to information contained in presentence investigation reports. The judge observed the defendant's false testimony firsthand, and his lack of honesty was relevant to a sentencing decision.

Roberts refused to cooperate with U.S. Attorneys who had indicted him on several drug offenses. They wanted him to give them information about his suppliers. After he was convicted the trial judge supported his sentence by noting that Roberts refused to help the government. The Supreme Court ruled in *Roberts v. United States* (1980) that the judge had not violated the Fifth Amendment privilege against self-incrimination when he considered the defendant's refusal to cooperate. In *United States v. Watts* (1997), a jury convicted Watts of drug possession with intent to distribute but acquitted him on using a firearm during the commission of the offense. During the sentencing hearing, the court found, by a preponderance of the evidence, that Watts possessed a firearm in connection with the crime. Based on this finding, under the federal sentencing guidelines, the judge enhanced (increased) Watts' sentence. The Supreme Court concluded that even though Watts was found not guilty on the firearm charge, the judge was not prohibited from considering the conduct underlying that charge, as long as it was proved by a preponderance of the evidence.

Another important difference between sentencing hearings and trials involves the admissibility of illegally seized evidence. Although it is inadmissible during the guilt or innocence trial, judges can admit evidence during a sentencing hearing that has been seized illegally. An exception to this rule would be if law enforcement officers illegally seized the evidence so it could be used at sentencing to enhance the defendant's sentence. *United States v. Brimah* (2000).

THE SUPREME COURT SIGNIFICANTLY CHANGES THE SENTENCING RULES

In 2000, the Supreme Court decided a very significant case about what evidence a judge can consider in making a sentencing decision – *Apprendi v. New Jersey*. Under the New Jersey hate crime statute, if a sentencing judge found beyond a preponderance of the evidence that an offender committed a crime purposely to intimidate an individual or group because of race, race color, gender, handicap, religion, sexual orientation, or ethnicity, the offender's prison term would be extended beyond the maximum term provided for the base offense. Apprendi pleaded guilty to various violent offenses. The judge found that his crimes were racially motivated and enhanced Apprendi's punishment beyond the statutory maximum. Apprendi appealed and argued the enhancement violated the Fourteenth Amendment's due process clause because there was no factual determination by a jury beyond a reasonable doubt that his crimes were racially motivated. In other words, he argued the finding of racial bias was a fact that should have been considered by a jury because it amounted to an element of the crime of which he was charged. The U.S. Supreme Court agreed with Apprendi, concluding that the New Jersey law was more than an enhancement statute. It required a judge to make a finding of fact that impacted the severity of a sentence based on the lower preponderance of the evidence standard.

The *Apprendi* decision sparked an intense debate about sentencing in states with laws similar to those in New Jersey. The debate soon expanded beyond a particular hate crime statute. In *Blakely v. Washington* (2004), the Supreme Court ruled on the constitutionality of the sentencing guidelines for the state of Washington. Blakely pleaded guilty to kidnapping. According to the state sentencing guidelines, the facts he admitted in his plea would result in a maximum sentence of 53 months. The judge imposed a 90-month sentence because he found that Blakely acted with "deliberate cruelty." Under the guidelines, a finding of "deliberate cruelty" was grounds for departing from the standard sentence. The issue for the U.S. Supreme Court was similar to the issue in *Apprendi*. The judge enhanced the defendant's sentence based on facts that were not found by a jury applying the reasonable doubt standard. The Supreme Court relied on the *Apprendi* precedent and ruled that Blakely's sentence violated his Sixth Amendment right to a trial by jury because the facts supporting the judge's decision to enhance his sentence beyond 53 months were not found by a jury.

The Court was careful to note that its' holding did not disturb the precedent established in *Williams v. New York* (1949). Judges are still permitted to rely on facts not presented to a jury when they decide on a sentence as long as they do not exceed the sentence provided by state law for the crime that led to the guilty verdict or guilty plea. The Washington guidelines violated the Constitution because judges were permitted to rely on facts not established during the trial or admitted in the plea bargain in order to increase a sentence beyond what state law allowed for the offense of conviction. For kidnapping alone, Blakely faced a 53- month sentence but the judge went beyond the maximum based on his finding of deliberate cruelty. In *Williams v. New York*, the judge made a fact-finding the jury had not made, but he used it to impose a sentence that was already within the range of punishment provided for that offense.

After the *Blakely* decision the controversy surrounding sentencing intensified. The focus shifted to the federal sentencing guidelines because they have provisions similar to those in the Washington State guidelines. Several federal district court judges ruled that the federal guidelines violated the Constitution, relying on the precedent set by the *Blakely* case. Federal criminal sentencing hearings were disrupted all over the country as the federal courts wrestled with what to do. Recognizing the serious situation, the U.S. Supreme Court fast-tracked a case, *United States v. Booker* (2005), in which a circuit court of appeals had ruled that the guidelines conflicted with the *Apprendi* and *Blakely* decisions. As with many Supreme Court opinions the *Booker* case raised as many questions as it sought to answer. A 5-4 decision, six of the nine Justices wrote opinions.

Booker faced a sentence within the range of 210-262 months for a drug conviction, but at the sentencing hearing the judge found additional facts by a preponderance of the evidence. The federal guidelines give judges the power to decide sentencing facts including such things as the amount of drugs involved in an offense and the severity of the crime. Under the guidelines they also have the power to use acquitted and uncharged conduct to increase the length of a sentence. In Booker's case, the judge found additional facts that caused him to impose a sentence between 360 months to life. Once the judge made the additional fact finding, the guidelines required him to impose the enhanced sentence. The guidelines did not allow the judge to exercise his discretion about whether the 210-262 month sentence should be enhanced. As a result, the sentence Booker would have received without the judge's finding was increased by ten years.

Five Supreme Court Justices concluded that the Sixth Amendment's right to a jury trial applied to the federal sentencing guidelines. Booker's additional ten-year sentence violated the Constitution because it resulted from a finding of facts conducted by a judge by a preponderance of the evidence. The Sixth Amendment requires that he should have been sentenced based on facts found by a jury or facts he admitted as part of a guilty plea. The Court ruled that the sentencing guidelines' mandatory requirement should be excised, meaning that the provisions requiring judges to impose enhanced sentences when they found certain facts exist should be struck down. When judges make fact-findings based on evidence and information that was not part of a guilty verdict or a guilty plea, the judge is no longer obligated to impose a certain sentence. In this way, federal judges are still free to consider information during the sentencing process that was not part of the guilt or innocence trial. What changed with the *Booker* decision is that when they determine such information is true, they are not required to impose a specific sentence based on the information. Use of the information is discretionary. Judges can decide the information they acquire after a conviction should result in an enhanced sentence, but they can also conclude that an enhanced sentence is not called for under the circumstances. That majority opinion stressed that judges must consider the sentencing guidelines when exercising their discretion, even though they may eventually decide against applying them in a particular case. Although the guidelines are now advisory, not mandatory, they remain the starting point for judges who are determining an appropriate sentence.

There are many unanswered questions left in the wake of the *Booker* decision. It may well take several years and several more appellate opinions before they are resolved. How many federal criminal cases will be affected? What will be the impact on past cases where sentences were finalized on appeal before *Booker* was decided? Will defendants with cases currently on appeal be able to challenge their sentences under *Booker*? What about defendants currently involved in the habeas corpus process? Most importantly, what factors can federal district court judges consider when they make sentencing decisions? To what extent can they exercise their discretion and depart from the federal guidelines?

GUILTY PLEAS AND GUILTY VERDICTS

In most states, trial judges decide the appropriate sentence for defendants in non-capital cases who have been convicted of or pled guilty to crimes. There are a few states that permit the jury to determine punishment for noncapital crimes.

Defendants can plead "guilty", "not guilty", and in some jurisdictions "*nolo contendere*" to the charges against them. A plea of *nolo contendere* means the defendant is offering no contest to the government's case. A guilty plea avoids the trial on guilt or innocence. A hearing is conducted where the formal plea is entered and a sentence is imposed. At this hearing the judge inquires about the nature of any plea-bargaining between the defendant and the prosecutor. The judge treats a "no contest" plea the same as a guilty plea. A guilty plea can be used as evidence in a civil lawsuit, however, a "no contest" plea cannot.

A "not guilty" plea triggers the beginning of the trial process. In a jury trial, the jury renders the verdict. In a bench trial the judge renders the verdict. After a guilty verdict is rendered, the sentence is imposed. In many states, the sentence is imposed after a sentencing hearing in which the prosecutor and the defendant present additional evidence relevant to the appropriate punishment. In most states, the sentencing judge also has a presentence investigation report prepared by the probation department to assist him or her in deciding on a sentence.

Plea-bargaining is an important part of the criminal justice system. Research shows that the vast majority of convictions result from guilty pleas (DuRose and Langan 2001). In many instances a plea is in the best interest of both the state and the defendant. Many defendants plead guilty in exchange for concessions from the prosecutor. Prosecutors can offer to reduce the seriousness of the charges against the defendant in exchange for a plea of guilt. They can also offer to dismiss or not file some of the charges. Finally, they can offer to recommend a specific sentence to the sentencing judge in exchange for a plea.

A Knowing and Voluntary Plea

The Supreme Court held in *Boykin v. Alabama* (1969) that a plea bargain is constitutional if the defendant made the plea knowingly and voluntarily. It is the trial judge's responsibility to make sure the defendant pleaded guilty of his own choice and that he or she knows and understands the ramifications of their plea. They have waived their right to remain silent under the Fifth Amendment, their Sixth Amendment right to a trial, and the right to confront the witnesses against them under the Sixth Amendment. A plea cannot be the result of threats, misrepresentations, or promises a prosecutor has no authority to offer. A guilty plea is offered in open court and on the record. The trial judge must ask the defendant certain questions about the plea in order to establish that the plea was voluntary and intelligent. Those questions include asking defendants if they understand the constitutional rights they are waiving by entering a guilty plea. A judge must also make certain defendants understand the nature of the charges against them. Just how extensive that questioning must be depends on the circumstances of a specific case.

Alford Pleas

One of the most troubling aspects of plea-bargaining is the prospect that, fearing conviction, a defendant will feel compelled to plead guilty to an offense they did not commit. The U.S. Supreme Court addressed that issue in *North Carolina v. Alford* (1979). Alford was charged with capital murder. He claimed his innocence, but the evidence against him was strong, and his attorney recommended he plead guilty to second-degree murder. Before his plea was entered, the court took testimony from a police officer who summarized the state's case and several other witnesses. There was no eyewitness testimony to the crime. Alford testified he had not committed the crime but was pleading guilty because he faced the death penalty if he was convicted. In response to the court's questions he acknowledged he understood the difference between first and second-degree murder and the rights he was waiving.

Alford appealed his guilty plea arguing it was invalid because it resulted from fear and coercion. In *Brady v. United States* (1970), the Supreme Court had ruled that a guilty plea is not necessarily involuntary because the defendant entered it in order to avoid the death penalty. Unlike Alford, however, Brady had not claimed he was innocent. Alford's guilty plea contradicted his assertion of innocence. The *Alford* case was especially important because state and lower federal courts were divided at that time over whether a guilty plea could be accepted if the defendant also claimed innocence. The Court ruled that Alford's plea should be viewed in light of the evidence against him, which strongly indicated his guilt. The trial record also showed that Alford's plea was made knowingly and intelligently. All of which led the Court to rule that the judge did not violate Alford's rights by accepting his plea.

As a result of the *Alford* case, many courts require that a factual basis for a guilty plea be put on the record before the plea is accepted. The factual basis helps establish the defendant is not pleading guilty to a crime they did not commit and the plea is truly voluntary. If he or she is pleading guilty, but claiming innocence, the factual basis helps the court determine whether the evidence indicates guilt. Other courts do not require that a factual basis for a guilty plea be established if the defendant does not claim innocence. In most jurisdictions, it is the judge's discretion whether to accept a guilty plea. If a plea is rejected and the defendant goes to trial, is found guilty, and receives a more severe sentence than was offered under the plea, appellate courts have generally found the trial judge did not abuse his or her discretion (Branham 2002).

Other Issues Regarding Guilty Pleas

Can the prosecutor threaten to reindict a defendant on more serious charges if he or she does not plead guilty to the charged offense? Do such threats constitute coercion, making the plea involuntary? In *Bordenkircher v. Hayes* (1978), the Supreme Court recognized the give-and-take nature of plea bargaining and ruled that so long as the prosecutor has probable cause to believe the defendant committed the crime, there is no constitutional violation. In *Alabama v. Smith* (1989), the Court decided the trial judge had not violated the Constitution when he imposed a more severe sentence after Smith appealed his original guilty plea and it was set aside. In that case the defendant pleaded guilty in exchange for the state dismissing a sodomy charge. He was given two 30-year sentences. After Smith won his appeal and his conviction was set aside, the state reinstated the sodomy charge, he was found guilty at trial, and the judge sentenced him to two life terms and a 150 year term for rape. According to the judge additional facts came to light during the trial. According to the Supreme Court, if there was a reasonable likelihood that the new sentences resulted from vindictiveness, they should be set aside. In that case, however, the Court concluded there was no evidence of vindictiveness in the judge's sentence.

What recourse does a defendant have when the government fails to keep a commitment concerning a sentencing recommendation in exchange for a guilty plea? The Supreme Court decided in *Santabello v. New York* (1971), that when a defendant enters a guilty plea based on an agreement with the prosecutor, the prosecutor is obligated to fulfill the agreement. Santabello pleaded guilty to a less serious offense than what he was indicted on in exchange for the prosecutor's promise he would not recommend a sentence. The offense he pled to carried a maximum prison term of one year. On the day Santabello was in court to enter his plea, a different prosecutor appeared and recommended one year of incarceration. Although Santabello's attorney objected and told the court about the plea agreement, the judge imposed one year based on Santabello's prior criminal record. The Supreme Court vacated the sentence because the prosecutor should have honored the original agreement not to recommend a sentence.

What recourse does the government have when a defendant breaches a plea agreement? In *Ricketts v. Adamson* (1987), the defendant, charged with first-degree murder, agreed to testify against two other people in exchange for pleading guilty to second-degree murder. The defendant testified at the trials of his codefendants, but their convictions were reversed on appeal and remanded for retrial. He refused to testify against them a second time. The government considered his refusal a breach of the plea agreement and charged him with first-degree murder. He was convicted and sentenced to death. The Supreme Court ruled the defendant could be tried without violating the double jeopardy clause because he had not fulfilled the terms of his plea agreement.

SUMMARY

For a large percentage of defendants the sentencing process is as important if not more important than the guilt or innocence phase of their case. Perhaps they have pleaded guilty. As we have seen, the majority of persons accused of committing a crime elect not to go to trial because they plead guilty. Perhaps they decide to go to trial but anticipate the real probability of a guilty verdict. What is sometimes an afterthought to a public that is focused on issues of guilt or innocence is often the most significant matter to the person actually charged with a crime. After the plea or after the verdict comes the decision that will determine whether they serve their time behind bars or in the community. If they are sentenced to prison, the decision will determine how long they will be incarcerated.

Disputes about what kind of sentencing laws best protect society and are fair to offenders raise critical issues. During the past several decades the state and federal governments have moved toward a more determinate sentencing model. That shift has had a tremendous impact on the criminal justice system. It has also had a tremendous impact on the lives of thousands of offenders and their families. Sentencing laws will be in a state of flux for some time as states struggle with the complex challenge of devising smart and safe ways to punish people who break the law. Compounding the struggle will be cases like *Apprendi v. New Jersey* (2000), *Blakely v. Washington* (2004) and *United States v. Booker* (2005) that attempt to make sure that sentencing statutes in the age of "get tough" do not violate the Constitution. On the other hand, cases like *Lockyer v. Andrade* (2003) and *Ewing v. California* (2003) give states significant leeway to experiment with sentencing laws.

Disputes about what rights convicted offenders should have during the penalty phase of their cases are also critical. The right to assistance from counsel and a judge's right to rely on out-of-court evidence when making sentencing choices are constitutional decisions that have real consequences to convicted offenders. Cases about plea-bargaining are obviously significant given the large percentage of guilty pleas entered every day in courtrooms all over the United States.

Sentencing is where it all begins, or ends – depending on your perspective.

The Death Sentencing Process

Death sentences are different than other types of punishment and so is the law that governs the death sentencing process. In *Gregg v. Georgia* (1976), the Supreme Court held that the death penalty for murder does not violate the cruel and unusual punishment clause, as long as the judge and/or jury is allowed to consider the aggravating and mitigating circumstances in making the death sentence decision and there is a review procedure to make certain the penalty was appropriate. The judge or jury making the decision must be guided in the exercise of their discretion by laws that require they be given relevant information, which is best done in a bifurcated process, meaning a separate sentencing hearing should be conducted after a defendant is found guilty of the capital crime.

The types of aggravating factors that apply in death penalty cases include: the defendant's prior criminal history and whether the homicide was a felony murder, involved the murder of more than one person, a police officer or other public official, was heinous or included torture, was a killing to avoid an arrest or an escape from custody. The mitigating factors can include the defendant's age or emotional and mental disturbance, lack of prior criminal history, and whether the defendant was a significant participant in the homicide. The Supreme Court has rendered many decisions that address the use of aggravating and mitigating circumstances – what circumstances are appropriate, how they should be weighted, whether the defendant's attorney is ineffective for failing to present mitigating evidence, and whether the judge or jury can consider circumstances not included in the statute. The law in this area is quite complex. In *Woodson v. North Carolina* (1976), the Court ruled that states cannot authorize the mandatory imposition of the death penalty for certain types of murder. Decisions to impose a death sentence must be based on the particular circumstances of the crime and the defendant who committed it.

In death penalty cases, the majority of jurisdictions require the jury to assess death, although there are a few in which the jury's decision is a recommendation to the trial judge who has the ultimate authority. The Supreme Court has ruled that in those few jurisdictions the Eighth Amendment does not require the judge to accept a jury's recommendation that a defendant in a capital case be sentenced to life (*Spaziano v. Florida* (1984)), nor does the Constitution require a state to define the weight a sentencing judge must give to a jury's advisory verdict in a death penalty case. (*Harris v. Alabama* (1995)).

Can death be imposed for any other crime than murder? In 1977, the Supreme Court ruled in *Coker v. Georgia* that the death penalty for the rape of an adult woman was grossly disproportionate to the crime and excessive under the Eighth Amendment. In reaching its decision, the Court noted that few states permitted death to be imposed for the crime of rape and, even in those states, few death sentences were being imposed for rape. In *Kennedy v. Louisiana* (2008), the Supreme Court struck down a Louisiana statute that allowed the death penalty to be imposed for the sexual assault of a child. Patrick Kennedy was sentenced to death for raping his step-daughter. The Court ruled that under the Eighth Amendment death is not a proportional punishment for the crime of child rape.

DISCUSSION QUESTIONS

1. Explain the differences between determinate and indeterminate sentencing and identify the forces that have moved the U.S. toward determinate sentencing during the last several decades.

2. Identify the different approaches jurisdictions have taken to create more determinate sentencing polices and practices.

3. Why is the right to counsel important even during the sentencing phase of a case? Why is counsel important even when a defendant pleads guilty?

4. Explain the legal issue that began with the Supreme Court's decision in *Apprendi v. New Jersey* (2000) and culminated most recently in *United States v. Booker* (2005).

5. How extensive are a defendant's rights when he or she enters a guilty plea?

SUGGESTED READINGS AND REFERENCES

Blumstein, Alfred et al. (1983). "Research on Sentencing: The Search for Reform." Washington, D.C. National Academy Press.

DuRose, Matthew R. and Patrick A. Langan (2001). "State Court Sentencing of Convicted Felons 1998." Washington, D. C.: Bureau of Justice Statistics.

Kittrie, N., Elyce H. Zenoff, and Vincent A. Eng (2002). *Sentencing, Sanctions, and Corrections: Federal and State Law, Policy, and Practice* (2d ed.). New York: Foundation Press.

Lubitz, Robin L. and Thomas W. Ross (2001). "Sentencing Guidelines: Reflections on the Future." Washington, D.C.: National Institute of Justice/ Office of Justice Programs.

Merritt, Nancy, Terry Fain, and Susan Turner (2003). "Oregon's Measure 11 Sentencing Reform: Implementation and System Impact: Report Prepared for the National Institute of Justice," Santa Monica, CA, RAND Corporation.

Sabol, William J., Katherine Rosich, Kamala Mallik Kane, David P. Kirk, and Glenn Dubin (2002). "The Influences of Truth-in-Sentencing Reforms on Changes in States' Sentencing Practices and Prison Populations." Washington, D.C.: Urban Institute Justice Policy Center.

Schiraldi, Vincent, Jason Colburn, and Eric Lotke (2004). "Three Strikes and You're Out: An Examination of the Impact of 10 years after Their Enhancement." Washington, D.C.: Justice Policy Institute.

Tonry, Michael (1999). "The Fragmentation of Sentencing and Corrections in America." Washington, D.C.: National Institute of Justice/Office of Justice Programs.

CHAPTER 3:

First Amendment Rights of Access to the Courts and Free Expression

INTRODUCTION

The need and desire to communicate do not end when a person is incarcerated. Maintaining communications with friends and family is important for offenders. Prisoners need emotional support. Many of them worry about remaining connected with spouses, parents, children, and friends. Prisoners also communicate with government officials - Governors, legislators, the President of the United States, and heads of government agencies and departments. They write letters to newspapers, magazines, and television reporters. They submit articles for publication. Sometimes they are interviewed by the print or television media. Simply put, prisoners communicate with a wide range of people and organizations. In prison, most communications with the outside world are accomplished through letter writing using the good, old-fashioned U.S. Postal Service. In some institutions, under certain conditions, prisoners can also communicate by telephone. Finally, prisoners can communicate face-to-face on visiting days.

There are a host of rules and regulations that govern when and how prisoners can communicate with people in the world outside of prison. There are also a host of different regulations that govern when and how prisoners communicate with their attorneys and the courts. Many prisoners appeal their convictions during their incarceration or file writs of habeas corpus, but they may also have other legal matters involving veterans' claims, workers' compensation claims, child custody or divorce proceedings. As is evident from the cases discussed in this textbook, prisoners file civil lawsuits against prison officials for alleged violations of their constitutional rights. They may still have business interests in the free world that require them to engage legal counsel. The rules that control communications with legal counsel are complex because the attorney-client privilege does not disappear just because the client is in prison. On the other hand, the prison environment where the communication takes place raises serious and important security issues that impact the privilege.

Complicating this discussion is the right of prisoners to access the courts. At first blush, guaranteeing the right to access the courts suggests guaranteeing the right of prisoners to file legal papers, communicate with counsel, or attend legal proceedings without interference from prison officials. Because many inmates no longer have a right to legal counsel in their criminal cases or are filing civil cases for which there is no constitutional right to counsel, it is very common for prisoners to proceed *pro se*, meaning they represent themselves. Acknowledging this fact and that prisoners are not free to take a trip to the local law library to do legal research, the Supreme Court has interpreted the right to access the courts rather expansively and, until recently (arguably), imposed an affirmative obligation on prison officials to provide access to meaningful legal resources.

Chapter 3 looks at the rights of prisoners to communicate with their attorneys and the courts and with all of the other "nonlegal" people in their lives, and addresses mail correspondence, telephone calls, and visiting. It discusses the mail that is sent by prisoners (outgoing mail) and the mail they receive (incoming mail). It also examines the Supreme Court decisions that try, sometimes confusingly, to delineate the right of prisoners to access the courts and the duties imposed on correctional institutions. The chapter covers a range of topics all related to prisoners' communications. Students need to keep in mind that courts analyze legal and nonlegal communications (whether by mail, telephone, or visits) differently under the Constitution. In addition, they need to understand that courts apply different legal standards to determine the constitutionality of regulations that impact incoming and outgoing nonlegal correspondence. The different standards applied in both these instances reflect the need to balance the constitutional rights of prisoners with the safety and security concerns that dominate the administration of a correctional facility.

ACCESS TO THE COURTS

Where in the federal Constitution is a right to access the courts? Such a right is not mentioned in the text of the original Constitution, in the Bill of Rights, or in any of the subsequent amendments! The First Amendment, however, grants to all citizens "the right to petition the government for a redress of grievances." The First Amendment is not the only constitutional provision that suggests there is such a right. Article I, section 9 of the Constitution protects our right to go to court to seek a writ of habeas corpus if we are unlawfully incarcerated. The right to due process of law, found in both the Fifth and Fourteenth Amendments, also supports the right to go to court to resolve legitimate complaints that involve violations of the law.

Before the prisoner litigation movement had successfully ended the "hands-off" era, the U.S. Supreme Court recognized the right of prisoners to gain access to the courts. Prisoners transact much of their legal business directly with the courts. It is quite likely they are representing themselves *pro se*. In 1941, the Court decided the case *Ex parte Hull*, which involved a prisoner in Michigan who had been prevented from filing legal papers. At that time, Michigan prison regulations required inmates to submit all of their legal documents to prison officials for screening. If the official felt the documents were in order, they would be passed on to a legal investigator, and then, only if the investigator deemed them "properly drawn," would they be forwarded to the appropriate destination. If the investigator determined the documents were not prepared according to court regulations, they were sent back to the prisoner. Michigan officials refused to mail Inmate Hull's petition for a writ of habeas corpus. Through his family, Hull was eventually able to file legal papers complaining about what had occurred. The Supreme Court ruled that the Michigan regulations were invalid and wrote, "the state and its officers may not abridge or impair petitioner's right to apply to a federal court for a writ of habeas corpus." The Court emphasized that only a court can determine if legal papers are properly prepared. In *Ex parte Hull* (1941) the Supreme Court specifically addressed prisoners filing writs of habeas corpus, however, courts have since recognized the right of prisoners to be free of interference from officials when filing direct appeals of their sentences and civil rights lawsuits challenging the conditions of their confinement.

Attorney-Client Communication

Being able to contact and communicate with an attorney is an important dimension of our right under the Constitution to access the court system. Although we have the right to represent ourselves in a court proceeding, in many cases the right of access is only meaningful if we are able to solicit the advice of trained legal counsel. For people living in the free world, communicating with your attorney is relatively easy. We make appointments and discuss our legal matters in a face-to-face confidential meeting in our attorney's office. We can speak with him or her by telephone or email in the same manner. We are able to assist our lawyer in preparing our case by helping to locate witnesses and documentary evidence. We can review the facts with our attorney as often as is necessary. All of our communications, both oral and written, are considered confidential under the doctrine of attorney-client confidentiality. Attorney-client confidentiality is an important principle of the American legal system. Lawyers are under an ethical obligation to keep communications with their clients completely confidential because strict confidentiality promotes open communications between an attorney and his or her client and allows an attorney to better represent a client and provide the best legal advice. Without confidentiality, some clients would refuse to share important information with their lawyer out of fear it would become public.

Prisoners enjoy little privacy in jail or prison because legitimate security concerns outweigh most of their privacy rights. Prisoners do not have privacy in their correspondence, both incoming and outgoing. As is explained in greater detail later in this chapter, officials have the right to read prisoners' mail. Why? Incoming mail may contain contraband that is illegal to possess in an institution, such as drugs. A prisoner may be corresponding with someone outside of prison about escape plans or plotting criminal activities. Does the loss of privacy include the correspondence prisoners have with their attorneys and their attorneys' staff? How do correctional institutions honor the attorney-client privilege and still address security concerns? Until prisoners started to challenge prison regulations in the courts in the 1970s, prison administrators generally treated legal mail the same way they treated nonlegal mail. The Supreme Court outlined the basic rules that control attorney and prisoner/client correspondence in *Wolff v. McDonnell* (1974), in which it evaluated the constitutionality of legal correspondence regulations used in the Nebraska state prison system. Nebraska did not allow correctional officers to read legal mail, including letters from attorneys and correspondence from the courts, but officers were permitted to open and inspect legal mail in the prisoners' presence. The regulation sought to balance attorney/client confidentiality with institutional security needs. Officers could make certain that there was no contraband hidden in the legal mail, but they were not permitted to read or even skim the contents of the correspondence. By requiring that legal mail must be opened in the prisoners' presence, prisoners could be assured that their confidentiality rights were not violated. The Eighth Circuit Court of Appeals ruled that legal mail could only be inspected by feel or with a fluoroscope, except in situations when officials had grounds to suspect the mail contained contraband. The Supreme Court, however, did not agree with the Eighth Circuit and instead upheld the constitutionality of the legal correspondence rules. The Supreme Court emphasized that Nebraska's rules prohibited officials from reading legal mail, which both protected the mail from censorship and assured prisoners their confidential communications remained private. The Court also upheld a Nebraska regulation that required correspondence from an attorney to be specially marked as originating from an attorney, including the attorney's name and address. The *Wolff v.McDonnell* decision has set the standard followed by prison systems nationwide. As in most areas of the law, after the *Wolff* case was decided, lower courts recognized the need for an exception to the basic rule. If prison officials can establish they have probable cause to suspect that the contents of specific legal correspondence includes discussion about matters that might threaten the security of the institution, officials are permitted to set aside the prisoner's confidentiality rights and read the mail. Written prison policies govern the procedures officials must follow before they can read legal correspondence.

Prisoners are also permitted to visit with their attorneys. According to the Supreme Court's decision in *Procunier v. Martinez* (1974), the right to legal visits includes visits with their attorney's legal staff—legal assistants, law school interns, and investigators. The attorney/client confidentiality privilege applies to those visits in the same way it does to correspondence. Correctional officers can be posted in the visiting areas to observe the visit and make certain there is no transfer of contraband, but they cannot stand close enough to the visitors to hear their conversations. Prisoners are not entitled to contact visits with legal counsel. Depending on the rules of the institution, some prisoners are only permitted to meet with their attorneys sitting opposite each other with a glass partition separating them.

What Constitutes the Right to Access the Courts?

Jailhouse Lawyers

What does access to the court system involve? As long as correctional officials do not interfere with legal mail going to and from courts or attorneys, have they met their constitutional obligations? In cases decided since *Ex parte Hull* (1941), the Supreme Court has addressed what access to the courts requires, beginning with cases involving prisoners appealing their convictions. In *Griffin v. Illinois* (1956), the Court held that States must provide trial records at no cost to inmates who could not afford them, and in *Burns v. Ohio* (1959) that indigent inmates are entitled to file appeals and habeas corpus petitions without payment of docket fees.

Not until 1969, however, did the Supreme Court decide the second landmark access to courts case since *In ex parte Hull* (1941). In *Johnson v. Avery* (1969), Johnson was a convicted rapist serving a life sentence who also functioned as a "writ-writer" or jailhouse lawyer. Prison regulations in Tennessee prohibited inmates from helping other inmates in preparing writs, and Johnson was disciplined for violating the regulation. Tennessee's prohibition was not unusual at the time. Jailhouse lawyers can use their special skills to gain undue power and influence over other prisoners. They can demand "payment" for their services. The only free legal service offered by the Tennessee state prison system to prisoners was notarization of their petitions. Sometimes prisoners were also allowed to examine the telephone books for attorney listings. Because indigent prisoners are not entitled under the Constitution to appointed counsel when they file petitions for writs of habeas corpus, they were virtually on their own in preparing and filing the necessary forms. The Supreme Court ruled that in the absence of a reasonable alternative to assist illiterate or poorly educated prisoners with their writs for post-conviction relief, a state may not enforce a regulation that absolutely bars prisoners from helping other prisoners with their legal work. In language that seems to enforce a constitutional right of prisoners to access the courts, Justice Douglas wrote in his concurring opinion:

> It is not unusual, then, in a subculture created by the criminal law, wherein prisoners exist as creatures of the law, that they should use the law to try to reclaim their previously enjoyed status in society. The upheavals occurring in the American social structure are reflected within the prison environment. Prisoners, having real or imagined grievances, cannot demonstrate in protest against them. The right peaceably to assemble is denied to them. The only avenue open to prisoners is taking their case to court.

The result is that prison officials must allow jailhouse lawyers to help other inmates or provide some sort of alternative legal assistance program. What did the Court mean when it wrote about alternative assistance programs? The Court observed that in some states public defenders are available to consult with prisoners about their writs of habeas corpus, while other states employ law students or invite volunteer attorneys through the state bar association. The Court refused to judge the value or viability of any particular alternative assistance program, only noting that their existence demonstrates alternatives exist if a state wants to pursue them. In states without alternative legal assistance, where jailhouse lawyers cannot be banned, officials can impose reasonable restrictions on the times and locations where prisoners can meet to discuss legal matters, including – and very significantly – officials can punish jailhouse lawyers who receive any type of compensation for their services. The right to regulate meeting times and locations and ban compensation are important tools to help officials limit the influence a jailhouse lawyer may enjoy (and potentially abuse) among fellow prisoners. The Court recognized the need to balance security concerns with the right of prisoners to have meaningful access to the courts. Importantly, in *Wolff v. McDonnell* (1974), the Supreme Court expanded its decision in *Johnson v. Avery* to include the right of jailhouse lawyers to assist other prisoners in preparing civil rights lawsuits. The Court acknowledged in *Wolff* that if prisoners, many of whom are illiterate or uneducated, are to have constitutional rights that can be protected by civil lawsuits, they need to be able to articulate those claims effectively.

Jailhouse lawyers were the focus of the Supreme Court's decision in *Shaw v. Murphy* (2001), which involved prison restrictions placed by the Montana State Prison on Murphy, an inmate law clerk. Murphy sent a letter to a maximum-security prisoner who was charged with assaulting a correctional officer, telling him he wanted to help him and advising him to plead not guilty. In his letter Murphy accused the correctional officer who was assaulted of homosexual advances. Murphy was charged with several disciplinary infractions and found guilty of insolence and interfering with a due process hearing. He filed a lawsuit alleging his First Amendment right to provide legal assistance was violated. The Supreme Court, however, refused to recognize that prisoners have a First Amendment right to provide legal assistance to other prisoners. Furthermore, the Court ruled that the constitutionality of the prison's restrictions on inmates providing legal assistance should be evaluated according to the four-part *Turner v. Safley* (1987) test, discussed in detail later in this chapter. The majority opinion emphasized the dangers that jailhouse lawyers can cause, including using legal correspondence to pass contraband and to communicate instructions about manufacturing weapons and distributing drugs. The Court opined that giving First Amendment protection to writ writers would undermine the ability of officials to address the complex problems of managing a prison.

Legal Resources

In 1977, the Supreme Court again expanded access to court rights, this time by imposing affirmative obligations on correctional officials to provide legal resources to prisoners. Whereas the cases *In ex parte Hull* (1941), *Johnson v. Avery* (1969), and *Wolff v. McDonnell* (1974) discussed things prison officials are prohibited from doing, in *Bounds v. Smith* (1977) the Supreme Court ruled that the right to access the courts requires prison officials to assist inmates in the preparation and filing of legal papers by providing them with law libraries or professional legal help. *Bounds* had a major impact on prisons and jails nationwide because correctional officials were forced, if they had not already done so, to devise systems to provide prisoners with either law libraries or professional legal assistance.

Bounds v. Smith (1977) was filed by prisoners in North Carolina who challenged the access to court program in that state's institutions. After considering the evidence, the District Court ruled that North Carolina did not have an adequate legal program to assist prisoners and ordered it to devise a plan to provide law libraries or help from legal professionals. In response, the state opened seven law libraries in several facilities throughout the state and provided prisoners with transportation to one of the libraries to work one full day, or longer if necessary, on their legal matters. The state also created a list of all the legal books, materials, and forms that would be made available in the libraries. The prisoners objected to the plan, arguing that a library should be available at every prison unit in the state and that legal counsel should also be made available. The District Court rejected the prisoners' objections and approved the state's plan, as did the appellate court.

The Supreme Court was called upon to consider the constitutionality of the North Carolina plan, which was originally devised under order from the District Court. North Carolina officials argued that its plan actually exceeded the Constitution's requirements because the only legal obligation was not to interfere with jailhouse lawyers giving advice to other inmates. The stage was set for the Court to determine how far the right to access the court system extends. Remember, prisoners do a great deal of their own legal work, putting them at a definite disadvantage in relation to their adversaries, who are most likely going to be represented by trained and licensed attorneys. They are not able take the day off and drive to the nearest law school or county law library to research their cases or locate the forms they need to complete. Also keep in mind that legal research and preparing legal documents can be tedious and time-consuming, especially for someone not trained in the law. From the other perspective, consider that law libraries are quite costly. Legal books are expensive and must be updated frequently to stay abreast of the most recent court decisions and changes in statutes. The Supreme Court ruled that the new North Carolina plan was constitutional and denied the prisoners' requests for more libraries and access to professionals. In that sense, the prisoners lost their case. But *Bounds* was less about the particular facts before the Supreme Court and more about trying to further define what is required to protect prisoners' right to access the courts. The Court wrote,

> We reject the State's claim that inmates are "ill-equipped to use" "the tools of the trade of the legal profession," making libraries useless in assuring meaningful access...We hold, therefore, that the fundamental constitutional right of access to the courts requires prison authorities to assist inmates in the preparation and filing of meaningful legal papers by providing prisoners with adequate law libraries or adequate legal assistance from persons trained in the law.

Just as in *Johnson v. Avery* (1969), the *Bounds* decision did not suggest what type or amount of professional legal assistance would be adequate to release officials from the obligation to provide access to law libraries. The Court mentioned that some states have trained prisoners to be legal assistants, used volunteer lawyers, or hired their own staff of attorneys to help prisoners, but left the issue open for local experimentation. Any plan, however, would have to provide adequate, meaningful assistance. After *Bounds* was decided, most correctional systems elected to provide law libraries, although many plans use alternatives to supplement libraries. Ultimately, law libraries provide more prisoners with the opportunity to access legal advice than other programs. It is difficult to provide adequate, ongoing, and consistent legal assistance to prisoners relying on volunteers or law students. Given the number of prisoners seeking legal counsel, it is also cost prohibitive to hire enough attorneys to do an adequate job. Although some correctional agencies train prisoners to be legal assistants, other agencies are not comfortable with that practice. An important part of the *Bounds v. Smith* case is the additional obligation the Supreme Court imposed on jail and prison authorities to provide indigent prisoners at state expense with the paper and writing instruments needed to draft legal documents and the stamps to mail them. Correctional officials have had to devise rules to make sure that these supplies get to only the prisoners who need them and are used for the intended purpose.

Bounds has generated many lawsuits with prisoners challenging different issues having to do with the adequacy of prison law libraries: the type and number of law books is insufficient; library schedules do not allow prisoners enough time to do their research; policies prohibit prisoners in administrative segregation to visit the library, forcing them to "borrow" a few books at a time for use in their cell; and libraries fail to meet the needs of illiterate prisoners or prisoners who do not speak and read English. There is significant variation in how the lower courts have decided these cases.

In 1996, the Court decided *Lewis v. Casey*, which resolved some (not all) of the legal issues that *Bounds* raised. In that case, prisoners in the Arizona Department of Corrections (ADOC) filed a class action lawsuit alleging First, Sixth, and Fourteenth Amendment violations because of inadequate law libraries, complaining that legal materials were not updated regularly, access to the library was generally insufficient but particularly for lockdown prisoners, the library staff was not trained, access to copy machines was inadequate, and non-English speaking and illiterate prisoners did not receive adequate assistance. The District Court found that the ADOC was in violation of the constitutional requirements outlined in *Bounds v. Smith* violation. The court appointed a special master to oversee extensive reforms and specified numerous changes that the Arizona Department of Corrections needed to make including create a course on videotape instructing prisoners about doing legal research. The court detailed the hours the library should be open, ruled that each prisoner is entitled to at least ten hours of access per week, and set minimum educational requirements for librarians. The District Court mandated ADOC provide direct legal assistance from attorneys or trained legal assistants for illiterate and non-English speaking prisoners and take special steps to train bilingual prisoners to be legal assistants. Finally, the court ordered that lockdown prisoners be given regular access to the library except on an individual basis when officials can demonstrate legitimate security or safety concerns. The Ninth Circuit Court of Appeals affirmed the District Court's judgment.

On appeal to the Supreme Court, ADOC maintained that before a court can mandate the sweeping system-wide relief that was ordered against it, prisoners must establish through evidence that they suffered widespread harm because the prisons' library facilities or legal assistance program was inadequate. In addition, in order for an individual prisoner to establish that the prison violated the requirements set forth in *Bounds*, the prisoner must establish through evidence that the inadequacies caused him or her direct harm. What kind of harm? Because of inadequate legal assistance perhaps the prisoner missed a deadline for filing legal papers or was unable to thoroughly research the issues which led to a poorly argued legal claim which caused his case to be dismissed. Obviously the stakes were high in this case for the Arizona Department of Corrections, but the legal issue involved was relevant for every correctional agency's access to court program.

Justice Scalia wrote the Court's majority opinion, which adopted the ADOC's legal analysis:

> Because *Bounds* did not create an abstract, free-standing right to a law library or legal assistance, an inmate cannot establish relevant actual injury simply by establishing that his prison's law library or legal assistance program is sub-par in some theoretical sense. That would be the precise analogue of the healthy inmate claiming constitutional violation because of the inadequacy of the prison infirmary. Insofar as the right vindicated by *Bounds* is concerned, "meaningful access to the courts is the touchstone," *Bounds*, 430 U.S., at 823 (internal quotation marks omitted) and the inmate therefore must go one step further and demonstrate that the alleged shortcomings in the library or legal assistance program hindered his efforts to pursue a legal claim.

According to majority opinion, the District Court had identified only two instances of actual injury. An illiterate prisoner and non-English speaking prisoner had inadequate legal assistance, prepared their own legal papers and the courts dismissed their lawsuits. Other than these two cases, the Court concluded there was no evidence that the violation was system-wide and impacted any other prisoners. The Supreme Court let it be known in *Lewis v. Casey* (1996) that federal judges must "accord adequate deference to the judgment of prison authorities." Although the Court has emphasized in many cases that judges need to defer to the expertise and experience of correctional officials, in *Lewis v. Casey*, the Court's majority opinion described the District Court's order, which was upheld by Court of Appeals as, "inordinately – indeed, wildly – intrusive." In his concurring opinion, Justice Thomas chastised the lower federal courts for trying to manage the reform of entire institutions without regard for the limits on judicial authority. Justice Thomas warned federal judges that the Constitution does not authorize them to make the policy decisions that state officials are entitled and qualified to make.

Justice Scalia also emphasized in the majority opinion that *Bounds* did not guarantee that prisoners would have "the wherewithal to transform themselves into litigating engines capable of filing everything from shareholder derivative actions to slip and fall claims." They require only the tools needed to file direct and collateral appeals of their sentences or lawsuits that challenge the constitutionality of prison and jail conditions.

Lewis v. Casey modified the *Bounds v. Smith* decision of twenty years earlier. The Court stated that *Bounds* did not create a prisoner's abstract right to use a law library. Instead, in order to establish a violation of his or her access to court rights, a prisoner must show that deficiencies in a prison's legal assistance program (which might include a library) adversely impacted their attempts to pursue a legal claim. It is not enough that prisoners allege a prison does not provide a law library or that a library is poorly maintained or has insufficient materials. Prisoners must have evidence of the injuries they suffered because there was no library access or the library was inadequate. The Court noted that some of the statements in the *Bounds* decision went beyond what the Court had previously recognized as a prisoner's right to access the courts. Several statements in *Bounds* suggested that prison officials must enable a prisoner to discover grievances and litigate them effectively. The Court wrote, "These elaborations upon the right of access to courts have no precedent in our pre-*Bounds* cases, and we now disclaim them."

Not only must an inmate prove he was harmed by a state's inadequate access to court program, according to *Lewis*, there is no such thing as a "free-standing right to a law library or legal assistance." Does this mean prison systems can close down libraries and legal assistance programs in operation since *Bounds v. Smith* was decided in 1977? Realistically, the lack of a legal assistance program or an inadequate program, will adversely impact the ability of prisoners to engage in the kind of research and preparation that filing a solid legal claim requires. Very soon, prisoners would have evidence to establish they were harmed, which is what *Lewis v. Casey* requires. Even after *Lewis*, correctional systems are obligated to provide prisoners access to some form of adequate legal assistance; however, those programs need not be so extensive that they "guarantee inmates the wherewithal to transform themselves into litigating engines capable of filing everything from shareholder derivative actions to slip-and-fall claims." Lynn Branham (2002) reports that since the *Lewis* decision, several prison systems have eliminated their law libraries and replaced them with legal assistants to help prisoners. Whatever approach a prison system adopts, assistance programs and libraries should be adequate enough to help prisoners prepare the documents needed to attack their sentence or challenge the conditions of their confinement.

NONLEGAL CORRESPONDENCE

Courts have given major consideration to the right of prisoners to free speech, including personal correspondence, telephone privileges, and communicating with the media. In a series of important decisions, the courts have concluded that prisoners' right to free speech can be restricted as long as the restrictions are reasonably related to legitimate penological interest, such as prison security and safety. For example, security issues such as the need to prevent the smuggling of contraband into or out of an institution and escape attempts justify inspecting and reading prisoner correspondence.

Procunier v. Martinez (1974) was one of the earliest Supreme Court cases concerning mail censorship in prison. In this case, the California Department of Corrections allowed censorship of prisoner mail. Prison regulations forbade inmate correspondence that "unduly complain[ed]," "magnif[ied] grievances," "express[ed] inflammatory political, racial, religious or other views or beliefs," or contained matter deemed "defamatory" or "otherwise inappropriate." California's regulations were not unusual. It was a common practice in America's jails and prisons, often approved in written regulations, for officials to read and censor prisoner mail for any variety of reasons. Censorship could include redacting certain portions of correspondence or denying delivery all together. In a class action lawsuit, California prisoners alleged that these regulations violated their rights under the First and Fourteenth Amendments. The District Court agreed with the prisoners, as did the Supreme Court on appeal. In a somewhat surprising opinion, the Supreme Court noted the Court was not going to decide the extent to which the censorship regulations violated prisoners' First Amendment rights. Instead, the Court emphasized that the constitutional problems with mail censorship went beyond prisoners' rights. The rights of individuals communicating with prisoners were adversely impacted. They were not permitted the right to read all of their loved one's communications. The Court concluded that censoring prisoner mail restricts the First and Fourteenth Amendment rights of those who are not prisoners.

After explaining that its' decision was founded on the rights of outside correspondents, the Court determined the proper standard for reviewing prison restrictions on prisoner correspondence. The Court adopted what is generally described as a "strict scrutiny" standard of review that requires the government to establish first through evidence (and not mere assertions) that the challenged regulations are necessary in order to help officials meet "substantial governmental interests of security, order, and rehabilitation." That interest must not be related to the desire to suppress free speech, meaning that officials can no longer censor mail merely because it offends them, criticizes them, or contains factual inaccuracies. The second part of the standard for review requires that whatever restrictions officials impose must be no greater than what is essential to protect the government's substantial interest. In other words, the restrictions cannot be too sweeping or broad. Under this two-pronged standard, California's regulations were deemed "far broader than any legitimate interest of penal administration demands...." Finally, the Court ruled that a decision to censor must be accompanied with minimal due process protections. Both the prisoner and the individual he or she was corresponding with must be notified in writing that a letter has been censored, and they must be given a reasonable opportunity to protest. Someone who was not originally involved in disapproving the correspondence should decide the protest.

Procunier v. Martinez (1974) only addressed mail censorship of correspondence between prisoners and nonprisoners. Thirteen years later, in *Turner v. Safley* (1987), the Supreme Court addressed inmate-to-inmate correspondence. In *Turner*, prisoners at the Renz Correctional Facility in Missouri, a coed prison facility, challenged a prison regulation that permitted correspondence between immediate family members who were prisoners at different institutions and between prisoners concerning legal matters, but allowed prisoners to correspond with other prisoners only if each inmate's classification/treatment team considered it to be in the best interests of both parties. The Supreme Court, in one of the most important decisions on prisoners' rights, ruled that Missouri's restrictions on inmate-to-inmate correspondence were constitutional. *Turner v. Safley* (1989) is the landmark case for establishing standards that other courts must use when they evaluate the constitutionality of prison and jail regulations that restrict prisoners' rights. In *Turner*, the Supreme Court stated that prison regulations that impinge on inmates' constitutional rights do not violate the Constitution if the regulations are "reasonably related to legitimate penological interests." The Court enumerated four factors for other courts to use when deciding if a regulation is so related:

1. Whether there is a valid rational connection between the prison regulation and the legitimate governmental interest that has been put forward to justify it;

2. Whether there are alternative means of exercising rights that remain open to the prisoners;

3. The impact that accommodating the asserted constitutional rights will have on officers, other prisoners, and on the allocation of prison resources generally; and

4. The absence of alternatives to the challenged regulation as evidence of the reasonableness of the regulation

Missouri officials instituted the ban on inmate-to-inmate correspondence because they were worried about the growth of prison gangs and prisoners using the mails to plan criminal activities. Officials split up the gangs by transferring gang members to different institutions and then restricting their right to correspond by mail. The Supreme Court applied the four-part test to the regulation and determined that: 1) there was a rational connection between the regulation and the government's interest in reducing the potential for prison violence; 2) prisoners retained the right to communicate with other groups of people; 3) to allow inmate-to-inmate correspondence would impact the liberty and security of other prisoners and the staff; and 4) there was no easy alternative to the regulation. Using the four factors, the Court ruled the regulation did not violate the Constitution – even though it impinged on the First Amendment rights of prisoners.

Notice that the Supreme Court did not rely on *Procunier v. Martinez* (1979) to help it evaluate the constitutionality of the Missouri mail restrictions. In the earlier *Procunier* case, the Court required the government to show a compelling interest for its regulation and establish there were no less restrictive measures that could have addressed the government's concerns. Instead, the *Turner* Court devised a four-part test that is far less strict on the government. *Turner* dealt with inmate-to-inmate correspondence, while the regulations at issue in *Procunier v. Martinez* involved prisoner correspondence with people outside of prison. Did the Supreme Court analyze the two cases so differently because the facts were different? The *Turner* Court refused to adopt the *Procunier v. Martinez* approach because it seemed to require a "least restrictive alternative" test that failed to give officials the opportunity to use their discretion to meet legitimate prison needs. Compared to the early prisoner rights cases decided in the 1960s and 1970s, it was clear with the *Turner* decision in 1987, that courts were moving in the direction of granting greater deference to the judgment of prison officials in matters related to institutional safety and security.

In *Thornburgh v. Abbott* (1989), the Court heard a case challenging Federal Bureau of Prison regulations that allowed federal prisoners to receive publications but authorized officials to reject those found to be detrimental to institutional security. The regulations prohibited officials from rejecting publications based solely on their religious, political, philosophical, social, or sexual content, or because they were unpopular or repugnant. Furthermore, officials were not permitted to establish a list of excluded publications. Each issue had to be reviewed separately. Prisoners and a group of publishers claimed the Bureau of Prison regulations violated their First Amendment rights under *Procunier v. Martinez* and specifically challenged the prison's exclusion of 46 different publications. The District Court upheld the regulations and did not address the 46 excluded publications, giving deference to the prison administrators' use of discretion. The Court of Appeals, however, followed *Procunier*, and ruled the regulations were invalid and remanded the case to the District Court to decide the constitutionality of the 46 excluded publications. The Department of Justice and the Bureau of Prisons appealed, and the Supreme Court granted certiorari in order to determine the appropriate standard for courts to use to review the regulations that were under challenge.

The Supreme Court agreed that the prisoners and the publishers had First Amendment rights in sending and receiving publications. The Court, however, refused to look to *Procunier v. Martinez* as legal precedent for its decision in this case. Instead, the Court held that the proper standard of review was the four-part standard set forth in *Turner v. Safley* (1987). Under the *Turner* test, the Court found the regulations were valid. The Court noted that the Bureau's regulations permitted prisoners to receive many other publications, leaving other forms of expression still open to them. The Court remanded the case back to the District Court for a case-by-case review of the validity of the regulations as applied to each of the 46 publications.

Of course the Supreme Court had to explain why it relied on *Turner v. Safley* instead of *Procunier v. Martinez* as precedent for how it should analyze the facts. Unlike *Turner*, the prisoners in the Federal Bureau of Prisons challenged a regulation that restricted their right to receive mail from outside of prison as opposed to their right to correspond with other prisoners. The facts of their case seemed more similar to the facts in *Procunier v. Martinez* than those in *Turner*. The Court, however, explained that it relied on *Turner* because the strict scrutiny standard applied in *Procunier v. Martinez* was not appropriate for evaluating regulations that are concerned with maintaining institutional order and security. As it did in *Turner v. Safley*, the Court expressed concern that the *Procunier v. Martinez* case could be interpreted to require courts to decide if officials should have used a least restrictive alternative to achieve their goal. Wrote the Court,

> Certainly, *Martinez* required a close fit between the challenged regulation and the interest it purported to serve. But a careful reading of *Martinez* suggests that our rejection of the regulation at issue resulted not from a least restrictive means requirement, but from our recognition that the regulated activity centrally at issue in that case – outgoing personal correspondence from prisoners- did not, by its very nature, pose a serious threat to prison order and security....

Furthermore, we acknowledge today that the logic of our analyses in *Martinez* and *Turner* requires that *Martinez* be limited to regulations concerning outgoing correspondence. As we have observed, outgoing correspondence was the central focus of our opinion in *Martinez*. The implications of outgoing correspondence for prison security are of a categorically lesser magnitude than the implications of incoming materials.

The Court did not overturn *Procunier v. Martinez*, but it limited its' holding to outgoing correspondence, mail that prisoners send from prison. In other words, the constitutionality of regulations that deal with outgoing mail must be evaluated under the strict scrutiny standard. Regulations, however, that deal with incoming mail must be evaluated under the four-part *Turner* standard. Why the difference? According to the Supreme Court, incoming mail has more potential than outgoing mail to create security and order problems inside a prison and a different standard is necessary. Officials will find it much easier to prevail under the *Turner* standard because it is purposely designed to allow greater deference (in comparison with the strict scrutiny test) to the judgment of prison officials and their use of discretion. *Thornburgh v. Abbott* was not a unanimous decision and reflects some of the controversy regarding protecting inmates' rights versus supporting prison officials. Three Justices dissented in this case and expressed their belief that the *Turner* standard provided inadequate protection for prisoners' First Amendment rights.

Visiting

One way that prisoners can visit with others is through telephone communications. Although the Supreme Court has not addressed this question, lower courts have determined that prisoners have a First Amendment right to telephone access; however, such access is subject to reasonable restrictions that are related to a legitimate security interests. The restrictions generally include rules that permit prisoners to make outgoing collect calls, with no right to receive incoming calls. Correctional institutions enter into contracts with telephone companies to help regulate the length of outgoing calls. The companies also set rates for the cost of telephone calls. Officials restrict the number of calls a prisoner can make over a certain time period. Officials monitor the telephone conversations, usually by taping them. Taped calls to legal counsel remain privileged communications and cannot be used by officials or in a courtroom. Pretrial jail detainees generally have greater access to telephone calls than prison inmates because they are immediate access to court needs.

Other than with legal counsel, do prisoners have a constitutional right to have face-to-face contact with visitors from outside the institution? Mail correspondence and telephone calls are helpful, but face-to-face visits can be critical for prisoners and their families. Complicating the situation is that prisons are often located in rural areas and transportation to a facility can be cost prohibitive for families traveling from urban communities who often rely on public transportation. Officials are not obligated to assign prisoners to institutions that are located near their homes. Because visiting raises legitimate security concerns, it is carefully regulated by a set of detailed rules that, among other things, schedule the days and times that prisoners can meet with their visitors. Visitors are prohibited from bringing gifts to prisoners. Prisoners can only visit with people whose names they have included on a visiting list, and visitors must present identification to officials when they arrive for a visit. Visitors are not permitted to visit if they are wearing revealing clothing. Prisoners in the highest security classifications may be placed in handcuffs or leg chains during a visit. Violations of a visiting rule by a prisoner or a visitor may result in a visit being terminated. Some visits occur in special areas with the prisoner seated on one side of a desk with a glass divider and the visitors on the other side, communicating through an opening in the glass or over a telephone. Depending on prison rules, some prisoners are permitted to have contact visits. Restrictions are then placed on how much contact can occur during a contact visit, including when and how often prisoners can kiss, embrace, or hold hands with their visitors. Some states have special visiting arrangements that allow prisoners to visit with their children in play area with relaxed contact rules. All visiting, both contact and noncontact, is supervised by correctional officers and camera surveillance. Very few states allow prisoners to have conjugal visits.

In *Kentucky v. Thompson* (1989), The Kentucky Department of Corrections had a policy that contained a list of reasons why certain visitors could be banned from visiting prison inmates. The regulation was written in such a way that the list was not exhaustive and officials were not required to ban such persons, they had the option to do so. A mother of an inmate was denied a visit with her son at the Kentucky State Penitentiary for six months because she brought a person with her on a visit who previously had been barred for smuggling contraband. Another prisoner's mother and friend were also denied visitation after the prisoner they had just visited was found with contraband. In both cases, the visits were suspended without a hearing. The prisoners argued the regulations required prisoners receive a due process hearing before visitation privileges could be suspended because they possessed a state created liberty interest in open visitation. (Refer to the discussion about state created liberty interests in Chapter 7). The Supreme Court decided differently. After examining the wording of the regulations, the Court concluded instead that because the list of visitors who could be banned was nonexhaustive and officials had discretion to impose a ban, meaning the ban was not automatically mandated by the regulations, prisoners did not have a liberty interest that needed due process protection. Under the Kentucky policy, visits could be banned without affording prisoners the opportunity to have a hearing.

In *Block v. Rutherford* (1984), also discussed in Chapter 9, the Court held that prohibiting contact visits to pretrial detainees is not excessive given the security risks involved. Contact visits increase the risk of drugs, weapons, and other contraband making their way into the jail. Although the case did not address regulations that ban contact visits for convicted offenders in state and federal prisons, it is obvious the Court indicated once again that prison authorities have a significant amount of discretion in fashioning regulations that govern visiting prisoners, including the discretion to impose significant restrictions on visiting.

In *Overton v. Bazzetta* (2003), the Supreme Court ruled on the constitutionality of a regulation enacted by the Michigan Department of Corrections. The department was concerned about security problems caused by a large increase in the number of persons visiting prisoners, which had put a significant strain on limited prison resources. Officers were finding it difficult to maintain order during visiting periods and were especially concerned about the potential for drug smuggling and trafficking. At the same time, substance abuse among prisoners was on the rise. Officials were also concerned about the large number of children visiting prisoners and believed they were at risk of seeing and hearing harmful things during visits and child visitors required additional supervision. The Michigan department revised its visiting rules to limit the number of visitors a prisoner could receive. Except for clergy and attorneys, visitors had to be placed on an approved visitors list. The list could include an unlimited number of family members and ten other individuals. Children under the age of eighteen could be on the list only if they were the children, stepchildren, grandchildren, or siblings of the prisoner. If a prisoner's parental rights had been terminated, the child was not permitted to visit. Former prisoners could not be included on the list unless they were members of the prisoner's immediate family and the warden granted prior approval. Prisoners who committed multiple substance-abuse prison violations were not permitted to receive visitors except for clergy and attorneys. A prisoner so restricted could apply to have his or her visiting privileges reinstated after two years. Prisoners, their friends, and family members claimed the new regulations violated their First, Eighth, and Fourteenth Amendments and filed a class action lawsuit. The alleged First Amendment violation was based on the right to association.

Both the District Court and the Court of Appeals ruled the regulations were invalid. The Supreme Court, however, disagreed. Wrote the Court:

> We do not hold, and we do not imply, that any right to intimate association is altogether terminated by incarceration or is always irrelevant to claims made by prisoners. We need not attempt to explore or define the asserted right of association at any length or determine the extent to which it survives incarceration because the challenged regulations bear a rational relation to legitimate penological interests. This suffices to sustain the regulation in question.

The Court applied the four-part test it announced in *Turner v. Safley* (1987) to determine the constitutionality of the Michigan regulations. Using the *Turner* test, the Court concluded the regulations restricting child visitors and requiring children who visit to be accompanied by a family member or guardian are reasonably related to the need to maintain internal security and protect children from harm. Excluding visits from minor nieces and nephews and children to whom parental rights have been terminated is also a reasonable means to reduce the growing number of child visitors. Prohibiting visits from former prisoners is a reasonable response to security concerns. Although the restriction is severe, banning visits for prisoners with multiple substance-abuse violations serves the legitimate goal of reducing drug and alcohol use inside the prisons. The Court described the regulation as a proper management technique that induces prisoners to comply with the rules because they do not want to lose their visiting privileges.

The Court concluded that prisoners have alternative means to exercise their constitutional rights. They can communicate with people who are not permitted to visit by sending messages through those who can visit, and they are able to communicate by letter and telephone. Although these are not ideal alternatives, they are available. Accommodating the prisoners' demands would require prison officials to reallocate financial resources and would impair their ability to provide a secure and safe prison environment.

In addition to the First Amendment claim, prisoners argued that the two-year restriction on visits for prisoners with multiple substance abuse violations amounted to cruel and unusual punishment in violation of the Eighth Amendment. In rejecting their argument, the Court commented:

> The restriction undoubtedly makes the prisoner's confinement more difficult to bear. But it does not, in the circumstances of this case, fall below the standards mandated by the Eighth Amendment. Much of what we have said already about the withdrawal of privileges that incarceration is expected to bring applies here as well. Michigan, like many other States, uses withdrawal of visitation privileges for a limited period as a regular means of effecting prison discipline. This is not a dramatic departure from accepted standards for conditions of confinement. Nor does the regulation create inhumane prison conditions, deprive inmates of basic necessities or fail to protect their health or safety. Not does it involve the infliction of pain or injury, or deliberate indifference to the risk that it might occur. If the withdrawal of all visitation privileges were permanent or for a much longer period, or if it were applied in an arbitrary manner to a particular inmate, the case would present different considerations.

The *Overton v. Bazetta* decision ended speculation that prison officials could not restrict prisoners' visiting privileges. Restrictions are allowed as long as they are reasonably related to legitimate security and safety concerns. Prisoners do not have a constitutional right to visitation.

Communicating with the Media

In three landmark cases the Supreme Court addressed prison regulations that restrict media access to prisoners. The Court found in all three cases that First Amendment restrictions on prisoners and the media can be justified for security reasons. Specifically, prisoners' access to the press can be restricted as long as prisoners have alternative means of communication, while the media enjoys no special access to prisons or jails greater than the access available to the general public.

In *Pell v. Procunier* (1974), four California prisoners and three professional journalists challenged the constitutionality of a prison regulation that prohibited media interviews with specific prisoners, although the press was allowed interviews with random prisoners. The regulation was passed after a violent prison episode that prison authorities believed was due in part to the former practice of free face-to-face prisoner-press interviews, resulting in a small group of inmates gaining notoriety and influence in the institution. The District Court held that the regulation impermissibly infringed on prisoners' First Amendment rights but dismissed the journalists' claims because the journalists were permitted to enter prisons and interview prisoners randomly. Prison officials appealed the part of the decision that upheld prisoners' First Amendment rights, and the journalists appealed the part that found the journalists' rights were not violated. The Supreme Court decided that regulations banning media-prisoner interviews do not violate prisoners' free speech protections, as long as they have other means of communication and the ban is applied in a neutral fashion, not based on the content of the speech. For example, if prisoners can correspond by mail with other persons, including the media, and if they are allowed visits with family, clergy, attorneys, and friends, they continue to enjoy personal contact and communication with the press and public. The Court noted the importance of personal contacts in assisting rehabilitation but also noted that it is important for prison officials to manage visiting so that it does not interfere with the security of the institution. Concerning the journalists' appeal, the Court wrote, "[T]he First Amendment does not guarantee the press a constitutional right of special access to information not available to the public generally."

In *Saxbe v. Washington Post* (1974), the Court upheld a similar Federal Bureau of Prisons regulation that banned press interviews with individual prisoners. In the Bureau's experience, prisoners who are chosen by the press for individual interviews often develop notoriety inside the institution, especially if they are the subject of repeated interviews. Their notoriety can lead to disciplinary problems if they develop a special status inside the institution. Inmates and even prison officials may be tempted to treat the prisoner differently than other prisoners. The Bureau justified its ban as necessary in order to prevent a prisoner from gaining this type of power or influence.

The third case addressing media access to prisons and jails is *Houchins v. KQED Inc.* (1978). In 1975, KQED, a San Francisco broadcasting company, was denied permission to inspect and photograph sections of a county jail. KQED had reported the suicide of a prisoner being held in a county jail. The broadcast included a jail psychiatrist's statement that conditions in the jail caused his patient-prisoners to become ill. One particular section of the jail was described as the scene of rapes, beatings, and adverse physical conditions. KQED reported that Sheriff Houchins denied the psychiatrist's allegation. After being denied access to the county jail, the broadcasting company and two branches of the NAACP filed a lawsuit against the sheriff, alleging that he had violated the media's First Amendment rights. KQED and the NAACP claimed that providing the media with access to information about jail and prison conditions is the most effective way to keep the public informed. The Supreme Court ruled that the First Amendment grants no special right of access to the press to government-controlled sources of information. The Court noted that the media and NAACP still possessed First Amendment rights to receive uncensored letters from prisoners and were free to interview legal counsel for prisoners, former prisoners, prison visitors, public officials, and institutional personnel. Chief Justice Burger stated in a footnote in the Court's opinion that "Inmates in jails, prisons, or mental institutions retain certain fundamental rights of privacy; they are not like animals in a zoo to be filmed and photographed at will by the public or by media reporters, however 'educational' the process may be for others".

The *Pell v. Procunier* and *Saxbe v. Washington* decisions have served as precedent for later courts faced with the interesting issue of televised executions. Because so many of the victims of the Oklahoma City bombings could not travel to the Indiana federal penitentiary to witness Timothy McVeigh's execution in 1997, U. S. Attorney General Ashcroft approved a closed circuit transmission of the execution for authorized survivors of the bombing and family members of those who were murdered. Entertainment Network, Inc. (ENI) requested permission to record and broadcast the execution over the Internet or for access to the live audiovisual transmission. The Bureau of Prisons denied ENI's request based on a federal regulation that prohibited the visual or audio recording of an execution. ENI filed a lawsuit in an Indiana federal court alleging the regulation violated the First Amendment because the regulation was not content neutral, meaning that the government was attempting to censor the content of communication.

The District Court denied ENI's request and upheld the regulation's constitutionality. The court relied on several cases to reach its decision, primarily on *Garrett v. Estelle*, 556 F.2d 1274 (5th Cir. 1977) in which the Fifth Circuit denied a request from a television news reporter to televise the first execution in Texas after the death penalty was reintroduced. State law prohibited the transmission and Garrett filed his lawsuit challenging the law under the First Amendment. The Fifth Circuit upheld the Texas ban, relying on the Supreme Court decisions in *Pell v. Procunier* and *Saxbe v. Washington*, which held that the press enjoys no greater First Amendment protections to access in prisons beyond that which is provided to the general public. The government does not have to give the press access to information that it is not required to give to the public. The Fifth Circuit decided that the Texas law was content neutral. The Supreme Court has not yet considered a case that has raised the question of televised executions.

SUMMARY

The First Amendment has played a major role in prisoners' civil rights litigation. In addition to protecting prisoners' freedom of religious expression, it protects – along with the due process clause – the right of prisoners to access the court system and their right to communicate with the world outside of the prison walls. The Supreme Court has had to reconcile a prisoners' right to rely on the confidentiality of communications with legal counsel and legitimate security concerns. The Court has also addressed when and how prison officials can censor or refuse to deliver prisoner nonlegal correspondence. In so doing, it created different standards of court review for mail coming into a penal institution compared to mail being sent out of the institution. It addressed the right of prisoners to receive legal counsel from jailhouse lawyers as well as the right of jailhouse lawyers to provide counsel. In two important cases decided almost twenty years apart, the Court discussed to what extent authorities must provide prisoners with access to law libraries or legal assistance programs. The Court examined the constitutionality of regulations that restrict prisoner-visiting programs and the First Amendment rights of the media to interview prisoners and have access to prison institutions. Prisoner communications covers a wide range of issues, each of which raises unique legal questions. As in other areas of constitutional rights, the Supreme Court has balanced First Amendment rights with security concerns. As is evident from the Court's decisions, the Court relies heavily on the expertise of prison officials and often defers to their professional judgment.

Many legal experts argue that the Supreme Court's decisions in this area indicate how conservative the Court has grown since the prisoners' litigation movement started in the late 1960s. In 1974, the Court imposed a strict scrutiny standard for reviewing regulations that censor prisoner correspondence. In 1977, it obligated officials to provide law libraries or legal assistance programs. By 1987, the strict scrutiny standard had been limited to outgoing correspondence and by 1996, the Court denied that prisoner have an abstract right to law library access and held inmates must show actual injury before they can establish they suffered an access to court violation. While it appears the Court has indeed grown more conservative over the past several decades, it has always extended judicial deference to the experience and expertise of prison officials.

DISCUSSION QUESTIONS

1. Explain the two different standards of review for incoming and outgoing prisoner correspondence and the Supreme Court cases that established the standards.

2. Why is prisoner communications with attorneys subject to different constitutional protections than other types of prisoner correspondence?

3. How did *Lewis v. Casey* change the Supreme Court's ruling in *Bounds v. Smith*?

4. Discuss the Supreme Court decisions that address prisoner visitation. Do prisoners have a constitutional right to visit with family and friends? How are visits with family and friends treated differently than visits with attorneys?

5. Does the press have a First Amendment right to demand interviews with select prisoners? What rights do the media have?

SUGGESTED READINGS AND REFERENCES

Bernstein, D. (1998). "Slamming the prison doors on media interviews: California's new regulations demonstrate the need for a First Amendment right of access to inmates." McGeorge Law Review 125: 163

Branham, L. (2002). *The Law of Sentencing, Corrections, and Prisoners' Rights* (6th ed.). West Publishing: St. Paul, MN.

Eisenberg, H. (1993). "Rethinking prisoner civil rights cases and the provision of counsel." Southern Illinois University Law Journal 17: 417-490.

Smith, C. (2000). Boundary changes in criminal justice organizations: The governance of corrections: Implications of the changing interface of courts and corrections. Washington, DC: National Institute of Justice.

CHAPTER 4:

First Amendment Rights: Freedoms of Religion and Association

INTRODUCTION

The First Amendment reads:

> Congress will make no law respecting an establishment of religion, or prohibiting the free exercise thereof; or abridging the freedom of speech, or of the press; or the right of the people to peaceably assemble, and to petition the Government for a redress of grievances.

It may surprise students to learn that over the years prisoners have filed many lawsuits about the First Amendment right to exercise their religious freedom. Maybe it is difficult to imagine hardened offenders so concerned about their right to worship that they would initiate lawsuits to protect it. In reality, some of the earliest and most influential prisoners' rights lawsuits addressed the Free Exercise Clause of the First Amendment. Think back to Chapter 1 of this textbook which examined the history of the prisoners' rights movement. The Supreme Court first recognized a prisoner's right to pursue a constitutional violation under section 1983 in *Cooper v. Pate* (1964), a lawsuit filed by Illinois state inmates who complained about restrictions on their right to worship as members of the Nation of Islam. Since then, a complex body of law has developed that deals with prisoners' rights to religious freedom

There are two clauses in the First Amendment that apply to religious freedoms. The Establishment Clause prohibits Congress from enacting laws that establish or endorse a religion or prefer one religion over another. This is the clause that led the Supreme Court to rule that the Constitution prohibits saying religious prayers in public schools. It is the clause at the center of such controversies as government aid to parochial schools, Christmas nativity displays set up in public parks, and the recitation of a prayer at public school graduations and sports events. The other part of the First Amendment that addresses religious freedom is the Free Exercise Clause, which prohibits Congress from enacting laws that interfere with our right to practice our religious convictions. Like the Establishment Clause, the Free Exercise Clause has also been at the center of important controversies. Because the Supreme Court has ruled that the First Amendment applies to the states through the Fourteenth Amendment's due process clause, the Establishment and Free Exercise Clauses restrain the actions of state and local governments as well as the federal government.

How does the Free Exercise Clause protect the First Amendment rights of persons who are incarcerated in jail or prison? Correctional officials encounter security and safety concerns totally unique to their environment. Prisoners' lives are necessarily structured around a routine imposed in an institution that houses hundreds, often thousands of people. A staff of correctional officers must observe prisoners as they come and go and engage in group activities. Prisoners live under rules that restrict what they can wear and how they groom their hair and clothes. They eat in cafeterias with limited food menus. Their nonlegal mail can be read and under certain circumstances censored.

Many of the religious freedoms available to people outside of prison and jail raise real security and discipline issues in the incarcerated world – issues related to following religiously mandated diets, wearing religious medals, wearing certain hair styles or having facial hair, receiving certain types of religious mail, supplying clergy to meet prisoners' needs, and worshipping on specific days and times in specific places. The courts have recognized that the Free Exercise Clause cannot be implemented in the prison world the same way it is implemented in the free world. A balance needs to be maintained between protecting prisoners' First Amendment rights while making certain the institution's security and safety are not compromised. That balance can be the source of much friction.

The Establishment Clause also raises important legal questions. On one hand, the Free Exercise Clause prohibits officials from interfering with prisoners' religious freedom. On the other hand, the Establishment Clause forbids the government from setting up a church or preferring one religion over another. How do prison officials facilitate the right of prisoners, who cannot leave prison to attend worship services, to practice their faith without aiding or funding (establishing) religion? Is providing a place of worship inside a public institution a violation of the Establishment Clause? Is it lawful for a correctional agency to hire prison chaplains and compensate them on the government payroll? If an agency hires and compensates chaplains, must it hire and compensate a chaplain of every faith represented by the prisoner population? Can a correctional agency participate in the creation, implementation, or operation of a faith-based rehabilitation program for offenders?

This chapter examines the important legal questions related to prisoners' rights under both the Free Exercise and the Establishment Clauses of the Constitution. The chapter concludes by examining two other First Amendment rights of prisoners "to peaceably assemble" and associate with organizations of their choice. As part of this right of free association, the chapter will examine the right of prisoners to marry while they are incarcerated.

FREEDOM OF RELIGION

Cruz v. Beto

In *Cruz v. Beto* (1972), the Supreme Court wrote a landmark First Amendment opinion involving a Buddhist prisoner. Cruz was serving 15 years in a Texas prison for robbery when he filed a civil rights lawsuit under section 1983 alleging that he had been discriminated against and persecuted by prison authorities because he was a Buddhist. Officials would not allow him to use the prison chapel, and placed him in solitary confinement on a diet of bread and water for two weeks for sharing Buddhist religious reading material with other prisoners. Cruz was also not allowed to correspond with his religious advisor in the Buddhist faith. According to Cruz, the prison system encouraged inmates to participate in traditional religious programs and employed Catholic, Jewish, and Protestant chaplains. The state also provided copies of Jewish and Christian Bibles, and allowed weekly Sunday school classes and religious services to be conducted. Cruz claimed that prisoners could earn good merit credits toward job assignments and consideration for early parole for attending conventional religious services.

In a per curiam opinion, the Supreme Court held that inmates holding less conventional religious beliefs are entitled to practice their religion in a manner similar to other inmates. Noting that the Buddhist faith has a long history, the Court found that discrimination against Cruz on the basis of his Buddhist faith amounted to discrimination, in violation of both the First Amendment and the

Fourteenth Amendment's Equal Protection Clause. It is important to note the Court's comments in a footnote to its opinion. In the footnote, the Justices stated they were not suggesting that every religious group in prison should be provided identical facilities or personnel. Officials are not required to provide a special place of worship for every faith regardless of the size of its membership or provide a chaplain or minister without regard to the extent of demand.

A *per curiam* opinion means "by the Court" and is not signed by an individual Justice and is generally short, although a dissenting opinion may be attached, as it was in the *Cruz v. Beto* case. The lone dissenter, Justice Rehnquist disagreed that the absence of Buddhist services at Cruz's prison impaired his religious freedom, suggesting that officials should be allowed discretion as to the number and type of religious services they elect to provide to prisoners. If there are too few inmates of a particular faith in a facility, officials would not be required to accommodate their requests to hold services.

Notwithstanding the dissent, *Cruz v. Beto* was a critical case in establishing that the First Amendment right to free exercise is not restricted to conventional, mainstream religions, even in the prison setting. The Court's ruling does not mean that places of worship for every religious faith have to be provided. Correctional officials are permitted to make one place of worship available for the various religious groups in the institution and are permitted to weigh the costs and benefits of providing clergy of different faiths. Officials must provide reasonable opportunities to all prisoners to exercise their religious freedom.

O'Lone v. Shabazz

In 1987, the Court considered a second significant case dealing with the Free Exercise Clause of the First Amendment, *O'Lone v. Estate of Shabazz*. This case was decided one week after the Court's decision in *Turner v. Safley* (1987), the landmark case that established standards for evaluating the constitutionality of prison regulations that restrict prisoners' rights (see Chapter Three). Many Supreme Court watchers were surprised when the Court applied the four-part *Turner* test to the alleged First Amendment violations in O'Lone.

O'Lone involved a challenge to prison regulations that impacted religious practices at New Jersey's Leesburg State Prison. In 1983, the New Jersey Department of Corrections issued a new policy that required inmates in maximum security custody status to spend time in an intermediate custody status before they could be reclassified to full minimum custody. The regulation also mandated that inmates in the intermediate custody status be assigned jobs outside the main prison building, due to serious overcrowding in the main building. Inmates in full minimum custody status were also required to work outside the main building. The changes mandated by the new regulations were implemented gradually. When they first went into effect, some Muslim inmates in intermediate custody were allowed to work inside the main prison building on Fridays so that they could attend Jumu'ah, a weekly Muslim afternoon service.

In 1984, as the new regulations were fully implemented, all intermediate custody inmates were directed to work outside the main building. Consequently, some Muslim inmates avoided reporting for work, and others found reasons, including wanting to attend religious services, to return to the main building during the course of the workday. According to officials, this movement created security risks and placed administrative burdens on prison officials because work details were supervised by only one guard. The whole detail was forced to return to the main gate whenever one prisoner desired to return to the facility. The returning inmate would be logged in and searched at the main gate, thus delaying all vehicle traffic.

Because of these issues, prison officials arranged to keep all inmates on outside work details at their work sites for the entire day. Lunch and medications were brought out to prisoners; doctor or social worker appointments were scheduled for late afternoons. When these arrangements proved insufficient, officials consulted with the director of social services, the director of professional services, and the prison's imam and chaplain, and issued a policy prohibiting inmates on outside work details from returning to the prison during the day except in the case of emergencies. This policy prevented Muslims from attending Jumu'ah. Muslim inmates requested that they either be allowed to work on weekends or on special inside details, but the officials refused the requests, explaining that special accommodations would adversely impact resources, prison security and discipline. Muslim inmates filed a lawsuit under section 1983, alleging that their first Amendment rights had been violated.

The Supreme Court decided in a 5-4 opinion that the prison regulations prohibiting inmates from returning to the building to attend religious services did not violate their religious freedom. The Court noted that the proper standard of review to be applied to prison regulations that are alleged to impair consti-tutional rights had been restated one week before in its decision in *Turner v. Safley* (1987). Using that test, the Court found that the new regulations were rationally related to legitimate governmental interests in maintaining institutional order and security. The Court also found that the policies reflected goals of rehabilitation because the outside work details simulated working conditions and responsibilities in society.

The Justices in the majority emphasized that they were not minimizing the importance of Jumu'ah to the inmates and noted that inmates could still congregate for prayer or discussion during off-work hours, and an imam was provided by the state and had free access to the prison. Further, Muslim prisoners' dietary needs were accommodated, as well as their needs during Ramadan, a month-long period of fasting and prayer, when early breakfasts and late dinners were provided. The Court reasoned that the restrictions with respect to Jumu'ah were reasonable in light of the other religious activities in which the prisoners could participate. The application of the *Turner* standards included considering the impact that accommodating the Muslim prisoners' rights would have on other inmates, on prison employees, and on prison resources. Accordingly, the Court accepted prison officials' testimony that if they were required to make special arrangements for one group of prisoners and allow them to avoid a work detail, other prisoners would perceive favoritism.

Prior to the *O'Lone* decisions, prison regulations that governed prisoners' religious practices had to pass a more exacting "strict scrutiny" standard. Using the *Turner* standard, the Court applied the "rational basis" test, which made it much easier for prison officials to prevail.

Congress Responds with the RFRA and the RLUIPA

The *O'Lone* decision was followed by a second controversial Supreme Court case that dealt with the Free Exercise Clause. This case did not involve prisoners, but its impact on what Congress did after the decision was significant for prison officials. The case of *Employment Division of Oregon v. Smith* (1990) involved a Native American drug rehabilitation counselor who was fired from his job because he used peyote in a religious ceremony. Even though the use of peyote is a recognized part of some Native American religious practices, his use violated Oregon state law. Because he was fired from his job for violating state law, he was unable to collect unemployment benefits, and he sued. The Supreme Court ruled that Oregon's Employment Division's regulations did not interfere with Smith's First Amendment right to practice his religious traditions. The Court concluded that Oregon's law was aimed at stopping the use of illegal drugs and was a reasonable response to that problem. Most importantly, the law was not designed to interfere with a person's religious freedoms. Smith and others must obey such a law even when it makes it impossible for them to engage in a recognized religious practice of their faith.

Many members of Congress, liberals and conservatives, were concerned about what they perceived was the Supreme Court's refusal to protect the rights guaranteed under the First Amendment. They sought to "restore" the heightened level of scrutiny courts were required to exercise when evaluating government regulations and practices that interfered with religious freedoms. In 1993, Congress enacted the Religious Freedom Restoration Act (RFRA). The RFRA mandated that the "government may substantially burden a person's exercise of religion only if it is in furtherance of a compelling governmental interest; and is the least restrictive means of furthering that compelling governmental interest." The law's intent was to make it very difficult for any government official to place burdens or penalties on individuals who are exercising the right to practice their religion. In order to do so, the official must establish a "compelling" reason and any type of burden or interference must be the least restrictive burden possible under the circumstances.

Many prison officials and the state attorneys who represented prison systems lobbied Congress, asking it to exclude prisoners from the RFRA. Prison officials preferred the four part *Turner* test that the Supreme Court had applied to Free Exercise issues in prison. They argued that legitimate security concerns required a different test be applied to prisoners than the strict "compelling" interest test mandated by the RFRA. Certain religious practices threaten the safety of inmates and staff. Officials also argued that the RFRA would open up additional claims for prisoners to litigate. Even though officials would eventually establish a compelling governmental interest in many of those lawsuits, the litigation would cost the agency valuable time and resources. The officials were not successful, and the RFRA was enacted without excluding prisoners, replacing the *Turner* test for use in religious freedom cases. The RFRA placed a much heavier burden on the government than the *Turner* test which essentially required judges to defer to the judgments of correctional officials. From 1993 to 1997, the test for alleged violations of religious practices was no longer the *Turner* test but the heightened standard required under the RFRA.

In 1997, the Supreme Court overturned the Religious Freedom Restoration Act in *City of Boerne v. Flores*, a case unrelated to corrections, ruling that Congress had violated the separation of power doctrine when it enacted the statute. Many states responded by enacting laws similar to the RFRA, but, of course, their jurisdiction was limited to the state where they were passed. In some of those states, prison authorities were able to convince the state legislators to exclude prisoners. Shortly after RFRA was overturned by the Supreme Court, then-President Clinton issued an Executive Order re-establishing the RFRA's compelling interest/least restrictive means test for federal agencies, making the RFRA's standard binding on the Federal Bureau of Prisons.

In 2000, Congress responded again and this time passed the Religious Land Use and Institutionalized Persons Act (RLUIPA) which reestablished the RFRA's compelling interest/least restrictive means test. Under the RLUIPA, government restrictions on religious practices must further compelling governmental interests such as safety, security, efficiency, and cost-effectiveness, and these compelling interests must be satisfied through the least restrictive means possible. In addition, the RLUIPA specifically mandates that the government cannot impose a substantial burden on the religious freedoms of people who are confined in or reside in an institution. Once again, prison officials must be more sensitive to inmate religious requests than they were under the *Turner* standard, as long as the religious requests are based on legitimate and sincere religious beliefs.

Section 2 of the RLUIPA prohibits the government from imposing a regulation on the use of land in a way that imposes a substantial burden of the free exercise of religion by a person, a group, or an institution. Section 3 protects the religious exercise of people who are confined to an institution and states:

(a) GENERAL RULE - No government shall impose a substantial burden on the religious exercise of a person residing in or confined to an institution, as defined in section 2 of the Civil Rights of Institutionalized Persons Act (42 U.S.C. 1997), even if the burden results from a rule of general applicability, unless the government demonstrates that imposition of the burden on that person-

(1) is in furtherance of a compelling governmental interest; and

(2) is the least restrictive means of furthering that compelling governmental interest.

(b) SCOPE OF APPLICATION – This section applies in any case in which –

(1) the substantial burden is imposed in a program or activity that receives federal financial assistance; or

(2) the substantial burden affects, or removal of that substantial burden would affect, commerce with foreign nations, among the several States, or with Indian tribes.

The Act defines the term "government" to include a state, county, municipality, or other governmental entity or a branch, department, agency, or official of a state, county, or municipality. By "religious exercise" the Act includes any exercise of religion, whether or not it is required by or central tenet of a religion.

Soon after the RLUIPA was enacted, lawsuits were filed challenging its constitutionality. Claims that it was unconstitutional were settled by the Supreme Court in 2005 in the case *Cutter v. Wilkinson*. The inmates who challenged the RLUIPA were members of the Satanist, Wicca (witchcraft or pagan), and Asatru religions (Norse heathen or neo-pagan) and the Church of Jesus Christ Christian (based on white supremacist views of the Aryan Nation). They complained the Ohio Department of Rehabilitation and Correction violated RLUIPA because it failed to allow them to worship, to have access to religious literature and ceremonial materials, to adhere to the dress requirements of their faiths, to have access to chaplains trained in their faith, and discriminated against them because they were members of nontraditional faiths. For purposes of the lawsuit, the Ohio agency did not challenge the sincerity of the inmates' religious beliefs or the legitimacy of their religions. The Sixth Circuit Court of Appeals held that RLUIPA violated the Establishment Clause of the First Amendment because it "impermissably advances religion by giving greater protection to religious rights than to other constitutionally protected rights." The appeals court found that the Act afforded religious prisoners more rights than nonreligious prisoners and encouraged nonreligious prisoners to become religious in order to gain those rights. The Supreme Court granted *certiorari* in order to determine whether the RLUIPA violated the Establishment Clause and to resolve the conflict among the Courts of Appeals who had split over the Act's constitutionality.

The Supreme Court recognized that there are "conflicting pressures" imposed by the Free Exercise and Establishment Clauses, but that its previous decisions had recognized "there is room for play in the joints between the Clauses." The Court concluded that the RLUIPA's provisions are compatible with the Establishment Clause because the Act lessens the burden government can place on a person's private exercise of faith. The Act's provisions accommodate the free exercise of religion without allowing the government to endorse or support religion. Properly imposed, courts must take into account the burden placed on how persons whose beliefs are not accommodated under the Act, and Judges must be satisfied that the Act is administered neutrally among different faiths. The RLUIPA protects persons held in state-run institutions like mental hospitals and prisons who must depend not only on the government's permission to practice their faith but on the government accommodating their exercise. As an example, the Court noted the federal government's lawful accommodation of religious practices of members of the military by hiring religious chaplains on the government payroll to serve those members. The Court was careful to also note that nothing in the RLUIPA elevates accommodating religious beliefs over an institution's need to maintain order and security. Courts must apply due deference to prison administrators' experience and expertise in establishing regulations and procedures that help maintain order and discipline. In addition, the RLUIPA does not differentiate among bona fide faiths because it does not confer special status on any particular religious group. The Court did not address how the RLUIPA applied to the particular claims made by the prisoners in the case. It ruled only that the RLUIPA is constitutional. It remanded the case back to the trial court to decide whether the Ohio Department of Rehabilitation and Correction established a compelling governmental interest to restrict the religious practices of the prisoners involved in the lawsuit.

A case decided by the Eighth Circuit Court of Appeals demonstrates the differences between the *Turner* test and the RLUIPA strict scrutiny test. A Missouri inmate, in *Murphy v. Missouri Department of Corrections*, 372 F.3d 979 (2004), belonged to the Christian Separatist Church Society (CSC), a religious group that believes Caucasians are blessed by God and must separate themselves from non-Caucasians. The inmate, Murphy, claimed the Missouri Department of Corrections violated his First Amendment rights because he and other Christian Separatist members were not allowed to worship together as a group, were denied religious funding and institutional air time for their religious videos, and the institution had censored a religious pamphlet they received in the mail. The appellate court first applied the *Turner* test to the alleged violations of Murphy's First Amendment rights. Under the *Turner* test, the court concluded that not allowing group worship because of concerns that racial segregation would spark violence was rationally related to the prison's security. The court also reasoned that Murphy could still practice his faith without group worship – study and pray in his cell, occasionally meet with clergy, and observe holy days. Murphy, however, also alleged that the prison violated his statutory free exercise of religion mandated by RLUIPA. Applying the requisite strict scrutiny analysis, the appellate court remanded the case back to the district court for trial during which Murphy would be required to show that his freedom to exercise his religion had been substantially burdened. Likewise, prison officials would have to provide evidence more than mere assertions that racial violence would result if they accommodated the Christian Separatists and that they had considered other alternatives before rejecting the inmates' right to group worship. Further, prison authorities would have to show that the solitary practice of the religion was the least restrictive means available in order to maintain security in the institution. Prison officials succeeded under the *Turner* test in their claim that denying the Christian Separatists right to worship as a group threatened prison security. In comparison, under the strict scrutiny analysis, the case was remanded back to the district court for trial. Prison officials would have to produce relevant evidence that the institution's security would be at risk if Murphy's group was permitted to worship. They would have to show through the evidence that nothing less than a ban on group worship would serve to keep the prison safe.

The Question of Legitimacy

Of course, what is a legitimate and sincere religion can be a difficult issue for correctional administrators, and both prison officials and the courts have been compelled to examine newly established religions for evidence of sincerity and a valid commitment to spiritual beliefs. A case decided by the Third Circuit Court of Appeals demonstrates the conflict prison officials face when deciding whether a belief system should be considered a religion. In *Sutton v. Rasheed*, 323 F. 3d 236 (3d Cir. 2003), inmates in a high-risk security unit challenged a policy of Pennsylvania's Department of Corrections which denied them access to Nation of Islam religious texts. The policy restricted the access prisoners in a high-security housing unit had to reading materials, including religious materials. It limited inmate access to a personal Bible and the Holy Koran, and the "religious equivalent" to these items. Inmate Richard Sutton, who belonged to the Nation of Islam, was confined to this unit. He and several other inmates requested and were denied access to texts written mainly by Fard Muhammad, Elijah Muhammad, and Louis Farrakhan. The Muslim chaplain, Imam Rasheed, denied that access because he believed the texts were not religious. Another prison chaplain reviewed the books and described them as racist and more of a political nature. Sutton questioned whether Imam Rasheed, a Sunni Muslim, had the authority to determine whether texts of the teachings of Elijah Muhammad were religious or not. The books at issue were characterized by a professor of Islamic Studies as "required reading" for followers of the Nation of Islam faith.

By October 2001, Pennsylvania had changed its policy and allowed inmates in the high security units to have a combination of written material as long as the reading material fit into a uniform sized records box. The new policy relieved prison officials of the responsibility to determine whether reading materials were religious or not.

The appellate court still had to decide if the prior policy was unconstitutional and whether Sutton was entitled to damages since he had been affected by the previous policy for several years. The appeals court acknowledged how difficult it can be to determine whether a belief is a religion and posited three distinct criteria for evaluating what constitutes a religion especially in light of increasing religious diversity in the U.S. It also acknowledged that there has not been a consensus as to whether the Nation of Islam is a religion. For guidance it turned to a previous appeals court decision that had set forth three criteria for evaluating whether a belief is a religion: (1) does the belief system attempt to address fundamental and ultimate questions; (2) is it a comprehensive belief system; and (3) are there formal and external signs like clergy and observance of holidays. Applying these criteria, the court concluded the Nation of Islam is a religion meriting First Amendment protection. The court next applied the *Turner* test to the former prison policies. The court concluded that the regulations did impermissibly violate the inmates' freedom of religion without a legitimate penological interest and that inmates did not have alternative means of practicing their religion. Further, accommodating the inmates would not have been burdensome in terms of prison resources. Thus, the prior regulations could not survive the *Turner* test.

Special Diets, Grooming Regulations, and Other Religious Practices

Over the years, inmates have filed lawsuits challenging regulations that restrict many different types of practices that impinge on the free exercise of religion. Most of those cases have not been heard by the U.S. Supreme Court. Lower appellate courts have developed a body of case law about these issues that, unfortunately, is not always consistent. Although it is possible to identify broad trends in the case law, lawyers representing prisoners and correctional agencies have to research court cases decided in their jurisdictions and consult applicable state laws to determine if specific regulations or practices violate the First Amendment.

Prisoners have filed numerous lawsuits demanding the provision of special religious diets. Most of those lawsuits have been filed by Muslim inmates who claim the right to eat either pork-free meals, including anything that came into contact with pork, or meals prepared according to a special ritual called hallal, and Jewish inmates who claim the right to kosher meals, which must be prepared in a special way. Inmates from other religious traditions have also sought special meals, usually vegetarian or vegan diets, which excludes dairy and egg products as well as meat. The trend in the case law is that under the correct circumstances, the Free Exercise Clause requires that prison officials must provide special meals.

It is not always clear, however, how correctional officials must respond to prisoners' demands. Preference for a certain diet is not sufficient; the prisoner must base his or her demands on their religious beliefs. Most courts have ruled that prisoners are not entitled to special diets that are not a part of their religious faith. In *Cape v. Crossroads Correctional Center*, 99 P.3d 171 (Mont. 2004), the Montana Supreme Court ruled that the correctional facility did not have to provide a Catholic prisoner with fish and unleavened bread on Fridays during Lent because the Catholic Church only requires members to refrain from eating meat on those days. In *Spies v. Voinivich*, 173 F.23d 398 (6th Cir. 1999), the court ruled a Buddhist prisoner who was provided a vegetarian meal, was not entitled to a vegan diet because it was not required by his faith.

Most courts have ruled that officials are not required under the First Amendment to comply with demands for special diets that are not based on a prisoner's sincerely held religious convictions, however, courts are often reluctant to inquire into a prisoner's religious sincerity. In *Jackson v. Mann*, 196 F.3d 316 (2d Cir. 1999), the court ruled that a prisoner who announced he was Jewish could not be denied kosher food even though the institution's Jewish Rabbi chaplain determined he was not Jewish. In contrast, however, in *Ramsey v. Coughlin*, 1 F. Supp. 198 (W.D.N.Y. 1998), the court denied the prisoner's claim for a kosher diet when there was no evidence he was Jewish.

Unlike special diets, prisoners have been less successful in challenging grooming and dress regulations based on religious grounds. Most courts have upheld regulations that require shaves and haircuts. Authorities justify the regulations based on health and sanitary concerns as well as security. Escape tools or weapons can be hidden in long hair and even beards. Officials also argue that inmates are easier to identify if they are clean-shaven with a uniform, short haircut. In *Cleveland v. Garner*, 69 F.3d 22 (5th Cir. 1995), the Fifth Circuit Court of Appeals ruled that the First Amendment did not protect a Rastafarian prisoner who refused to cut his dreadlocks and beard on religious grounds because the grooming requirements were reasonably related to the legitimate interests of officials to maintain security and be able to easily identify inmates. In *Pollock v. Marshall*, 845 F.2d 656 (6th Cir), a Lakota Indian prisoner refused to cut his hair because he believed it was sacred and his religious beliefs would not allow him to cut it. The appeals court accepted the legitimacy of the prisoner's beliefs but upheld the grooming requirements, finding that the regulations served reasonable penological purposes.

In *Standing Deer v. Carlson*, 831 F.2d 1525 (9th Cir. 1987), the appeals court considered a claim by Native American inmates at the U.S. Penitentiary at Lompoc who challenged regulations that banned the wearing of headgear, including headbands, hairnets, or hats, in the inmate dining hall. Officials claimed the ban was necessary for sanitary and security reasons and was imposed across the board. Native American prisoners argued that the ban infringed on their First Amendment right to wear headbands that reflected their religious convictions and that an exception to the ban should be made on their behalf. The Eighth Circuit supported prison officials and upheld the constitutionality of the blanket ban.

A Native American inmate filed a lawsuit against Missouri prison officials who refused to allow him access to a sweat lodge or to conduct sweat lodge ceremonies. For many Native Americans, the sweat lodge ceremony is very important to their religious practice and allows them to purify their spirit. A sweat lodge is a small structure constructed with poles made from trees and covered with animal hides and blankets. Heated rocks inside the lodge are drenched with water, creating steam. Participants enter the lodge nude where they remain for several hours and sweat and pray. While inside the lodge, they stoke the fire that heats the rocks with an ax or shovel. In *Hamilton v. Schiro*, 74 F.3d 1545 (8th Cir. 1996), the Court of Appeals decided that despite the importance of the sweat lodge ceremony, the Native American prisoners were not entitled under the First Amendment to build and use sweat lodges even though the inmates had introduced evidence that other state prison systems allowed access to sweat lodges. Officials had agreed to consider allowing the prisoner to conduct a modified ceremony outside of a sweat lodge, but he had refused. The court noted that the prisoners were allowed to carry medicine bags and had access to a ceremonial pipe and a certain type of tobacco.

Faith-Based Corrections

The role of religious organizations in corrections has changed considerably during the last decade. Early in his presidency, President George W. Bush issued several Executive Orders encouraging the federal government to enlist and enable faith-based organizations in providing social services. The President's efforts built on a movement that was already developing in both institutional and community based corrections. Provisions of the Charitable Choice Act, enacted in 1996 and amended several times, encourage states to involve community and faith-based groups in providing federally funded social services. The government can enter into contracts with religious providers of social services. The religious organizations are not required to jettison their religious message as a condition to receiving the funds. They are permitted to retain their religious message and employ their faith as part of the delivery of social service programs. They are, however, not permitted to discriminate against recipients of their services based on their religion, and recipients cannot be forced to engage in religious activities in order to receive assistance.

Prison Fellowship, a not-for-profit Christian organization that ministers to prisoners, ex-prisoners, victims, and their families created a program in 1997 called InnerChange Freedom Initiative, a faith-based program that operates currently in prisons in six states – Arkansas, Minnesota, Missouri, Texas, Iowa, Kansas, and Minnesota. It is a Christ-centered program designed for inmates who are within 18 and 24 months of release. The program continues for six to twelve months after the prisoner is released into the community. It is an entirely volunteer program and, although it is Biblically-based, it is open to all inmates. In 2002, the Federal Bureau of Prisons (BOP) issued guidelines for piloting several faith-based programs in federal prisons, called Life Connections. It is a voluntary, 18-month residential program for inmates within 24-60 months of release. The BOP's multi-faith program contracts with religious leaders of five faiths – Catholic, Jewish, Muslim, Native-American, and Protestant – to meet the spiritual needs of prisoners from many different faiths. It matches released inmates with volunteer mentors in the community from appropriate faith groups. In addition to institution-based programs, many faith-based organizations operate community-based treatment programs for substance abusers who are ordered to enter the programs as part of the disposition of their criminal cases.

Do these faith-based corrections programs violate the Establishment Clause of the First Amendment? In 2007, the Eighth Circuit Court of Appeals decided the case *Americans United for Separation of Church and State v. Prison Fellowship Ministries*, 509 F.3d 406 (8th Cir. 2007) which challenged the constitutionality of the InnerChange program that had opened its doors in the Iowa Department of Corrections in 1999 at the Newton correctional facility, in units that formerly housed honor inmates. In order to understand the Eighth Circuit's decision, it is important to know some of the details about how InnerChange operated in Iowa. Like the other InnerChange programs active in state prisons, participation in the program was entirely voluntary and did not lead to reduced sentences or early parole. Inmates who joined were well advised in advance that the program was based on Christian values and contained religious content, although an inmate did not have to be a Christian to participate. Inmates were free to quit the program at any time without fear of penalty. The program consisted of a four-week orientation which included Bible studies. After orientation, inmates entered Phase I for 12 months which consisted of days filled with prayer, classes, and Bible study. Phase II followed for six months of more prayer and Bible study and meetings with a volunteer mentor form outside of prison whose role was to help prepare the inmate live a Christian life once they were released. Mandatory classes in Phases I and II included classes on the Old and New Testaments, substance abuse treatment, anger management, victim impact, financial management, and marriage/family/parenting, all of which, according to InnerChange had religious content. For example, the substance abuse curriculum was based on the premise that only Jesus Christ can cure addiction. The only secular class was computer training. Inmates who failed to meet the spiritual expectations of the program staff could be dismissed. InnerChange staff supervised the inmate activities, classes, and recreation, including issuing disciplinary reports, without the assistance of the department of corrections staff.

The Iowa DOC contracted with InnerChange for the program and reimbursed InnerChange for non-religious costs and expenses. In the first year of the contract, the state DOC paid InnerChange $229,950. In year two, the DOC paid InnerChange $191,625 and then again in year three. These funds came from the Inmate Telephone Rebate Fund, which by law could be used at the discretion of the DOC for the benefit of inmates. In 2002, the Iowa legislature appropriated $172,591 to the department of corrections for a values-based treatment program at Newton. Those funds were used to expand InnerChange to the Newton Release Center. Following that appropriation, the legislature appropriated additional funds ($310,000 in 2003 and $310,000 in 2004). In 2005, the legislature switched its funding from cost reimbursement to a per diem payment. State funds accounted for 30 to 40 percent of InnerChange's operating costs and were supposed to cover only the non-religious aspects of the program; however, evidence presented during the trial in District Court suggested it was often difficult to separate religious from non-religious expenses.

The three judge panel of the Eighth Circuit Court of Appeals upheld the federal district court's decision in 2006 and ruled that the Iowa InnerChange program violated the Establishment Clause of the First Amendment. It concluded that even though the state of Iowa did not intend to advance religion when it entered into a contractual arrangement with InnerChange, the payments made by Iowa directly to InnerChange were used for religious purposes and resulted in governmental indoctrination. In addition, in order to use the state funds inmates had to participate in a Christian-based program, meaning that government funds were not allocated based on neutral criteria on a nondiscriminatory basis. Iowa's contract with InnerChange had the effect of advancing or endorsing religion, and the direct government aid to InnerChange violated the Establishment Clause. Switching to a per diem payment structure did not change the fact that the state was endorsing religion.

What does this mean for faith-based corrections programs in the future? Much depends on whether and how the U.S. Supreme Court will eventually address the issue. The Eighth Circuit decision does not put an end to all faith-based programs. It suggests that programs that are not tied to one religious belief system may have better success in passing constitutional muster. It also warns government officials to structure funding to faith-based programs in such a way that public monies not be used to support or maintain religious related activities or events.

FREEDOM OF ASSOCIATION

Inmate Organizations

Protecting inmates' First Amendment freedom of association rights illustrates the continuing balancing act between upholding inmates' constitutional rights and legitimate penological concerns of prison administrators. The "right to assemble peaceably and petition the government to rectify grievances" is specifically implicated in the issue of prison unions.

Inmate labor unions were the focus of the Supreme Court's decision, *Jones v. North Carolina Prisoners' Labor Union, Inc.* (1977). The North Carolina Prisoners' Labor Union was formed in 1974 in order to promote charitable labor union purposes, seek through collective bargaining to improve working conditions, and serve as a mechanism for hearing and resolving inmate grievances. By early 1975, the union had attracted some 2,000 inmate "members" in 40 different prison units throughout North Carolina. Prison officials believed the union was a threat to prison security. North Carolina inmates alleged that their right to freedom of association was violated when officials implemented regulations that prohibited inmates from holding union meetings, soliciting other inmates to join the labor union, and receiving bulk mailings of union materials. The Supreme Court ruled that because prisoner unions can be detrimental to prison order and security, the North Carolina regulations were reasonable and necessary and did not violate the Constitution. North Carolina allowed inmates to be members of a union, the restrictions were imposed on group activities or solicitation of new members that could interfere with the operation of a safe prison system. The Court concluded that the restrictions were rationally related to the functioning of a safe system and did not violate the inmates' right to free speech. The inmates' right to free association was implicated by the regulations, however, prison authorities had the right to curtail their freedom of association because they could show such activities were likely to disrupt the order and stability of the prison system and interfere with legitimate penological objectives. Importantly, the Court cautioned the lower courts to recognize the expertise of prison officials and defer to their decisions involving security and safety matters unless it can be shown officials abused their discretion. The prisoners in the Jones case also claimed their Fourteenth Amendment equal protection rights were denied because the North Carolina prison system allowed the Jaycees, Alcoholics Anonymous, and, in one institution, the Boy Scouts to have meetings and distribute bulk mailing material. The Supreme Court noted that prison administrators must make legitimate distinctions between those types of organizations, which work in conjunction with the goal of rehabilitation and do not threaten prison order, and unions which are more adversarial in nature. Jones is the only case decided by the Supreme Court dealing with inmate unions. Prisoner unions were popular in the 1970s, but have largely been abandoned.

The Right to Marry

Turner v. Safely (1987) is one of the Supreme Court's most important decisions regarding prisoners' rights. As already discussed in Chapter 3, in that case the Court created a four-part test for lower courts to apply in lawsuits that challenge the constitutionality of a prison regulation. The broad pronouncement in *Turner* is that officials must demonstrate that a regulation which impinges on inmates' constitutional rights has a legitimate penological purpose. More specifically a court must examine: 1) whether there is a rational connection between the regulation and a legitimate governmental interest, 2) whether there are alternative means by which inmates can exercise the rights that is being restricted, 3) the impact of accommodating the right on officials and other inmates and on prison resources, 4) the absence of a ready alternative to the regulation may be evidence of its reasonableness, however, officials are not obligated to implement the least restrictive means to achieve a legitimate goal.

Chapter 3 discusses the regulation that restricted the right of prisoners to correspond with other Missouri prisoners through the mail system. Prisoners in the *Turner* case also challenged a regulation that permitted them to marry only if they had permission from the prison superintendent, to be granted only if there were compelling reasons to do so. The marriage regulation failed to define what was meant by compelling reasons, but officials testified that generally only pregnancy or the birth of an illegitimate child would be considered compelling enough for a superintendent to grant permission. Officials supported the regulation by citing security concerns raised when inmate marriages create love triangles that lead to violence. In terms of rehabilitation, officials claimed that many female inmates were subject to abuse and over dependence on men, which was often related to their criminal activity. Female prisoners needed to use their prison time to learn new skills and develop greater self-reliance. Getting married while incarcerated might sabotage those goals. The state argued that these compelling governmental interests were the source of its authority to restrict the fundamental right that all people have to marry.

The Supreme Court did not agree and ruled the marriage restriction violated the Constitution because it was too broad in scope. Officials failed to show that before the regulation was put into effect, there had been the sort of problems they claimed existed. The regulation seemed to target female inmates marrying male inmates or ex-felons, and officials failed to explain why other types of marriages were also banned. Although officials can certainly regulate the time, place, and circumstances of when a marriage can take place, the regulation in question was not reasonably related to legitimate penological purposes. The Court suggested that there might well be a situation when a superintendent could ban a marriage for specific, demonstrable prison security or public safety reasons.

While the Supreme Court has recognized the right of inmates to marry, it is clear that their right to freedom of association is extremely limited. Prison officials can exercise their discretion to restrict the types of organizations that can actively function inside a correctional institution. A prisoner is free to identify himself or herself as a member of a particular organization and adopt that organization's agenda or goals, but officials can ban inmates from soliciting membership and refuse requests to hold meetings if they can demonstrate a security or safety rationale for the ban. *Jones v. North Carolina Prisoners' Labor Union, Inc.* (1977) was decided by the Supreme Court ten years before *Turner v. Safely* (1987). Beginning with the *Turner* case, prison regulations that restrict prisoners' right of assembly or free association must be evaluated under the four-part test to determine if the regulations serve a legitimate penological purpose.

SUMMARY

Lower courts generally defer to the discretion of correctional administrators when limitations on religious freedom are based on grounds of institutional security. The rule of thumb is when officials allow one religious group to engage in a particular activity, the same right must be accorded all other religious groups within the institution. In general, correctional administrators support inmates' religious practices, reflecting the belief, supported by some research, that religion has a positive effect on inmates' behavior (deGroot, 1997). However, vexing issues remain for prison administrators due to the proliferation of unconventional or nontraditional religions. Obviously, a burgeoning prison population over the past few decades will result in prison officials being faced with increased numbers of "fringe" religions and myriad requests for accommodations. State RFRA laws and the RLUIPA require officials to accord greater sensitivity to religious requests than the less strict standards allowed by the four-pronged *Turner* test.

Alleged violations of freedom of assembly or association rights are evaluated under the *Turner* test, and inmates have a hard time sustaining such allegations. Restrictions on the freedom to associate and assembly rights can generally be easily justified in a prison setting because of security issues. The Supreme Court noted in *Jones v. North Carolina Prisoners' Labor Union, Inc.* (1977) that freedom of association rights under the First Amendment are obviously curtailed by the act of confinement.

DISCUSSION QUESTIONS

1. Discuss the extent to which First Amendment religious freedom rights apply to inmates.

2. To what extent does the First Amendment freedom of association apply to inmates?

3. How do organizations such as the Jaycees and Boy Scouts differ from inmate unions? What types of organizations would you allow in your prison? Why?

4. Select an unconventional religion such as the Christian Separatist Church Society, Asatru, or Wicca and research its basic tenets and requirements. Discuss legitimate security concerns, if any, that would face correctional administrators in accommodating the particular religion you have examined.

5. Review Pennsylvania's Department of Corrections Religious Activities Policy (Policy Number DC-ADM 819-1) at the Pennsylvania DOC Internet site.

6. Evaluate the policy from an inmate's point of view. Is this policy reasonable? Why or why not? Next evaluate the reasonableness of the policy from an employee's point of view.

SUGGESTED READINGS AND REFERENCES

de Groot, G. (1997). "Supreme Court Invalidation of RFRA Could Reduce Frivolous Litigation by Inmates." *On the Line*, 20(4):1-2.

Palmer, J. W. (1997). *Constitutional Rights of Prisoners*. Cincinnati, OH: Anderson Publishing.

Welch, Michael. (1996). *Corrections: A Critical Approach*. NY: McGraw-Hill.

CHAPTER 5:

Fourth Amendment Rights

INTRODUCTION

The Fourth Amendment bars "unreasonable searches and seizures." Exactly what constitutes an unreasonable search or seizure is a topic that has been much addressed by the U.S. Supreme Court. The Supreme Court has determined that the protections of the Fourth Amendment apply whenever a person has a "reasonable expectation of privacy." The Court has explained that this expectation of privacy varies depending on where the individual is located—a person has a very high expectation of privacy in their home, but a lesser expectation of privacy in their automobile, and an even lesser expectation of privacy in public.

Not surprisingly, a person's expectation of privacy is greatly reduced in prison. What is considered a reasonable expectation of privacy in free society is quite different from what is considered a reasonable expectation of privacy in prison. Inmates are generally subject to searches of their person, belongings, and cells without a search warrant or even the existence of probable cause. Correctional officers and visitors also enjoy a lessened expectation of privacy inside prisons. Courts recognize that the unique security needs of the institution outweigh the individual rights of the inmate, employee, and visitor. In this chapter we examine the application of the Fourth Amendment to the prison setting. Searches of inmates, correctional officers, and visitors are covered, as well as current issues such as cross-gender searches.

CELL SEARCHES

In free society, police officers must have probable cause or a search warrant in order to search a person or place. Probable cause refers to the amount of particularized evidence the police have. Police officers may not randomly search people without justification. In prison, however, the situation is very different. The Supreme Court, in *Hudson v. Palmer* (1984), held that inmates do not have a reasonable expectation of privacy in their cells. In the words of the Court, the Fourth Amendment does not apply "within the confines of the prison cell." Consequently, correctional officers may search cells without a warrant, probable cause, or even reasonable suspicion that the prisoner is engaged in criminal activity or violations of prison rules and regulations.

Palmer was an inmate in a Virginia state prison. Hudson, a correctional officer in the prison, conducted a "shakedown search" of Palmer's cell, looking for contraband. During the search a ripped pillowcase was discovered, and Palmer was charged with destruction of state property and found guilty in a prison disciplinary proceeding. Palmer filed a lawsuit, alleging that Hudson violated his Fourth Amendment right to be free from unreasonable searches and seizures because Hudson conducted the search without probable cause and for the purpose of harassing Palmer, and that during the search Hudson destroyed some of Palmer's personal property.

In *Hudson v. Palmer*, the Supreme Court held that the Fourth Amendment does not apply to cell searches. The Court explained that its decision was based on a balancing of the competing interests of the inmate and the prison administration. While inmates obviously have a preference for privacy in their cells and their personal belongings, this preference is outweighed by the interests of prison officials. Prisons are dangerous places, and maintaining institutional security is an overriding concern. The unique security needs of a prison outweigh the individual rights of inmates. Prison officials must be able to control the flow of weapons, drugs, and other contraband into prisons, and searches are a necessary part of this process.

The Court also noted that destruction of an inmate's personal property during a search, even if the destruction is intentional, does not create a due process violation as long as there is a mechanism by which inmates can seek reimbursement for their property. Inmates may also invoke the Eighth Amendment prohibition against cruel and unusual punishment when alleging the intentional destruction of their personal property.

Inmates do not have the right to observe correctional officers' search their cells.

The Supreme Court, in *Bell v. Wolfish* (1979), upheld a policy at a federal detention center that permitted correctional officers to search the cells of pretrial detainees without the inmates being present. Officers conducted random, unannounced "shakedown searches." Cell occupants would be removed from the area and while officers conducted the search of the cells and surrounding areas. In *Block v. Rutherford* (1984), the Supreme Court reaffirmed its decision in *Bell v. Wolfish*, holding again that conducting random, irregular shakedown searches of cells of pretrial detainees in the absence of the cell occupants is a reasonable response by officials to legitimate security concerns. The Court noted that "proper deference to the informed discretion of prison authorities demands that they, and not the courts, make the difficult judgments which reconcile conflicting claims affecting the security of the institution, the welfare of the prison staff, and the property rights of the detainees."

SEARCHES OF INMATES

Inmates are regularly and routinely searched in prison. Prison officials search inmates primarily to control the flow of weapons, drugs and other contraband. Inmate searches may occur at designated places or times, or randomly. There are several different forms of searches. These include pat down searches, strip searches, body cavity searches, searches with equipment (such as metal detectors), and scientific testing (such as blood tests). Courts give prison officials board authority and discretion to conduct inmate searches.

Types of Searches	
Searches of Inmates	**Degree of Suspicion Needed**
Pat down searches	None
Body cavity searches	None
Digital body cavity searches	Reasonable suspicion
Searches with equipment	None
Scientific testing	None

A pat down search involves a correctional officer running his or her hands over the outside of the inmate's clothing. The officer may remove and examine any items he or she feels during this examination of the inmate's clothing. Pat down searches are routinely conducted when inmates are going to or from work, recreation, or lunch, or when they are being transferred to another part of the institution. Courts uphold pat down searches unless there is evidence that the search was conducted purely to harass the inmate. Cross-gender pat down searches are becoming more common as the number of women in the corrections workforce increases. (Legal issues surrounding cross-gender searches are discussed later in this chapter).

A strip body cavity search involves a correctional officer conducting a visual examination of a nude inmate, including the body cavities, where contraband might be secreted. Obviously, these searches are conducted less frequently than pat down searches. They are most frequently used when an inmate enters the prison from the outside or after a contact visit. Prisoners in maximum and supermaximum security housing areas generally experience body cavity searches more frequently than other prisoners in an institution. Courts uphold the use of body cavity searches as necessary for preventing the flow of contraband into and out of the prison. As with pat down searches, courts will not permit correctional officers to use body cavity searches to humiliate or harass inmates.

The Supreme Court, in *Bell v. Wolfish* (1979) upheld a jail policy permitting body cavity searches of any person housed in the facility, including pretrial detainees, after the detainee had a contact visit. The jail argued that the interests of institutional security outweighed the privacy interests of the pretrial detainees, and the Supreme Court agreed. Obviously, if the Supreme Court is willing to permit body cavity searches of pretrial detainees, it would uphold similar searches conducted on prison inmates.

In addition to body cavity searches, under certain circumstances officials are permitted to go a step further and conduct a physical examination of the inside of an inmate's body cavities. This is generally accomplished by a finger probe, also known as a digital examination. Such searches are not conducted on a random basis, but only when there is some evidence of wrongdoing on the part of the inmate. Courts have upheld digital probe searches, so long as they are conducted in a sanitary manner, usually by medical personnel, and no unnecessary pain is inflicted. Courts permit such searches so long as there is reasonable suspicion that justifies the search and there is no evidence the search was conducted solely to harass or humiliate the inmate.

Searches with equipment involve a correctional officer using some form of technology to search an inmate. This technology may be a metal detector, a heat measurement device, an X-ray machine, or some other machine that allows a correctional officer to uncover hidden contraband. Searches with equipment may be used when an inmate enters a prison from the outside, during a transfer, or any time there is suspicion the inmate is hiding contraband on his person and it can only be detected via use of this equipment (as when an inmate is suspected of swallowing drugs). Courts have routinely upheld searches conducted with equipment, as these are seen as less intrusive and non-humiliating than other searches.

Scientific tests may be used to search inmates suspected of having ingested drugs or who may have a contagious disease. Tests typically include urinalysis and blood tests. Such tests may be conducted randomly, or be part of a mandatory testing program. While these sorts of tests are generally upheld by the courts, as they are relatively painless and non-humiliating, courts have found against correctional personnel who improperly disclosed the results of the tests. Thus, a prison may have mandatory HIV/AIDS testing, but the results of these tests generally may not be revealed to other inmates or non-medical staff.

While courts generally uphold searches of inmates, the more intrusive the search, the more closely courts will scrutinize it. So long as the search is not conducted to harass or humiliate the inmate, courts will generally permit the search in the interests of institutional security.

SEARCHES OF VISITORS

One of the consequences of a criminal conviction is the restriction of individual rights. Inmates have a number of their constitutional rights restricted in order to maintain institutional security. The Fourth Amendment is just one example. But how does the need to ensure institutional security impact on the constitutional rights of those not convicted of a crime, such as correctional officers and visitors? In general, anyone who enters a prison or other correctional facility has a lessened expectation of privacy. Correctional institutions typically have a policies stating that entry into the institution is conditioned on the visitor's consent to be searched.

Courts have held that prisons and jails may, in the interests of institutional security, conduct routine searches of any visitors. These searches may include the use of technology, such as metal detectors, as well as pat down searches and searches of any items the person brings with them (such as purses, backpacks, or briefcases). Courts have upheld more intrusive searches, such as strip searches and body cavity searches, only upon a finding of at least reasonable suspicion that the visitor is in possession of contraband. Such information may come from an informant or through personal observation by a correctional officer.

Visitors may be searched both when they enter the prison and when they are leaving it, in order to prevent the flow of contraband either into or out of the prison. If a visitor does not wish to be searched, he or she may refuse and simply leave without entering the institution. By entering a prison, visitors implicitly consent to being searched before they leave the prison.

SEARCHES OF EMPLOYEES

Just as visitors to a correctional facility enjoy a lessened expectation of privacy, so do correctional personnel. Correctional institutions typically have policies providing that employment is conditioned on the employee's consent to be searched. These searches may include the use of technology, such as metal detectors, as well as pat down searches and searches of any items the employee brings with them (such as purses, lunchboxes, or backpacks), as well as any areas under the employee's control, such as their locker or desk. More intrusive searches are permitted only upon reasonable suspicion. Many jails and prisons limit the types of belongings that employees and visitors can bring into the institution. For instance, Texas requires that correctional officers bring their lunches in clear containers, so the contents are visible at all times.

CROSS-GENDER SEARCH ISSUES

A cross-gender search involves the search of an inmate by a correctional officer of a different gender—either a male officer searching a female inmate, or a female officer searching a male inmate. As more women enter the corrections workforce, the issue of cross-gender searches receives greater attention from the courts.

Historically, courts did not look favorably on the complaints of female inmates regarding cross-gender searches, as judges were unwilling to require corrections administrators either to hire more female officers or prevent searches of female inmates by male officers. In recent years, however, a number of lower courts have considered lawsuits by male inmates challenging the constitutionality of cross-gender searches. The courts are split on this issue.

Several courts have upheld cross-gender searches on the ground that inmates have a reduced expectation of privacy, and this includes the possibility that females will either observe them or conduct pat down or body cavity searches upon them. Forbidding correctional faculties from conducting cross-gender searches would, these courts assert, impose a tremendous burden on administrators in terms of hiring and scheduling staff. Searches may need to be conducted immediately, on the spot; if prison staff had to wait for an officer of the same gender as the inmate, the search might be delayed and institutional security unduly compromised. Additionally, several courts have held that forbidding cross-gender searches would violate employment discrimination laws. In general, a person cannot be barred from a job on the basis of their gender unless there is compelling evidence that their gender makes them unable to perform the task.

Other courts have ruled in favor of inmates who have complained about cross-gender searches. In most of these cases, the courts relied on the Eighth Amendment rather than the Fourth Amendment. These courts agreed with the inmates that cross-gender searches were a form of cruel and unusual punishment because they violate the inmates' religious beliefs that they should not to be touched in intimate areas by persons of the opposite sex.

While the issue of cross-gender searches has not been resolved by the Supreme Court, most lower courts defer to the needs of prison administrators and permit cross-gender searches. Most institutions will make some effort to reduce the need to conduct cross-gender searches, but will not, as a matter of policy, forbid the practice. To do so would create an undue burden on the institution.

SUMMARY

Inmates have a greatly reduced expectation of privacy in prison. In fact, their expectation of privacy is reduced almost completely. Prison officials may conduct random searches of inmates, their belongings, and their living areas without a warrant, probable cause, or even in most circumstances, reasonable suspicion. This interference with the privacy interests of inmates is justified by the institution's need to be safe and free from contraband. Searches are a means to this end; so long as searches are not used as a subterfuge for harassment or humiliation, they will be upheld by the courts.

Not only inmates have a reduced expectation of privacy. Visitors to the institution and employees also have reduced expectations. Although their Fourth Amendment rights are not as severely limited as the inmates' rights, by virtue of entering a correctional institution, they, too, forfeit some of the rights they enjoy in the outside world. They can be subjected to pat down searches and their purses, briefcases, and knapsacks can be searched all without probable cause or reasonable suspicion. They can be required to walk through metal detectors. The courts have not had a difficult time deciding cases involving the Fourth Amendment protections afforded to jail and prison inmates because the security concerns are so clearly apparent.

DISCUSSION QUESTIONS

1. To what extent, if any, does the Fourth Amendment apply to inmates? To correctional officers? To visitors to the prison?

2. What are the different types of searches that may be conducted on an inmate?

3. What level of suspicion is required to search an inmate?

4. In your opinion, what kind of protections should be given to inmates with respect to cell searches?

5. What recourse, if any, is available to an inmate if their personal property is intentionally damaged by corrections officials?

6. Do you think that a compulsory blood test of an inmate to obtain DNA information would violate the Fourth Amendment? Why or why not?

SUGGESTED READINGS AND REFERENCES

Belbot, Barbara, and del Carmen, Rolando (1991). "AIDS in Prison: Legal Issues." *Crime and Delinquency* 37(2): 134-153.

Branham, Lynn S. (2002). *The Law of Sentencing, Corrections, and Prisoners' Rights*. St. Paul. MN: West.

Fliter, John A. (2001). *Prisoners' Rights: The Supreme Court and Evolving Standards of Decency*. Westport, CT: Greenwood.

Gardner, Martin (1985). "Hudson v. Palmer: Bright Lines but Dark Directions for Prisoner Privacy Rights." Journal of Criminal Law and Criminology 76: 75-115.

Hemmens, Craig, Belbot, Barbara, & Bennett, Kathy. (2004). *Criminal Justice Case Briefs: Significant Cases in Corrections*. New York: Oxford University Press.

CHAPTER 6:

Use of Force

INTRODUCTION

The Eighth Amendment is the focus of this chapter dealing with use of force in correctional institutions. Prison officials and correctional officers are permitted to use reasonable force to maintain discipline and for protection. Indeed, the reality of prison life is that force is frequently employed by correctional officers as a means of enforcing prison rules and regulations, protecting themselves and others, and to maintain control over large groups of people, many of whom have committed violent crimes. The question is not whether correctional officers can use force, but when and how much force? The short answer is that the force must be reasonable under the circumstances. Thus, officials may be justified in using extreme force, even deadly force, if the situation warrants it.

The first part of the chapter traces the use of force from its early roots, through English common law, to the present conception of the "proper" use of force in the correctional setting. The second part of the chapter examines the legal issues surrounding the use of force in corrections. The chapter focuses on the Eighth Amendment's prohibition on "cruel and unusual" punishment, and the different standards of review used by the courts in cases involving prisons and jails. There are only a few United States Supreme Court cases involving the use of force in corrections. Most Supreme Court decisions involving corrections have dealt with other issues, such as freedom of religion, due process, and general "conditions of confinement."

THE HISTORY OF THE USE OF FORCE IN CORRECTIONS

Use of Force In Ancient Times

Throughout history, the use of force, most often through the imposition of punishment, has taken many forms. Non-legal punishment was practiced long before the "legal" use of force ever developed. Prior to the advent of written legal codes, the victim (or general public) was largely responsible for the punishment of the offender. From the Middle Ages through the early modern period in England and Western Europe (roughly the late 1600s), punishment became more formalized and ceremonial. Specifically, certain procedures began to develop for using force against offenders that made the process of punishment less erratic and more routinized. Given that American guidelines surrounding use of force policies in corrections are rooted in the English experience, it is important to examine the development of punishment during this period in England.

The use of force in early modern England was corporal, public, and carried out by the state. Common punishments included mutilation, branding, whipping, and torture. These punishments were most often public displays aimed at the education of the citizenry; thus punishment efforts were carefully staged, proper, and dignified undertakings. Regardless of its form or stated intent, however, after late 1600s, the English tradition (as well as the rest of continental Europe) placed the authority over the use of force in the hands of the state (Clear, Cole & Reisig (2006).

Use of Force at Common Law

Until the late 1600s, punishment was delivered by both the monarch and the church; each maintained authority over separate domains of criminal behavior. In the wake of the division of religious and civic (political) authority in England, John Locke's notions of individual rights and the "social contract" gathered considerable momentum.

Locke argued that the authority to govern was created through collective agreement between the government and the governed and that the state should exist only to protect the "natural rights" of individuals. As such, the state's mandate was to prevent individuals from arbitrarily exercising coercive force over one another; thus the state should, as a matter of law, have sole control over the use of force. This "social contract" perspective shaped the common law development of the authority over the use of force in England, which, in turn, influenced the rest of Western Europe and the United States.

Use of Force in America

The use of force in the early American period (up until the mid-1800s) was largely based on the English model of punishment: for the stated purpose of retribution. Whether viewed through the lens of *lex talionis* (the doctrine of an "eye-for-an-eye"), or the current language of "deserved punishment," retribution suggests that the punishment is necessary simply to balance the scales of justice. During this early American period (1650-1830) the form of the punishment remained, as in England, public and corporal -- prison was rarely used as an instrument of punishment.

This model of criminal justice was eventually replaced, however, by the rise of the utilitarian philosophical tradition in the 1800s. Utilitarian philosophy held that punishment should not be an end in and of itself (as it is in retribution or revenge), but rather punishment should be used as a means of achieving a larger goal, such as controlling criminal behavior. For example, Ceasar Beccaria's utilitarian theory of the relationship between punishment and crime, "deterrence," can be summarized as follows: crime should decrease as the swiftness, certainty, and severity of punishments increase. Given this assumption, Beccaria advocated a system where the severity of punishments should be slightly greater than the severity of the crime. While this "theory" may sound rather simple now, it was a radical departure from the conventional wisdom of the past. The implementation of this more "enlightened" view of crime and punishment required a more rational approach to the use of force against the offender.

From Public Punishment to the Prison

Beginning in the mid 1800s, antiquated forms of public corporal punishment -- such as beheading, stoning, public hanging, breaking on the wheel, live burials, drowning, stocks and pillories, burning, and quartering -- lost their public appeal. The development of the prison as a means of punishment and social control was a natural outgrowth of Americans' understanding of the causes of deviance. The prison, or penitentiary, was created to remove the so-called "dangerous classes" from society and to provide them with the opportunity (solitary confinement) to reflect on their misdeeds. The penitentiary movement began with the opening in 1817 of Auburn Prison in New York and Eastern Penitentiary in Pennsylvania (Welsh, 1996).

The prison soon became the primary punishment method as it was better suited to deterrence because it was easily scaled to the seriousness of the offense. As a replacement to the almshouses, poorhouses, and mental hospitals of the early Nineteenth Century, the prison became the primary institution where the use of force for punishment purposes took place.

Despite the shift from public view to private incarceration, corporal punishment was still very much a part of corrections. A note--as used here, the term corporal punishment refers to the infliction of physical pain on an inmate for discipline or restraint. Now hidden from public view and therefore somewhat immune from public accountability, prison officials routinely inflicted a variety of corporal punishments on inmates. Examples include flogging inmates with a rawhide whip, or a "cat" made of wire strands, and physical beatings. Use of solitary confinement, or the "hole" also became common (Young, 1996).

Although many states officially prohibited corporal punishment by 1900, Delaware's prisons employed whipping until 1954, and the law sanctioning it remained on the books until 1972. In 1968 the Eighth Circuit Court of Appeals, in *Jackson v. Bishop*, 404 F.2d 571 (8th Cir. 1968), held that whipping inmates as a means of enforcing prison rules violated the Eighth and Fourteenth Amendments. The opinion (written by future Supreme Court Justice Harry Blackmun) noted that corporal punishment was "easily subject to abuse in the hands of the sadistic and unscrupulous."

Corporal punishment has fallen out of favor in corrections and correctional administrators acknowledge that the practice is inappropriate. While prison officials are permitted to use force when necessary to enforce prison regulations, courts have generally followed the rationale of *Jackson v. Bishop* in holding that corporal punishment is no longer acceptable under the "evolving standards of decency" approach to interpreting the Eighth Amendment. While many states currently have no statute explicitly prohibiting corporal punishments in prison, the courts have clearly rejected it.

In *Hope v. Pelzer* (2002), the Supreme Court held that handcuffing an inmate chain gang member to an iron rail for seven hours at a work site as punishment for being disruptive and disobeying an order was a violation of the Eighth Amendment. The Court found no legitimate penological interest in the infliction of unnecessary pain and suffering in this case. The purpose of punishment has also changed over time, from revenge, to deterrence, to rehabilitation. Current goals of corrections include all of the above. Despite the plurality of positions regarding the overriding goal of corrections, today there is consensus that the punishment aspect of prison is the deprivation of liberty, and further punishment is not necessary or a legitimate exercise of state authority. Even so, the revival of practices such as "chain gangs," which mirror the prison labor practices of the early 1900s, indicates that the use of force in corrections has not fully broken from its common law/corporal punishment roots.

THE EIGHTH AMENDMENT AND "CRUEL AND UNUSUAL" PUNISHMENT

The Eighth Amendment prohibits "cruel and unusual" punishment. Ideas about what is cruel and unusual have changed as society has evolved. At various times, the U. S. Supreme Court has defined what is cruel and unusual as punishment that is disproportionate to the offense, punishment which "shocks the conscience," and punishment which is not in accord with "evolving standards of decency." The Court has analyzed the prohibition against cruel and unusual punishment in the context of a variety of situations in corrections, including the death penalty, corporal punishment, and the use of force (both deadly and non-deadly) to control inmates, protect other inmates, or to repel an assault by an inmate.

The courts have employed three main standards, or tests, to determine whether a punishment is cruel and unusual: (1) whether the punishment shocks the conscience of a civilized society; (2) whether the punishment goes beyond legitimate penal aims; and (3) whether the punishment is unnecessarily cruel and unusual. Two things should be clear about these three tests. First, they are all relatively vague and subject to much interpretation by the lower courts. Second, they are subject to change over time. What is common practice today may be "shocking or unconscionable" years from now. Certainly, the common practices of the early colonial times (drawing and quartering) would be shocking if attempted today.

Yet, the courts have moved beyond these general tests, and it is now relatively clear as to what constitutes unnecessary force by corrections officers. The courts have defined both the situations in which force is permitted, and the amount of force that is proper. The majority of inmate use of force lawsuits target prison administrators and guards and seek monetary damages. A review of inmate cases suggests that use of force cases are among the most costly of inmate suits. Thus the legal standards associated with the use of force are critical for both administrators and correctional officers to understand.

In general, every prisoner has the right to be free of both offensive bodily contact and the fear of offensive bodily contact. Prison officials are permitted to use reasonable force to enforce discipline and protect themselves and others. The key here is that the force must be reasonable under the circumstances--thus prison officials may be justified in using extreme force, even deadly force, but only if the situation warrants it.

USE OF FORCE

Corrections personnel may lawfully use force against inmates in one of five situations. These include:

(1) in self-defense

(2) in defense of others

(3) enforcement of prison rules and regulations

(4) to prevent criminal activity within the prison

(5) to prevent escape

Self-Defense

Principles of self-defense permit an individual who reasonably fears for his safety to use force to protect himself from assault. This is true in society generally; it is also true for correctional officers. Correctional officers may use the amount of force necessary to repel an attack and subdue an inmate. Correctional officers may not use any amount of force they deem proper, rather they must use only so much force as is necessary under the circumstances to protect themselves. Furthermore, once an officer no longer fears for his or her safety, they may no longer be justified in using force against the subdued inmate. An officer cannot inflict additional injury as a means of punishing the inmate who attacked him.

Obviously it is difficult to determine in the heat of the moment how much is "just enough" force. Consequently, courts provide correctional officers with some degree of flexibility, and will not substitute their judgment of reasonableness unless the use of force is clearly greater than that which is necessary, or appears to have been, in the words of the Supreme Court, "malicious and sadistic."

While the Eighth Amendment prohibits cruel and unusual punishment, this does not mean that anytime an inmate is injured by correctional personnel that a constitutional violation has occurred. Instead, there must be evidence that the injury occurred when the correctional officer used more force than was reasonable under the circumstances of the case. This is a factual determination, thus each case is different and must be considered separately.

Defense of Others

Correctional officers may also use whatever force is reasonable in defense of others, including fellow officers, other inmates, and visitors. Essentially, the correctional officer may use the same degree of force as the third party (the one being attacked or threatened) could use. This is similar to the general free world rules of self-defense and defense of others.

It is worth noting that most correctional institutions have policies warning visitors that they enter at their own risk, and that correctional personnel will not negotiate any differently with inmates who take visitors hostage. This policy is intended to deter inmates from taking visitors hostage during a disturbance. Nothing in such a policy prevents a correctional officer from using force, even deadly force if necessary, to protect a visitor, however.

Enforcement of Prison Rules and Discipline

Without rules and regulations, maintaining control of an inmate population would be impossible. And if correctional officers were unable to force recalcitrant inmates to obey these rules and regulations, it would be likewise be impossible to maintain order in the prison. Thus courts have consistently recognized that correctional officers may use force to insure inmates comply with institutional rules. This force must of course be reasonable under the circumstances.

Inmates who refuse to leave their cells may be forcibly removed. Most correctional institutions do this with a special cell extraction team, trained to control and remove the inmate without being harmed. Inmates may be injured when the team piles on them, but courts have generally upheld this practice of removing inmates.

Prevention of Criminal Activity

Correctional personnel have a duty to prevent inmates from engaging in criminal conduct. This criminal activity may take the form of direct harm to an inmate (as in an assault), or it may take the form of an indirect harm to an inmate (as in criminal activity such as drug sales or extortion). In *Farmer v. Brennan*, 511 U.S. 825 (1994), the Supreme Court reviewed a case involving a preoperative transsexual federal prisoner who had been housed sometimes in male facilities, sometimes in segregation. After his transfer to a federal penitentiary that houses more troublesome inmates, Farmer was assigned to a male housing block and within two weeks was beaten and raped by another inmate. He sued authorities alleging they had assigned him to the general population knowing the facility he was transferred was populated with violent offenders and that he was vulnerable to sexual assault. He alleged their decision violated his Eighth Amendment right to be free from cruel and unusual punishment. The Supreme Court ruled that prison officials violate the Eighth Amendment when they are deliberately indifferent to a substantial risk of serious harm to an inmate. Deliberate indifference occurs when officials are subjectively aware of the risk and disregard it, failing to take reasonable steps to avoid it. Prison officials have the duty to protect prisoners from injury at the hands of other prisoners. They are only liable, however, if the injured inmate can show that officials had knowledge of the risk of injury. Their knowledge is a question of fact that will depend on the circumstances of the case. The risk need not be from a specific source. Neither does it matter if the inmate faced the risk for reasons peculiar to him or if all prisoners in his situation faced the risk. The Court was careful to emphasize that officials will not be held liable if they can prove they were not aware of the risk or if they took reasonable steps to avert it, but the steps failed.

Prevent Escape

Correctional officers are permitted to use force to prevent escape, or to recapture an inmate who has escaped. Deadly force may be permitted, depending on the circumstances. While the Supreme Court in *Tennessee v. Garner* (1985) limited police use of deadly force to instances involving the apprehension of a dangerous felon, the high court has never issued a ruling on the appropriate degree of force permitted to prevent inmate escape.

A number of lower courts have permitted the use of deadly force to prevent an inmate from escaping, on the ground that attempting to escape is often classified as a felony, and under the common law fleeing felon rule, deadly force could be used to apprehend any fleeing felon, regardless of the severity of the felony. Because the Supreme Court has held the fleeing felon rule unconstitutional in the context of police seizures, however, this rationale is suspect.

Other courts have permitted the use of deadly force to prevent escape, following the standard for the use of excessive force established in *Whitley v. Albers* (1986), as long as the correctional officers' goal in shooting the inmate was to prevent his or her escape, and not to "sadistically" cause harm. Deadly force is defined by the courts as force which does, or is likely to cause death or serious bodily injury. The use of certain weapons, such as firearms, will always be considered a use of deadly force.

Reasonable Force

The general rule for use of force in corrections is that a corrections officer may use such force as is necessary under the circumstances. This means that every use of force is judged on the particular facts of the case—no two uses of force are the same, just as no two inmates (or correctional officers) are alike. Courts look to a number of factors in determining whether the use of force in a specific instance was appropriate. These factors include the amount and type of force used by the inmate, as well as the amount and type of force used by the correctional officer and the perception of the correctional officer. Would a reasonable person in the correctional officer's position have used the same degree of force? This test combines subjective and objective components. The subjective components consider the officer's own point of view. The objective components include the use of the "reasonable person" standard.

Standard of Review in Use of Force Cases

Until recently, courts rarely even considered use of force claims by inmates. But as the "hands off" doctrine fell out of favor, prisoners filed more and more claims of excessive force. Courts examined the claims under the Due Process Clause of the Fourteenth Amendment and the "shocks the conscience" test. Force was deemed excessive and violation of the Constitution only if the conduct seemed so outrageous and inappropriate that it literally "shocked the conscience" of the court. This standard proved difficult to define.

In *Whitley v. Albers* (1986) the Supreme Court clarified the standard for examining excessive force claims in corrections. In *Whitley*, the inmate was shot and seriously injured by a correctional officer during a prison riot. During the riot a hostage was taken by a group of inmates, and a number of inmates refused to return to their cells. Captain Whitley was part of a team of correctional officers who attempted to enter the cellblock where the hostage was being held. Albers, an inmate on the cellblock who was not part of the group of rioters or hostage takers, attempted to run up the stairs when the officers entered the cellblock. He was shot by an officer who thought he was trying to reach the hostage to harm him. Albers was seriously injured and filed a lawsuit alleging the use of deadly force was excessive, in violation of the Eighth Amendment prohibition of cruel and unusual punishment.

The primary issues before the Supreme Court were: (1) determining whether the Eighth Amendment applied, and (2) determining what amount of force may be used in the correctional setting. In its decision, the Court held that any time there is an unnecessary and wanton infliction of pain the Eighth Amendment is implicated. In determining the degree of force that could be used, the Court focused on the intent of the correctional officer using the force. The Court held that only when force was used "maliciously and sadistically for the very purpose of causing harm" was the Eighth Amendment violated. If officers, however, used force in good faith for the purpose of maintaining order and security, they did not violate the Constitution. The Court listed five factors to be considered in determining whether a correctional officer has acted in good faith in using force:

1. the need to use force
2. the relationship between the need to use force and the amount of force that is used
3. the severity of the injuries caused by the use of force
4. the harm faced by inmates and correctional staff at the time the use of force occurred
5. the steps taken to limit the amount of force used

The Court determined that in the *Whitley* case, the use of force was appropriate because correctional officials were attempting to stop a riot and obtain the safe release of a hostage.

It was unclear whether this subjective standard, focusing on the mindset of the officer, was the appropriate standard for review of all claims of excessive force, including instances where the injury did not occur during a riot and when the injury was relatively minor. In *Hudson v. McMillan* (1992), the Supreme Court applied the *Whitley* standard to a situation involving only minor injuries to an inmate. In *Hudson,* a Louisiana inmate being transferred to a different cellblock was punched and kicked by the officer moving him. He did not physically resist, in fact he was handcuffed and shackled at the time of the beating. The inmate suffered bruises, facial swelling, loosened teeth, and a cracked dental plate. The trial court awarded the inmate some $800 in damages; the court of appeals set aside the verdict and declared that the Eighth Amendment applied only to "significant" injuries. The Supreme Court reversed the court of appeals, holding that the severity of an inmate's injuries is largely irrelevant in Eighth Amendment claims. In doing so the court made clear that that the test included both an objective and subjective component: the force must be "reasonable (objective) and not "malicious" or sadistic" (subjective).

The Court also made clear that the extent of the inmate's injuries is just one factor in the inquiry. Just because injuries are "minor" does not mean the use of force was not cruel and unusual punishment. There must, however, be some degree of injury, not every use of force amounts to a potential constitutional violation. In the words of the Court, not "every malevolent touch by a prison guard gives rise to a federal cause of action."

The obvious question is, if an injury must be more than a shove, but does not need to be serious, how is a correctional officer to know when a violation has occurred? The Court declared that the Eighth Amendment "excludes from constitutional recognition *de minimis* [minimal] uses of physical force, provided that such use of force is not repugnant to the conscience of mankind." Although this is still a not clear standard, it suggests even a *de minimis* use of force may be a violation if it is "repugnant" but that generally there must be some injury.

SUMMARY

In *Whitley v. Albers* (1986), the Supreme Court finally addressed the standard by which uses of force in corrections should be analyzed. If the force was used sadistically and maliciously with the intent to harm the prisoner, the action violated the cruel and unusual punishment clause of the Eighth Amendment. If force was used in a good faith effort to maintain order or restore discipline, it did not violate the Constitution. As we saw in *Hudson v. McMillan* (1992), even uses of force that cause minor injuries can violate the Constitution if they were malicious or sadistic.

Since the 1970s, correctional agencies throughout the country have implemented extensive policies and procedures addressing the proper use of force. Officers receive training in when and how force can be used, including the use of chemical agents. When a use of force incident occurs, written reports are required from the officers involved, witnesses (including employees and inmates), and the prisoner or prisoners against whom the force was used. In some agencies, all use of force incidents are reviewed by an internal affairs division. If there is reason to question whether the force was proper, the investigation deepens. Many agencies require uses of force to be videotaped if at all possible. The video tape becomes a part of the official record. The goal is that videotaping will both encourage officers to use only the force appropriate for the incident as well as help reduce frivolous inmate lawsuits. Uses of force are examined to ascertain whether the force was necessary, and if it was necessary, whether the amount of force was excessive.

It is important that correctional officials use appropriate force not only in order to reduce the number of lawsuits that inmates can file, but also because using appropriate force legitimizes the officials' control of the institution. It is challenging to control a large number of people who do not want to be in incarcerated, some of whom are violent. Security and safety are the primary goals in institutional corrections. Using force to abuse inmates or using more force than is necessary undermines the authority of officials in the long run. In Chapter 7, students will study how correctional authorities control inmate conduct by means that do not involve force.

DISCUSSION QUESTIONS

1. What standards did *Whitley v. Albers* establish regarding use of force by correctional officers?

2. The dissent in *Whitley v. Albers* supported allowing civilian juries to decide if a correctional officer's use of force was reasonable, even if no malicious intent was present. Discuss the pros and cons of such an arrangement.

3. Research the use of force policy in your state's department of corrections. How does it differ from what you have learned in this chapter?

4. The Supreme Court has held that the death penalty is constitutional in certain circumstances. How do you reconcile the Supreme Court's determination that killing someone is constitutional with the lower courts' holding that corporal punishment is unconstitutional?

5. The Supreme Court has upheld the corporal punishment of schoolchildren. How do you reconcile the corporal punishment of children with the claim that it is unconstitutional to whip inmates?

6. If every state had a law that allowed corporal punishment of inmates who violate prison rules, would this be constitutional? How might this consensus of opinion affect the Supreme Court's resolution of the issue?

SUGGESTED READINGS AND REFERENCES

Bennett, Katherine and Del Carmen, Rolando V. (1997) 'A Review and Analysis of Prison Litigation Reform Court Decisions: Solution or Aggravation?' *Prison Journal* (77)4: 405.

Branham, L. (2002). *The Law of Sentencing, Corrections, and Prisoners' Rights* (6th ed.). West Publishing: St. Paul, MN.

Clear T., Cole, G. & Reisig, M. (2006). *American Corrections, Seventh Edition.* U.S.: Thomson/Wadsworth.

Smith, C. (2000). *Boundary changes in criminal justice organizations: The governance of corrections: Implications of the changing interface of courts and corrections.* Washington, DC: National Institute of Justice.

Welsh, W.N. (1996). History of Prisons: The Jacksonian Era. In *Encyclopedia of American Prisons* (eds. Marilyn McShane and Frank P. Williams III). New York & London: Garland Publishing, Inc.

Young, V. (1996). Corporal Punishment. In *Encyclopedia of American Prisons* (eds. Marilyn McShane and Frank P. Williams III). New York & London: Garland Publishing, Inc.

CHAPTER 7:
Due Process Rights: Prisoner Discipline and Classification

INTRODUCTION

The Due Process Clause in the Fifth Amendment to the Constitution only restricts the activities of the federal government. In 1868, the Fourteenth Amendment extended due process to the states by requiring that no state can deprive a person of life, liberty, or property without due process of law. The meaning of due process, however, was purposefully left vague. Each state decided what types of procedures were required when life, liberty or property were restricted. How extensive those procedures were, how much protection they afforded were matters for the states.

As discussed in Chapter 1, in the 1960s, the United States Supreme Court ushered in the "due process revolution." In a series of landmark decisions addressing the rights of criminal suspects, the Warren Court, led by Chief Justice Earl Warren, re-wrote the law of due process. The Supreme Court favored the "incorporation doctrine" which used the Fourteenth Amendment's Due Process Clause to "incorporate" many protections in the Bill of Rights to state proceedings. The due process revolution that so significantly impacted the rights of criminal defendants soon had its impact on the rights of convicted offenders. In 1972, the Court considered the liberty interests of a convicted offender on parole. In *Morrissey v. Brewer* (1972), it ruled that parolees have a liberty interest in remaining free from incarceration as long as they abide by the conditions of their parole. Before their parole can be revoked, they are entitled to certain due process procedures (discussed further in Chapter 10). The Supreme Court grounded the offender's liberty interests in the Fourteenth Amendment's Due Process Clause. With *Morrissey*, the Court charted a course that eventually led to the "state-created liberty interest doctrine," a doctrine that evolved overtime and dominated due process analysis in prisoners' rights litigation for over two decades. In 1995, the Supreme Court dramatically revamped the doctrine, leaving the lower federal courts with the task of deciding what it now means.

This Chapter is the story of the due process revolution as it occurred in the prisoners' litigation movement. Its focus is due process and 1) the prisoner disciplinary system, and 2) inmate classification. It is in these two often-related settings that due process has its most meaningful impact on the daily lives of inmates. Discipline and classification decisions are the two most important means of controlling prisoners. Protecting prisoners involved in these processes was the major issue in a number of lawsuits filed early in the prisoners' rights movement, and it remains a major issue even today.

PRISONER DISCIPLINE

The need for discipline in a correctional institution is obvious. Prisons house hundreds, sometimes thousands, of individuals who are being incarcerated involuntarily for substantial periods of time. Prisons are coercive organizations (Etzioni 1969). During their incarceration, inmates live under severe restrictions. They cannot move around at will. They are told when and where to eat, work, sleep, and exercise, all of which happens within a relatively small space. Prison officials create disciplinary regimens to keep order and provide security among the involuntary "residents." Prison discipline includes the policies and procedures that detail how inmates are housed, assigned jobs, admitted into programming activities, and are moved from one location to another within and outside an institution. There are rules that regulate visiting privileges, correspondence, and access to commissary goods. Correctional officers follow specific procedures for opening access to cells, cellblocks, and dayrooms. Prison management is the task of keeping a diverse group of offenders in a safe, orderly, and predictable environment (Austin 1983).

Creating an effective prison regimen is not easy. Throughout the history of prisons in the United States, there has been tremendous debate about what works best. The American colonists did not rely on prisons to punish individuals convicted of crimes. Instead they sanctioned offenders with corporal punishment, banishment from the colonies, or fines. The first penitentiary in the United States was the Walnut Street Jail in Philadelphia, built in 1790. Considered by some as the "cradle of the penitentiary" (Teeters 1955), the Walnut Street Jail tried to implement a regimen that became known as the separate system. Inmates lived in their own cells, isolated from each other and from guards. They were allowed to labor alone in their cells. The separate system sought to encourage prisoners, protected from the bad influences of their fellow inmates, to contemplate their crimes and repent. Little external discipline was needed other than isolation itself because prisoners did not interact with each other or the staff. There were few rules and regulations to govern everyday activities.

Although the separate system was instituted in a few penitentiaries in the 1800s, it could not realistically compete against its rival – the congregate system. The congregate system developed at the Auburn penitentiary in New York State in 1819. In the congregate system, prisoners slept alone in small cells at night, but during the day they worked together in large industrial shops. They also ate meals together in large mess halls. In order to keep order among groups of incarcerated offenders, the creators of the congregate system devised a severely restrictive day-to-day regimen. Prisoners were forbidden to speak to each other. In order to enforce this silence, rules prohibited them from looking directly at each other or at the officials guarding them. They marched from place to place in lockstep. Disobedience to any of a myriad of prison rules generally resulted in corporal punishment, often a whipping with a leather strap. As new penitentiaries were built, the congregate system soon dominated the prison regimens. By the mid-1800s, the separate system died in the few institutions where it was initiated. Under the congregate system prisoners were able to staff very productive and income-generating industrial plants that paid for the institution's operations and often resulted in profit for the state.

The debate about effective prison regimens continued into the second half of the Nineteenth Century as the members of a fledging but growing corrections profession began to exchange ideas about different correctional practices. Despite lots of rhetoric and attempts to change the strict, regulated environment ushered in by the congregate system, prisons regimens remained quite harsh in the United States well into the Twentieth Century.

Implementing a Prison Regimen

In order to implement a prison regimen, officials have to enforce the rules and regulations that the regimen requires. Some of the rules regulate the activities of the correctional staff. If a staff member fails to follow the rules, they are subject to discipline, ranging from a verbal reprimand to termination. There are even rules that, if not followed, can result in a staff member being criminally prosecuted. Most of the rules, however, address the conduct of the prisoners themselves. Even though today's prisoners are permitted to communicate with each other and do march in lock step, they follow a host of regulations that govern almost every aspect of their daily lives. Each state prison system, the federal prison system, each local jail and corrections halfway house provide inmates with a detailed list of the disciplinary offenses in that system, analogous to a sort of "institutional criminal code." Prison systems divide infractions into more serious and less serious categories. More serious offenses (often called "major" offenses) result in more serious penalties, less serious offenses ("minor") result in less severe punishment.

Some of the offenses are obvious: escape, attempting escape, and failure to return from a furlough. Other obvious offenses include such behavior as possession of a weapon, fighting or assaulting a staff member or another offender with a weapon, fighting or assaulting without the use of a weapon, extortion, theft, sexual abuse, possession of drugs, destroying state property, and inciting a riot. Many of these disciplinary offenses are also violations of the criminal code in the jurisdiction where the facility is located. Prisoners who commit these offenses can be administratively disciplined for violating a prison regulation and criminally prosecuted in a free world court for violating the criminal law.

Many of the disciplinary offenses or infractions that inmates can commit, however, would not be considered free world crimes. Nonetheless, enforcing these regulations is necessary to create a prison regimen that fosters a safe and orderly living environment. Many of the rules restrict what prisoners are allowed to possess. They are not permitted to possess, distill, or brew alcoholic beverages or possess intoxicating inhalants. Since the mid-1990s, in many corrections facilities, they are not permitted to possess tobacco products. They are not permitted to gamble or possess dice or playing cards. They are not permitted to possess any item that institutional authorities think might hinder the successful operation of the facility. They are not permitted to alter items they are allowed to possess in a manner that jeopardizes the facility's security. They are not permitted to possess money, books or magazines that have not been approved for them to have, or clothes that have not been approved. Other rules restrict many of their personal choices and freedom to move about. In some jurisdictions, they must comply with specific grooming standards. They cannot refuse a housing/cell assignment. They cannot refuse to work. If they are enrolled in an educational or vocational program, they cannot refuse to attend school, report late to class, or refuse to do their assignments. If they are enrolled in a treatment program, they cannot refuse to attend. They are not permitted to walk freely throughout the institution. Their movements are restricted to certain areas of the facility at certain times of the day. There are regulations that make it an offense to create a disturbance or refuse or fail to obey a legitimate order from a staff member. They cannot exert authority over another inmate. Their relationships with the staff are also subject to regulation. They are not allowed to establish or attempt to establish an inappropriate relationship with a staff member or employee or solicit money or gifts from a staff member. Prisoners must follow the safety regulations required by their job assignment, whether wearing safety equipment or operating equipment in a particular manner.

When a prisoner fails to follow a prison regulation, he or she is charged with a disciplinary violation or infraction. Next to deciding what regulations should be enforced to create a prison regimen, deciding what happens when a regulation is violated is the next important consideration. For over a century, and well into the 1960s and early 1970s in some parts of the country, corporal punishment was a common and popular form of disciplining inmates who violated prison rules. As discussed in Chapter 6, gradually corporal punishment was supplemented and finally replaced with other forms of discipline. Solitary confinement, cell restriction, restrictions on recreation, possession of personal property or commissary purchases, and extra work duties have become standard means for disciplining inmates who violate the rules. Solitary confinement is generally reserved for offenses categorized as more serious. Another form of discipline reserved for more serious offenses is to take away the good time or earned time that a prisoner has accumulated. Almost every state prison system and the federal system awards good conduct time to prisoners who follow the rules. In some systems, inmates can also earn good conduct time for participating in certain programs. Good time shortens the amount of time that inmates must be incarcerated, allowing them to be conditionally released prior to serving their full term. In many jurisdictions, prisoners who violate a rule in the more serious category may have some or all of their good time revoked. In some systems, inmates found guilty of serious infractions can also have their custody or security classification changed as a sanction. This means they can be assigned to a more restrictive classification category, which often has a direct impact on their housing and job assignments or the amount of good time they can accumulate.

Related to the type of discipline an offender should receive for an infraction is the manner in which the facts surrounding the violation and the discipline should be determined. Did the accused prisoner actually engage in the violation that was charged? Are there extenuating circumstances that might mitigate the seriousness of the violation? Were there witnesses whose version of the event should be considered to insure accuracy and fairness? A prison disciplinary regimen must address not only the regulations necessary for its implementation and the punishment that should be meted out for specific categories of offenses. It must also address the process that must be followed to determine that an infraction has occurred.

Wolff v. McDonnell and its Progeny

By the early 1970s, it was clear the same due process revolution that had dramatically changed the rights of criminal suspects, was going to have an important impact on the rights of incarcerated offenders as well. The Fourteenth Amendment's Due Process Clause provides:

> No State shall make or enforce any law which shall abridge the privileges or immunities of citizens of the United States; nor shall any State deprive any person of life, liberty, or property, without due process of law ...

Due process guarantees that when engaging in certain activities, government officials will follow a specific set of procedures. The greatest amount of due process protection is afforded to suspects and defendants in criminal cases, who are facing possible conviction under a criminal statute. Such a conviction has serious ramifications, including loss of freedom, loss of life, a monetary fine, a criminal record that impacts their right to vote and qualify for certain occupational licenses. The stakes are so high that criminal suspects and defendants have extensive protections under the Constitution. Prison discipline, on the other hand, is an administrative process that deprives prisoners of the use of their property, further restricts their already restricted liberty, or extends their terms of incarceration by taking away good time they have accumulated. In the 1970s, the issue became: does prison discipline trigger due process protections, and, if so, how extensive are they. In *Wolff v. McDonnell* (1974), the U.S. Supreme Court addressed this complicated issue for the first time.

Nebraska awarded good time credits to inmates who had satisfactory behavior, which shortened their terms of incarceration. According to Nebraska prison regulations, an inmate who violated a major disciplinary rule could lose some or all of those credits and could also be assigned a term in solitary confinement. In *Wolff*, an inmate filed a complaint that challenged the procedures by which he was found guilty of a major infraction that resulted in his good time credits being reduced. He alleged he should have had greater procedural rights than he was afforded, as guaranteed by the Fourteenth Amendment's Due Process Clause. In response, the State of Nebraska argued that a prisoner has no Fourteenth Amendment protections.

The Supreme Court rejected the legal arguments of both the prisoner and the state. The Court decided that the U.S. Constitution does not provide a guarantee of good time credit, however, Nebraska had provided a right to good time in its state statutes. Having created that statutory right and providing in the disciplinary regulations that good time could only be forfeited for serious misconduct, the prisoner had a liberty interest that needed protection against arbitrary action by state officials. Even though the liberty interest was created by a state statute and not the federal Constitution, the Court found it was protected by due process. Determining whether an inmate engaged in serious misconduct is critical in a system that allows for good time credits to be forfeited in the event of a guilty decision. The Court described the inmate's interest as a state-created liberty interest.

The *Wolff* decision went on to consider the type of due process the Nebraska inmates should be afforded when they are charged with a major disciplinary infraction. The Court acknowledged the reality of disciplinary processes in prison and the need to avoid unnecessary confrontations and the possibility of retaliation between charged inmates and those who provided evidence against them. It would be unwise, concluded the Court, to require prison proceedings to abide by the same due process requirements as criminal trials. Such an adversary proceeding might increase the likelihood of confrontation between inmates and staff and would undermine the goal of rehabilitation. In fact, prisoners involved in the disciplinary system are not entitled to the same rights afforded to offenders facing probation or parole revocation. A more flexible approach is needed to accommodate the needs of correctional institutions.

The Court outlined a list of minimum due process protections to be afforded prisoners facing charges on serious infractions:

1. Advance written notice of the alleged violations including a statement of the evidence on which the allegations are based and the reasons the disciplinary action was initiated.

2. The written notice of charges must be provided to the prisoner in order to allow him or her to prepare a defense, therefore, it must be provided no less than 24 hours prior to the disciplinary proceeding.

3. Inmates facing disciplinary charges should be allowed to call witnesses and present documentary evidence in their defense in those circumstances when permitting such will not threaten the safety and security of the institution. Although the Court specifically noted that it was not requiring disciplinary committees to state in writing the reasons for refusing to call a witness, the Court commented that this practice would be useful. Because confrontation and cross-examination of those who provide evidence against an inmate might present additional dangers to institutional security, it is not required by due process.

4. The Court stated it was not prepared to hold that inmates have a right to either retained or appointed counsel in disciplinary hearings, noting that inserting lawyers into these proceedings would increase their adversary nature and reduce their utility.

   When an illiterate inmate is charged with a serious infraction or the complexity of the charge will make it difficult for the prisoner to collect and present evidence, the prisoner should be able to seek the help of a fellow inmate, or if that is not permitted, to have adequate substitute aid from the staff or an inmate designated by the staff.

5. Inmates must be provided a written statement of the findings on which the disciplinary decision was based. Written records are important in the event the inmate appeals the disciplinary authority's decision

through an internal grievance system or in court and when the inmate comes up for parole.

6. Disciplinary charges must be considered and decided by an impartial board or party; however, the Court did not hold that such a board must be composed of a person or persons from outside the prison system. A board can be composed of responsible prison employees as long as they were not involved in the specific incident that resulted in the charge against the inmate.

The *Wolff* case is significant on several levels. It outlined in fairly explicit language the manner in which prison disciplinary hearings should be conducted. Prison officials were now in a position to implement changes in their disciplinary systems under the direct guidance of the Supreme Court. State authorities drafted forms for disciplinary committees to complete in order to meet the requirements for notice and written findings of fact. Other forms provided checklists for officials to use to make certain all the *Wolff* standards were met. Officials involved in operating the inmate disciplinary system, frequently selected from the ranks of correctional officers, were trained in the *Wolff* requirements. States initiated counsel substitute programs to assist inmates using either other inmates or staff. Due process was breathed into prisoner disciplinary systems throughout the country. On yet another level, the *Wolff* case introduced the state-created liberty interest doctrine. By applying this doctrine to the legal issues surrounding prisoner discipline, the Supreme Court opened the door for the doctrine's use in the future. The state-created liberty interest very quickly became one of the most controversial legal doctrines in the field of prisoners' rights. This chapter catalogs that controversy, but before it does, there are other important cases concerning inmate discipline that soon followed *Wolff*.

The *Wolff* Court refused to hold that attorneys should be provided to inmates in disciplinary hearings, but the issue was urged again in *Baxter v. Palmigiano* (1976). Palmigiano was charged with inciting a prison disturbance in a Rhode Island penitentiary and told that authorities might also prosecute him under state law. He was advised to consult an attorney for the state criminal case but told the attorney would not be permitted into the administrative disciplinary hearing. He was also advised he could remain silent during the disciplinary hearing but his silence could be used against him. Palmigiano did not testify during his disciplinary hearing, was found guilty, and given 30 days in punitive segregation. He filed a lawsuit alleging his due process rights were violated, maintaining that his silence should not have been used against him in the disciplinary hearing. He also maintained that where there is a realistic possibility an inmate would face criminal charges; he or she should be able to have counsel assist him during the administrative hearing.

The Court quickly disposed of both Palmigiano's arguments. The fact that he might also be involved in a criminal case involving the same matter did not give him a constitutional right to retained or appointed counsel during the disciplinary hearing. The Court drew a bright line separating the right of counsel for criminal defendants and no such right for prisoners charged with prison infractions. It is of no consequence that an inmate may be facing both administrative discipline and a criminal indictment. The Court drew a second bright line between the Fifth Amendment's protection against self-incrimination for criminal defendants whose silence can never be used against them and prisoners whose silence can be used against them in the prison disciplinary process. In *Baxter v. Palmiagiano*, the Supreme Court ended any speculation that the due process protections first afforded by *Wolff* would be expanded. The Court did note, however, that if an inmate is compelled to testify in a disciplinary hearing and furnishes evidence that might incriminate him in a later criminal case, he must be offered whatever immunity is constitutionally required.

In *Superintendent of the Massachusetts Correctional Institution at Walpole v. Hill* (1985), the Supreme Court decided the degree of evidence that is needed to support a guilty verdict in a prison disciplinary matter. This issue had not been raised in *Wolff*. Is the "beyond a reasonable doubt" standard used in criminal cases the applicable standard in a disciplinary court? Or is the civil "beyond a preponderance of the evidence" standard more appropriate? Hill was found guilty of assault based on the testimony of a correctional officer who heard a commotion, ran to investigate, found the assaulted inmate, and saw Hill and two other prisoners running from the area. No other inmates were in the area. Hill and the other two were found guilty, and Hill lost good time and was placed in solitary confinement. His lawsuit alleged there was insufficient evidence to support the finding of guilt. On appeal from the Massachusetts Supreme Judicial Court, the U.S. Supreme Court agreed that good-time credits constitute a protected liberty interest and cannot be forfeited without some evidence of guilt. According to the Supreme Court, the relevant question was whether there was *any* evidence in the record to support the disciplinary finding of guilt. The Court agreed the evidence in this case might well be characterized as meager, certainly none of it was direct, nevertheless the record was not so devoid of evidence as to suggest the finding was arbitrary or could not be supported. In the *Hill* case, the Supreme Court announced that neither the criminal nor civil burdens of proof are required in the prison context. A finding of some evidence is all that is necessary to provide minimum due process.

The same year the Court issued the *Hill* opinion, it also decided *Ponte v. Real* (1985). Real was found guilty of fighting and forfeited good time credit after a disciplinary hearing during which he was not permitted to call witnesses. The Massachusetts Supreme Judicial Court agreed that Real was entitled to have a written reason entered into the hearing record as to why his request for witnesses was denied. The U. S. Supreme Court decided otherwise, ruling that due process requires officials to state their reasons for denying witnesses either in the administrative record of the disciplinary hearing *or* by presenting testimony in court if the prisoner later challenges the decision in a lawsuit. The Court again refused to expand the *Wolff* requirements. As had been stated in *Wolff,* noting a reason for denying a witness in the record may be a good practice, but it is not constitutionally required.

By the mid-1980s, the due process revolution had revolutionized the inmate disciplinary system. In *Wolff v. McDonnell* (1974), the Supreme Court outlined a set of directions for officials to follow concerning the procedural due process that must be afforded offenders facing serious disciplinary charges. Correctional institutions nationwide revamped their disciplinary procedures to meet the Supreme Court's interpretation of what the Constitution required. Despite attempts to expand due process protections in *Baxter v. Palmigiano,* the Court refused to go beyond the extensive revisions it ordered in *Wolff.* Prison disciplinary hearings are administrative matters, not criminal trials. The prison environment is unique; and many of the due process protections provided in the criminal context are inappropriate and counterproductive in a correctional facility.

DUE PROCESS COMES TO PRISONER CLASSIFICATION

Since the 1970s, prisoner classification systems have evolved to become the primary management tool for prison administrators. Austin (1993; 1986) went so far as to describe a properly functioning classification system as the "brain" of prison management. It controls inmate movement, housing, and program participation, which directly impact staffing and budgetary needs. Classification is a sophisticated mechanism that assesses the risks inmates pose to the public and to other inmates as well as their treatment and program needs. In the ideal situation, prisoners are assigned to institutions and housing arrangements that reflect both of these concerns. Given the impact that classification decisions have on the daily lives of prisoners, it is not surprising that classification issues are the basis of many inmate lawsuits (Belbot and del Carmen 1993). At issue are the conflicting interests of prisoner officials in operating efficient and safe institutions and the prisoners' interests in being assigned to facilities, housing areas, and jobs that are amenable to them. The growing population of prisoners with special needs – elderly inmates, inmates with long sentences, inmates with physical or mental health concerns – makes classification an even more important management tool.

A well-designed and implemented classification system can reduce tension among prisoners and officials. Along with the disciplinary system, it is a correctional agency's formal mechanism of social control, by which it can respond to a prisoner's past behavior and threaten consequences for future misconduct. Classification systems "reward" good behavior by providing that inmates with good institutional records be assigned to less restrictive housing areas, be permitted to engage in more programming opportunities, and qualify for more interesting jobs. Inmates who misbehave are sanctioned by classification assignments that place them in restrictive housing, limits their privileges and the availability of programs. Prisoners who are found guilty of committing disciplinary infractions often face the possibility of being reclassified to a more restrictive custody or security level, either as a part of their disciplinary punishment or in a separate, additional administrative action. The disciplinary and classification systems complement each other, both central to the prison regimen officials rely on to create prisons that are safe and secure.

In a series of separate cases in the 1970s - *Holt v. Sarver*, 309 F.Supp 362 (E.D. Ark. 1970), aff'd 442 F.2d 304 (8th Cir. 1971), *Gates v. Collier*, 349 F.Supp 881 (N.D. Miss. 1972), aff'd 501 F.2d 1291 (5th Cir. 1974), *Pugh v. Locke*, 406 F. Supp 318 (M.D.Ala. 1976), aff'd, 559 F.2d 283 (5th Cir. 1977) and *Palmigiano v. Garrahy*, 443 F. Supp 956 (D.R.I. 1977) – federal courts concluded, among other findings, that the state prisons involved in those lawsuits failed to classify prisoners properly. As a result, serious offenders were housed with first time offenders, violent inmates were assigned to live in dormitories, mentally ill prisoners were not identified and placed in appropriate housing, and stronger inmates were allowed to prey on weaker inmates. The courts responded in these early prisoner rights cases by establishing two important principles: 1) effective prisoner classification systems are required in order to provide prisoners with their constitutional right to a reasonably safe and secure living environment, and 2) classification systems must be implemented in a constitutional manner, meaning they must rationally, fairly and equitably classify prisoners according to legitimate characteristics logically relevant to where they should be housed, assigned work, and how they should be supervised.

Since those early cases, one of the most frequently litigated areas related to classification has been the due process rights provided to prisoners involved in the process. The central issue has been the scope of due process protections that inmates should be afforded. How much due process is required? With the exception of transfer to a mental health institution, the Supreme Court has consistently rejected claims that prisoners are entitled to constitutionally mandated due process during classification. Although the Constitution requires prisoners have a safe living environment and a rational and fair system is necessary to realize that requirement, the Constitution's Due Process Clause does not mandate classification procedures. Instead, the due process rights of prisoners involved in classification matters has been analyzed according to the state-created liberty interest doctrine. The doctrine the Court applied in 1974 to the inmate discipline in *Wolff v. McDonnell* became the basis for evaluating due process and classification.

In one of the first cases dealing directly with prisoner classification issues, *Meachum v. Fano* (1976), the Supreme Court distinguished between due process protections that originate in the Constitution and those created by state statute. Several prisoners who were suspected of setting fires were transferred from a medium security institution to a maximum-security institution where the living conditions were substantially less comfortable. They alleged that the hearing they were given prior to their transfers was constitutionally inadequate. The Supreme Court ruled the Constitution does not guarantee an inmate will be assigned to any particular prison if a state has more than one facility. The decision to assign an inmate to a particular institution does not initiate due process protection even if life in one prison is less agreeable than life in another. Neither does the Constitution protect a prisoner against transfer from one institution to another within the prison system. The Court examined the state law where the inmates were incarcerated to see if it created a liberty interest for inmates to remain in any particular institution. The Court concluded that state law gave officials a broad grant of authority to assign and transfer prisoners under a wide variety of circumstances, and, as worded, did not confer a liberty interest requiring constitutional protection.

The Supreme Court decided *Montanye v. Haymes* (1976) on the same day as *Meachum v. Fano*. Haymes was removed from his assignment as a prisoner clerk in the law library at Attica in New York and transferred to another facility. According to prison officials, he was removed because he violated the regulations governing prison use, however, no disciplinary infraction was charged against him. Haymes alleged he was removed in retaliation for providing legal assistance to other inmates. The Supreme Court determined that it did not matter why Haymes was removed because the Constitution's Due Process Clause does not require a hearing even if a transfer resulted from an inmate's behavior or if the transfer was labeled disciplinary or punitive. The Court also decided that New York State law did not give Haymes the right to remain at a particular institution.

The third Supreme Court case to address transfer involved an inmate who was transferred from the Hawaii State prison to a mainland facility. In *Olim v. Wakinekona* (1983), the Court reinforced its earlier position. Wakinekona did not have a constitutional due process right to remain incarcerated in a specific state. Neither did Hawaii law create a liberty interest in his remaining in that state because it did not put substantive limits on official discretion to decide which prisoners should be transferred.

In *Meachum v. Fano*, *Montanye v. Haymes*, and *Olim v. Wakinekona*, the Supreme Court established that just as with the disciplinary system, the due process afforded to prisoners involved in classification is created by a statute, administrative rule, or policy that limits the state's discretion in an area where otherwise the state would be free to operate without restraint. The Constitution itself does not mandate due process. Nonetheless, in the three cases it analyzed, the Court decided that state law did not create such an interest, so that no particular classification procedures were mandated.

Johnson v. California (2005)

The Supreme Court's decision in *Johnson v. California* (2005) addressed where prisoners are housed after they first arrive in the California Department of Corrections (CDC) or after they are transferred from one CDC facility to another CDC facility. At issue was the constitutionality of an unwritten CDC policy of racially segregating prisoners in double cells in reception centers for up to 60 days each time they arrived at a new correctional institution. The CDC also subdivided inmates within each racial group. Japanese-American inmates were housed separately from Chinese-Americans. Hispanic inmates from northern California were housed separately from Hispanics from southern California. CDC officials justified the policy as necessary to prevent racial gang-related violence, and supported the policy with testimony from numerous prison administrators about the seriousness and prevalence of racial violence. The 60 day period gave officials time to observe the inmates' conduct and evaluate whether they posed a danger to other inmates. Only the housing blocks in the reception centers were racially segregated. The rest of the facility was fully integrated.

The inmate who filed the lawsuit alleged that the policy violated the Equal Protection Clause of the Fourteenth Amendment because it was based on race. He argued that all racial classifications imposed by the government must be analyzed under a strict scrutiny standard. California prison officials maintained that the segregation policy should be analyzed under the four-part *Turner v. Safely* (1987) test, discussed in detail in Chapter 3. According to officials, under the *Turner* test the policy was rationally related to the legitimate government purpose of maintaining prison security. The fact that inmates were segregated for a short period of time was evidence that the policy did not deprive inmates of their constitutional rights. Not enforcing the policy put the safety of other inmates and the staff at risk.

The Supreme Court decided that the strict scrutiny standard should be applied in deciding the constitutionality of the CDC policy under the Equal Protection Clause. Strict scrutiny requires the government prove that the racial classification is narrowly tailored and is necessary to further a compelling governmental interest because all racial classifications are immediately suspect. Even though all inmates are racially segregated under the CDC policy, the Court concluded that strict scrutiny is required because such a policy can never be neutral. In addition, the Court cited research that suggests racial integration in prison leads to less violence. The Court relied heavily on its decision in *Lee v. Washington* (1968), in which it struck down Alabama's policy of racially segregating its prisons, which had also been justified as necessary to maintain security. The Court concluded that the *Turner* test is not appropriate for evaluating racial classification policies since, "The right not to be discriminated against based on race is not susceptible to the logic of *Turner*."

The Court did not decide whether the CDC segregation policy violated the Constitution. It remanded the case back to the lower courts to review the policy under the strict scrutiny standard. The Court agreed there may be situations where a narrowly drawn policy of racial segregation serves a compelling governmental interest.

THE STATE-CREATED LIBERTY INTEREST DOCTRINE MATURES

In 1983, the Supreme Court outlined the state-created liberty interest doctrine in much greater detail than it had in its previous inmate discipline and classification cases. *Hewitt v. Helms* (1983) involved a prisoner who was removed from general population and placed in administrative segregation following a riot in a Pennsylvania correctional institution. Inmate Helms argued that the informal due process procedures afforded him were constitutionally inadequate, and he had been held in segregated status without proper safeguards.

The Supreme Court analyzed Helms' claim from the perspective of two possible sources of liberty interests – the Due Process Clause and state law. The Court concluded that the Constitution did not provide Helms with an interest in remaining in the general population. Administrators have broad discretion in managing inmates. As long as the conditions of confinement are constitutional and within the sentence imposed, due process is not violated. Moreover, every prisoner can expect to be assigned to administrative segregation at some point during incarceration. Such an assignment was within the term of Helms' sentence. The Court, however, ruled that the state had created a liberty interest by enacting statutes and regulations governing the use of administrative segregation that restricted official discretion. The state went beyond simple procedural guidelines by using explicitly mandatory language requiring that certain procedures "shall," "will," and "must" be employed. The regulations also provided that placement in administrative segregation would not occur in the absence of legal justifications, such as the need for control or threat of a serious disturbance. Even though the Court acknowledged that prisoners had a state-created liberty interest in not being placed in administrative segregation, the Court declined to hold that Helms had a right to more procedural protections than he had already been afforded. The Court decided the informal, nonadversarial procedures used in Helms case were adequate to protect his state-created liberty interest.

Hewitt v. Helms was an important opinion for several reasons. On one level, it established that an informal hearing was sufficient to protect an inmate's state-created liberty interest to remain in the general population. In making these determinations, states were not required to provide the same scope of protections afforded inmates facing allegations of violating a serious disciplinary rule. There was a significant difference in the two liberty interests. On another level, the case is important because it attempted to clarify the state-created liberty interest doctrine. The Supreme Court announced in *Hewitt v. Helms,* that lower federal courts faced with deciding whether a state had created a liberty interest for prisoners needed to examine the state's statutes and regulations for explicit language, specifically words like "shall," "will," and "should." These words denote a mandate to state officials. They require officials to take or refrain from certain actions and restrict the use of discretion. For example, statutes or regulations that simply set forth a set of criteria establishing under what circumstances a prisoner can be transferred, classified, or reclassified, have not created liberty interests. To create such interests, the language of the statutes or regulations must also mandate that administrators "must," "shall," "will," or "should" take certain steps under those circumstances. Terms such as "may" or "can" do not limit administrative discretion and tend not to create liberty interests. If a liberty interest has been created by state law or regulation, an agency must provide adequate due process in the form of notice and a hearing to make certain the agency abides by the limitations set in its own criteria and procedures. The statute, rule, or policy limits the state's right to choose and requires the state agency to follow procedural due process to assure it makes a decision that is consistent with the limits it has imposed on its own discretion.

VITEK V. JONES

Case law is clear: the Constitution's Due Process Clause fails to protect prisoners in matters pertaining to classification. The one exception is when an inmate is transferred involuntarily to a mental health institution for treatment. In *Vitek v. Jones* (1980), the Court concluded that transfer from a correctional institution to a mental hospital is not within the range of confinement justified by a prison sentence. Commitment to a mental hospital imposes qualitatively different adverse consequences than does punishment, including social stigma and the possibility of mandatory participation in behavior modification programs. Ordinary citizens are entitled to Due Process Clause protections before being transferred involuntarily to mental hospitals, so do inmates enjoy the same constitutional due process rights. Prisoners retain a liberty interest in not being arbitrarily or inappropriately transferred to a mental institution. Such transfers require: 1) adequate, advance written notice to the inmate that a transfer is under consideration; 2) an adversarial hearing where prisoners have the opportunity to present evidence and witnesses, and where, if security permits, cross-examination of the agency's witnesses; 3) an independent decision maker; and 4) a written statement by the decision maker outlining the evidence relied on and the reasons for the decision. Although four of the five Justices in the majority believed the prisoner should have a right to counsel, there was no majority agreement that counsel was constitutionally required. Justice Powell held instead that inmates have the right to some competent help during the process.

In a case similar to *Vitek v. Jones* (1980), in *Washington v. Harper* (1990), the Supreme Court considered procedural protections for prisoners who the state wants to treat involuntarily with antipsychotic medication. Following *Vitek*, the Court grounded the inmate's liberty interest in the Constitution's Due Process Clause. Both cases recognized that a criminal sentence does not permit the state every intrusion into a prisoner's liberty. Both decisions concluded that issues concerning mental health treatment are qualitatively different from issues involving length of custody or conditions of confinement.

THE STATE-CREATED LIBERTY INTEREST DOCTRINE REDEFINED

Although the scope of due process rights is central in the disciplinary and classification systems, it is also relevant in other prison contexts. In *Kentucky v. Thompson* (1989), two inmates were denied visits with family members because the visitors were suspected of smuggling contraband into the institution. In both cases, visiting privileges were suspended without a hearing. The prisoners filed a lawsuit alleging their due process rights were violated. The Supreme Court dismissed any notion that the Constitution provides inmates with a liberty interest in visitation, finding that denying visitation was to be expected as part of a prison sentence. As long as the conditions of confinement are within the sentence, the due process clause does not apply. The Court then examined Kentucky state law and polices to determine if they created a liberty interest for inmates in visitation, thereby triggering due process protection. Building on its reasoning in *Helms v. Hewitt* (1983), the Court concluded that although the state's visitation policies listed certain criteria for officers to follow in deciding whether visits should be restricted, the policies lacked mandatory language. They failed to require a specific result when one or more of the criteria were met. Officers were not required to exclude visitors when one of the events on the criteria list occurred, and, on the other hand, officers could exclude visitors for reasons not included in the list of criteria. A state-created liberty interest cannot exist without mandatory language. In *Kentucky v. Thompson*, the Supreme Court applied a doctrine it had used primarily to analyze due process for prisoners involved in the discipline and classification systems to an entirely different matter. The state-created liberty interest doctrine had permeated the debate about the extent of inmates' rights.

Meanwhile, the lower federal courts were applying the doctrine in a large number of lawsuits prisoners were filing, lawsuits claiming their liberty interests were infringed without due process. They claimed liberty interests in remaining in the general population, in being considered for particular job assignments, programs and activities, in receiving regular meals instead of sack lunches – to describe just a few of the more frequent claims (Belbot 1998). The courts were charged with deciding whether the liberty interest existed and, if so, what due process inmates should be afforded. The lower courts worked toward refining the doctrine. As applied, the doctrine reduced the opportunities officials had to exercise arbitrary authority based on facts or criteria that were not relevant to the issue at hand. It was not, however, a doctrine that was easy to apply and the lower court judges were not hesitant to recognize its many limits.

In 1995, the Supreme Court decided *Sandin v. Connor*, which significantly restricted when and how the state-created liberty interest doctrine could be used.

Connor was serving 30 years in a maximum-security institution in Hawaii. During a strip search, he used angry and foul language to the correctional officer and was charged with several disciplinary infractions. One of the charges was for "high misconduct" and could result in up to 30 days in disciplinary segregation. Connor requested several witnesses at his hearing, but the hearing officer deemed they were unavailable. Connor was found guilty and given 30 days of confinement in solitary, which he served. Nine months after his hearing, pursuant to his administrative appeal, the deputy administrator found that the high misconduct charge was unsupported and removed it from his record.

Before his appeal was decided, however, Connor had filed a lawsuit complaining that he had been deprived of due process at his disciplinary hearing. The federal District Court dismissed his case. The Ninth Circuit Court of Appeals reversed that decision and concluded that Connor had a liberty interest in staying out of disciplinary segregation based on the language of the Hawaii statutes and regulations. Citing *Kentucky v. Thompson* the appellate court ruled the Hawaii regulations created explicit standards for officials to follow, including a requirement that a disciplinary committee could not reach a guilty finding without substantial evidence of guilt. The court then decided there was a real and important issue as to whether Connor was deprived of his right to call witnesses and present documentary evidence in his defense. The case should be sent back to the District Court to examine that issue.

On appeal to the U.S. Supreme Court, Chief Justice Rehnquist's majority opinion (5-4 decision) dramatically altered the state-created liberty interest doctrine. The majority was especially critical of the *Hewitt v. Helms* decision because it failed to examine whether the liberty interest in question was one of real substance, but instead focused on the regulation's language. Wrote Rehnquist,

As this methodology took hold, no longer did inmates need to rely on a showing that they suffered a 'grievous loss' of liberty retained even after sentenced to terms of imprisonment (citation omitted) …. For the Court had ceased to examine the 'nature' of the interest with respect to interests allegedly created by the State.

This shift in focus from the nature of the deprivation to the language of the regulation encouraged prisoners to search regulations for mandatory language on which to claim rights. This approach strayed from the real concerns of the liberty interest doctrine first recognized in *Wolff v. McDonnell* (1974). According to the majority, states can create liberty interests, however:

[T]hese interests will be generally limited to freedom from restraint which, while not exceeding the sentence in such an unexpected manner as to give rise to protection by the Due Process Clause of its own force, *see, e.g., Vitek* … nonetheless imposes atypical and significant hardship on the inmate in relation to the ordinary incidents of prison life.

Prisoners can expect to be held accountable for violating a disciplinary infraction sometime during their term of incarceration. Punishment for such a violation is not an atypical or significant hardship compared to the ordinary circumstances under which a prisoner lives. Connor's 30 days in disciplinary segregation was not atypical or significant. Conditions in solitary were similar to conditions in administrative segregation and protective custody, found the Court. Connor did not suffer a major disruption to his environment while he was in solitary. His time in solitary would not impact his overall length of incarceration. The Supreme Court ruled that Connor did not have a liberty interest in remaining out of disciplinary segregation that would entitle him to the type of due process set forth in *Wolff v. McDonnell.*

The majority opinion highlighted the important policy considerations in its legal analysis. It attacked the state-created liberty interest doctrine on the grounds it encouraged states to not draft written standards and policies out of fear the rules would actually spawn inmate litigation. Prisoners would comb the rules looking for mandatory language to use as the basis for a liberty interest lawsuit. Just as significant for the majority was concern that the doctrine had led federal courts to become overly involved in the daily operations of prisons. Judges failed to defer to correctional administrators and allow them the flexibility they needed to manage effectively. The old liberty interest doctrine had also burdened federal courts with too many prisoner lawsuits that lacked merit.

Sandin v. Connor (1995) re-wrote the state-created liberty interest doctrine. However, the Court's opinion provided little guidance for determining what amounts to an atypical and significant hardship on an inmate that exists outside of the ordinary circumstances of being incarcerated. How should lower federal courts apply this new standard to future cases? Both Justices Breyer and Ginsburg dissented to the *Sandin* majority and made note that the new version of a state-created liberty interest is so general as to create greater uncertainty than what existed under the old version. What exactly is atypical? What is a significant deprivation? While the Court resolved those issues for Inmate Connor, it would be up to future courts to apply the revised doctrine to cases prisoners filed after *Sandin*, where the facts are different and arguments can be fashioned on both sides. A court must find that an inmate has been subjected to an atypical or significant hardship before the state-created liberty interest doctrine is triggered. In those cases where it is triggered, a court then considers the appropriate scope of the prisoner's due process rights and whether they were afforded.

The federal courts of appeal went in several different directions interpreting the *Sandin* version of the state-created liberty interest doctrine, especially as it related to classifying prisoners into administrative segregation, which, unlike solitary confinement, frequently involves a long-term placement (Goldman 2004). The Supreme Court finally clarified this issue in *Wilkinson v. Austin* (2005). In that case, prisoners housed in the Ohio State Penitentiary (OSP), a supermaximum facility that was built in 1998 to house up to 504 of the state's most dangerous inmates, filed a class action lawsuit challenging the procedures by which they were assigned to the special facility. Conditions in the OSP are the most restrictive in the state prison system, including death row and other administrative control units. Prisoners in the OSP remain in single cells 23 hours a day with a light on at all times. They are allowed to leave their cells one hour a day to recreate in an indoor recreation cell. The cells doors are solid metal with metal strips along the sides and bottom to prevent communication. All meals are served in the cell and visits are limited. Prisoners are assigned to the OSP for an unlimited period of time, limited only by their sentence.

Inmates are assigned to the OSP if they are classified as level 5 in the state's security classification system. Level 5 inmates are considered serious security risks based on any number of factors including criminal history, escape history, gang affiliation, and institutional conduct. Classification to level 5 can occur when an inmate enters the prison system or during his incarceration. A prison official begins the process of assigning an inmate to the OSP by preparing a three-page form that details the reasons for requesting the inmate's classification to level 5. A three member Classification Committee reviews the request and conducts a review hearing. At least 48 hours before the hearing, the prisoner is provided written notice summarizing the conduct that triggered the request along with the more detailed three-page form. He can attend the hearing and offer information and explanation and submit a written statement. He may not call witnesses.

If the Committee recommends placement in the OSP, it sets forth its reasons in writing to the warden where the inmate is currently housed. If the warden agrees with the assignment to OSP, he or she provides reasons in writing to the state level Bureau of Classification for a final decision. The inmate is given notice of the recommendation made by the Classification Committee and the warden, and has 15 days to file written objections to the Bureau of Classification. If the Bureau agrees to the OSP assignment, the prisoner is so assigned. Assignment to OSP only occurs if the Classification Committee, the warden, and the Bureau of Classification approve it.

Inmates assigned to the OSP have their assignments reviewed within 30 days their assignment. After that, placement in OSP is reviewed on an at least annual basis according to the same three-step process that resulted in the prisoner's initial assignment.

The class of prisoners in *Wilkinson v. Austin* (2005) argued that the procedures by which they were assigned to the OSP violated their due process protections. The Federal District Court and the Sixth Circuit Court of Appeals both agreed that the prisoners should be provided additional procedural protections including providing inmates with an exhaustive list of the grounds that justified placement at OSP and the right to call witnesses at the Classification Committee review hearing.

The U. S Supreme Court began its analysis by first considering whether inmates assigned to the OSP have a protected liberty interest in not being so assigned. A unanimous Court wrote:

> The *Sandin* standard requires us to determine if assignment to OSP 'imposes atypical and significant hardship on the inmate in relation to the ordinary incidents of prison life.' ... In *Sandin*'s wake the Court of Appeals have not reached consistent conclusions for identifying the baseline from which to measure what is atypical and significant in any particular prison system... This divergence indicates the difficulty of locating the appropriate baseline, an issue that was not explored at length in the briefs. We need not resolve the issue here; however, for we are satisfied that assignment to OSP imposes an atypical and significant hardship under any plausible baseline.

The Court described the severe restrictions placed on inmates housed in OSP and concluded, "While any of these conditions standing alone might not be sufficient to create a liberty interest, taken together they impose an atypical and significant hardship within the correctional context." The Court's analysis did not end here. With the liberty interest established, the Justices had to decide what process is due an inmate who is facing placement in OSP. Here the Court disagreed with the two lower courts that Ohio must expand its procedural protections. Instead it ruled that the procedures Ohio already had in place sufficiently protected the prisoners' constitutional due process rights. The Court recognized the need to have a supermaximum security unit and the ability to place prisoners in that unit for extended periods of time. It concluded that multiple levels of review reduced the risk of erroneous placement and that security concerns argued against an inmate's right to present witnesses at a review hearing. The Court was satisfied that prisoners were provided timely and adequate notice of the reasons for the assignment and the grounds for the decision.

In *McKune v. Lile* (2002), the Supreme Court had the opportunity to apply the *Sandin* holding to a somewhat unique set of circumstances. Lile was convicted of rape, aggravated sodomy, and aggravated kidnapping, but maintained during trial that the sexual encounter was consensual. He was ordered to participate in a special sex offender treatment program while incarcerated in Kansas. The program required inmates to admit responsibility for their offense and complete a history of their prior sexual misconduct, including activities that had not resulted in criminal charges. The information in their history could be used against them in future criminal proceedings. Lile refused to participate because he argued that doing so would violate his privilege against self-incrimination under the Fifth Amendment. According to the rules of the program, when an inmate refused participation, his work assignment, visitation rights, commissary, earnings, and access to television could be affected, and he risked transfer to a maximum-security facility. Lile filed a lawsuit and the District Court issued an injunction that prevented officials from reducing his privileges or transferring him. The court of appeals affirmed, and Kansas officials went to the Supreme Court.

The Court decided that a mandatory prison-based sex offender treatment program that requires offenders to admit sexual misconduct for which they have not been charged or convicted does not violate the Fifth Amendment even though inmates who refuse to participate are penalized. Officials are not required to offer inmates immunity from prosecution based on the information they provide as part of their history of sexual misconduct. Treatment professionals designed the program this way in order to emphasize the seriousness of sexual misconduct. The program is rationally related to legitimate penological purposes. The types of penalties imposed on prisoners who refuse to provide a history – transfer to a more secure institution and limits on work and privileges – are not the types of things that compel inmates to provide incriminating information and, in essence, testify against themselves. And here is where the *Sandin* case enters the picture. The Court reasoned that *Sandin* held that prison conditions do not violate the Due Process Clause unless they are atypical and significant hardships. The Supreme Court Justices decided that the penalties Lile faced were neither. They did not include extending his sentence, taking away good time, or affecting his parole eligibility. Transfer to another prison unit is not punishment, and the Constitution gives officials significant discretion to restrict privileges. According to the *Lile* opinion, an inmate cannot argue successfully that he was compelled to incriminate himself when he is threatened with a punishment that is not atypical or significantly harsh.

The *Sandin* case will continue to raise new legal issues. The *Wilkinson v. Austin* opinion resolved the liberty interest issue only as it relates to assignments to severely restrictive housing units. How the Court's decision in *Wilkinson* will impact placements in less restrictive environments still remains to be seen. Even acknowledging the atypical hardship of an assignment to OSP, the Court did not extend the prisoners' due process rights beyond what Ohio already provided. It's apparent that the state-created liberty interest doctrine, which provided prisoners many due process protections since its introduction in *Wolff v. McDonnell* (1974) through its evolution in cases like *Hewitt v. Helms* (1983) and *Kentucky v. Thompson* (1989), has changed and will continue to evolve – this time in the direction mandated by *Sandin v. Connor*. Prisoners have never had an easy time arguing that they possessed a state-created liberty interest. Courts have not been reluctant to find that the doctrine did not apply. The *Sandin* decision increases that likelihood. Critics of the decision allege it sends a message to prison administrators that their policies and procedures are less likely to be subject to court oversight.

SUMMARY

Due process as it affects the prisoner disciplinary and classification systems has been an evolving and sometimes confusing story. The due process revolution transformed these two systems of social control. It is an excellent study in how law develops overtime and adapts to changing social attitudes and priorities. The story, however, has not yet ended. What constitutes due process in a prison setting will never be easy to delineate. Legitimate needs for security and control make it difficult to determine the parameters of procedural due process. Once it is determined that some due process must be afforded, rights like confrontation of witnesses, the minimum burden of proof, and advice of counsel raise complicated issues when they are considered in the context of prison. The Supreme Court decided that for many reasons, due process in prison could not be as comprehensive as due process in a court of law.

Before deciding what type of due process must be extended, the Court had to create a standard or methodology for deciding if due process was even required. The methodology was designed for the lower courts to use in pending litigation and to guide prison officials as they devised rules and regulations. As cumbersome as it was, the state-created liberty interest doctrine evolved through a series of Supreme Court cases and came to dominate due process analysis for over twenty years. The doctrine is still alive, but the significant revisions that resulted from *Sandin v. Connor* (1995) make it a very different doctrine that lowers the minimum procedural due process protections prisoners must be afforded. To some it heralds a major retrenchment to a time when inmates had few due process rights. To others, it was a necessary adjustment to a doctrine that had been misinterpreted and resulted in an over-involved federal judiciary, burdened by thousands of nonmeritorious lawsuits.

Summary of Due Process Protections for Prisoners

Disciplinary Hearings

Wolff v. McDonnell (1974)

1) advance written notice of the charges and evidence relied on at least 24 hours before hearing
2) right to call witnesses and introduce documentary evidence unless security may be jeopardized
3) right to counsel substitute for illiterate inmates or inmates facing serious, complex charges that would make it difficult for them to collect and present evidence
4) written statements of findings upon which decision is based
5) decision by impartial board or hearing officer
6) no right to confront or cross-examine witnesses

Baxter v. Palmigiano (1976)

No right to counsel during disciplinary hearing even if criminal charges could result

Hearing officer can make an adverse inference from prisoner's decision to remain silent during hearing

Superintendent v. Hill (1985)

Only "some" evidence is constitutionally required to support a guilty finding

Ponte v. Real (1985)

Prison officials are not required to state their reasons for denying an inmate's request for a witness during a hearing

Transfer to another Prison Facility

Meachum v. Fano (1976)

No due process afforded to prisoner being transferred to a prison with a less favorable environment

Montana v. Haymes (1976)

No due process afforded to prisoner being transferred to another prison as a result of misconduct.

Viet v. Jones (1980)

Due process required in order to transfer a prisoners to a mental health hospital, including

1) written notice of a hearing
2) opportunity to present evidence
3) written reasons for the decision
4) an impartial decision maker – not necessarily a judge

Summary of Due Process Protections for Prisoners (cont.)

Transfer to Disciplinary or Administrative Segregation

Hewitt v. Helms (1983)

Inmates assigned to administrative segregation may have a state-created liberty interest based on state laws or regulations that require limited due process be afforded.

Sandin v. Connor (1995)

Inmates assigned to disciplinary segregation do not have a state-created liberty interest based on state laws or regulations that afford them due process protections because such an assignment is not atypical or a significant hardship.

Wilkinson v. Austin (2005)

Assignment to a severely restrictive housing unit is an atypical and significant hardship which gives rise to a liberty interest protected by limited due process.

DISCUSSION QUESTIONS

1. Why are due process protections different for criminal suspects and defendants versus already incarcerated offenders?

2. What about the prisoner disciplinary process in particular lends itself to fewer due process rights than those afforded in a criminal trial?

3. Outline the various Supreme Court cases that addressed prisoners' state-created liberty interests. How did each case build on the case that came before it?

4. What about the *Sandin v. Connor* case dramatically changed the state-created liberty interest doctrine?

5. Why is prisoner classification so important to both officials and to prisoners and what kind of due process rights do inmates have as a part of that process?

6. What is the working relationship between the prison disciplinary and classification systems?

7. How has the Supreme Court addressed the right to counsel in the inmate disciplinary and classification processes?

SUGGESTED READINGS AND REFERENCES

Austin, J. (1983). "Assessing the new generation of prison classification models." *Crime and Delinquency 29*: 561-76.

Austin, J. (1993). "Objective prisoner classification systems: A review" in *Classification: A Tool for Today's Offenders*. Laurel, Md.: American Correctional Associaton.

Belbot, B. (1998) "Where can a prisoner find a liberty interest these days? The pains of imprisonment escalate" *New York Law School Review* 42 (1) : 1-69.

Belbot, B. and Rolando del Carmen (1993). "Legal issues in classification," in *Classification: Tool for Managing Today's Offenders.* Laurel, Md.: American Correctional Association.

Etzioni, A. (1969) *Complex Organizations: A Sociological Reader*. New York: Holt, Rinehart and Winston.

Goldman, M. (2004). "*Sandin v. Conner* and intraprison confinement: Ten years of confusion and harm in prisoner litigation." *Boston College Law Review*: 45, 423- 466.

Robbins, I. 1980. "The cry of *Wolfish* in the federal courts: the future of federal judicial intervention in prison administration. *Journal of Criminal Law and Criminology* 71: 211-225.

Smith, C.E. (2000). "The governance of corrections: Implications of the changing interface of courts and corrections." In Boundary Changes in Criminal Justice organizations. Vol. 2. 113-166. Office of Justice Programs or the NIJ.

Teeters, Negley K. (1955). *The Cradle of the Penitentiary: The Walnut Street Jail at Philadelphia, 1773-1835*. Philadelphia: Temple University.

Thomas, J. et al. (1991). "Exacting control through disciplinary hearings: "making do" with prison rules," Justice Quarterly: 37.

CHAPTER 8:

Eighth Amendment

INTRODUCTION

Chapter 8 begins with a discussion about the Eighth Amendment's cruel and unusual punishment clause and how it has been interpreted in prisoners' rights cases. This very short amendment reads, "Excessive bail shall not be required, nor cruel and unusual punishment inflicted." Noticeably absent is an attempt to define what constitutes cruel and unusual punishment. Historically, the amendment has been applied to the sentence imposed after an individual has been convicted of an offense. The legal issues have involved whether the sentence was cruel or unusual. Students will discover that with the advent of the prisoner's rights revolution, the Eighth Amendment has received a "face-lift." The Supreme Court significantly expanded the amendment's meaning to include the living conditions an offender experiences while they are incarcerated pursuant to a sentence that is itself clearly constitutionally legitimate. Chapter 8 examines the prison condition cases before the Supreme Court that have raised the Eighth Amendment. It also looks at the controversy surrounding judicial activism and federal judges who have relied on the cruel and unusual punishment clause to reform correctional institutions and the complex remedies they have designed to implement and monitor the reform.

Finally, the chapter ends with an examination of some of the unique legal issues associated with providing inmates with adequate medical care. Prisoners generally come from populations who are underserved by the health care system in the U.S., further complicated by the fact that they bring with them a high level of drug, tobacco and alcohol abuse. Health care costs have risen dramatically in the last decade, and the percentages of state budgets dedicated to inmate health care have expanded accordingly, making some of the legal issues more controversial than ever. Why discuss correctional health care in a chapter about the cruel and unusual punishment clause? As students will see, the Supreme Court has interpreted that clause to require the delivery of adequate medical care to prison and jail inmates – whether they have been convicted of crimes or are still waiting to go to trial.

EARLY PRISONERS' RIGHTS CASES AND THE EIGHTH AMENDMENT

Penologist John P. Conrad (1989) described the deplorable living conditions he observed when he visited the Mount Meigs Correctional Institution in Alabama where he served as an expert witness for the prisoner plaintiffs in the class-action lawsuit *James v. Wallace*, 406 F. Supp 318 (M.D. Ala.1976), which was eventually consolidated into the case *Pugh v. Locke*, 406 F. Supp 318 (M.D.Ala. 1976), aff'd, 559 F.2d 283 (5th Cir. 1977). Conrad wrote about a dormitory designed for new arrivals:

> There were double bunks, mattresses on the floor, and two mattresses installed over the bank of urinals that lined one wall of the dorm.... Except for meal times and one morning off for showers and recreation, these men – new arrivals in the Alabama prisons – stayed there day and night. No effort was made to sort them out. The vulnerable were jammed in with the depraved and violent. Prisoners chose their bunks and could change them as they, or sexual predators, pleased. No officer ever intruded at night, and inspections by day were infrequent. (p.308).

He went on to visit the cell-blocks:

> During my tour, I observed a filthy hospital and a callously overcrowded cell block on which three or four men were locked into spaces designed for one. A mattress was laid under the bottom bunk, and the third man could squeeze into this cramped space, though not comfortably. Less fortunate was the fourth man, who had to sleep on the floor between the toilet and the front of the cell. Control of population movement at night was impossible; none of the locks on the cells were operational (p.309).

Conrad described the infamous "doghouse" designed for disobedient prisoners located at the Draper Correctional Center in Alabama:

This was an unlighted, unventilated building, architecturally similar to the conventional doghouse, located outside the main prison. Prisoners under this discipline were packed six to a cell, with a bucket or a hole in the floor serving as a toilet. Shocked, I asked the associate warden acting as my guide whether this adjunct was really necessary to the maintenance of discipline. He assured me that it was, adding that these cells had been approved by the Department of Corrections for the occupancy of eight prisoners (p.309).

James v. Wallace (1976) and *Pugh v. Locke* (1976) were filed by Alabama prisoners. Inmate James complained that during the 25 years he had been incarcerated in Alabama, he had received no rehabilitative services. Inmate Locke claimed he had been attacked in the dormitory by a group of inmates who left him unconscious and crushed part of his skull. The consolidated case, *Pugh v. Locke* (1976), alleged that the totality of living conditions in the Alabama prison system violated the cruel and unusual punishment clause of the Eighth Amendment. Testimony at the trial established that the Alabama facilities were grossly overcrowded and understaffed and that officials tolerated widespread inmate-on-inmate violence. Testimony from a sanitation expert described dirt and rodents throughout the institutions, unsanitary food preparation areas, overflowing and nonfunctioning toilets, broken showers, and generally filthy conditions. Federal District Court Judge Frank Johnson's order mandated that Alabama make significant changes in its penal system. Initially he appointed a Human Rights Committee to assist in the implementation of his mandate, followed in 1983 by an Implementation Committee to oversee compliance and address particular problems associated with the state's overcrowded jails. John Conrad was one of two distinguished penal experts to serve on the Implementation Committee, which exercised its oversight for six years. Judge Johnson's opinion emphasized that the Eighth Amendment's cruel and unusual punishment clause protected inmates from the kind of conditions found in the Alabama prisons. His ruling and the extensive orders he issued to remedy the problems were based on the constitutional protections provided by that amendment. The Fifth Circuit Court of Appeals upheld Judge Johnson's orders with a few minor changes.

Judge Johnson helped blaze new legal territory when he relied on the cruel and unusual punishment clause as grounds for finding that prisoners in Alabama were incarcerated in unconstitutional living conditions. According to Feeley and Rubin (1999), as late as 1965, few judges, prisoner advocates, or prison officials imagined that the prisoners' rights movement would go beyond courts recognizing that inmates had specific, narrowly-defined constitutional rights. Not until the late 1960s was there an indication that federal judges would rely on the Eighth Amendment to address challenges to the totality of conditions under which inmates were living. Judge Johnson was not the first judge to interpret the

Eighth Amendment in such a way. Inmates in Arkansas filed *Holt v. Sarver*, 309 F.Supp 362 (E.D. Ark. 1970), aff'd 442 F.2d 304 (8th Cir. 1971), which resulted in a federal court finding that inmates were living in deplorable conditions that violated the Eighth Amendment. In *Hutto v. Finney* (1978), the U.S. Supreme Court upheld the Federal District Court's finding that, in light of the conditions under which inmates lived while in punitive segregation, confining them in that status for longer than 30 days violated the Eighth Amendment. The Supreme Court also agreed with the District Court's conclusion that, taken as a whole, conditions in the isolation cells at Cummins violated the Eighth Amendment. As many as eleven inmates were assigned to a filthy cell that had no furniture and a toilet that could only be flushed from outside the cell. Inmates were placed on a special diet of "gruel" that essentially starved them.

Judge Johnson's trail blazing in Alabama, however, was especially significant. He not only declared that the living conditions in the state prisons were unconstitutional, he ordered the prison system to make a list of specific and detailed reforms, which he titled "Minimum Constitutional Standards for Inmates of the Alabama Penal System." The reforms were extensive and included mandating that cells should have at least 60 square feet of living space and how they should be equipped, the rights of prisoners in solitary confinement to showers and three meals a day, and how correctional officers should be deployed throughout the institution. Officials were ordered to provide inmates with clean towels and linens weekly, toothpaste and soaps, cleaning supplies for their cells, a bed off the floor and a mattress and blankets. He went so far as to require that at least one toilet should be maintained in working order for every 15 inmates. He also ordered the state to create a plan for classifying inmates and put the Director of the Center for Correctional Psychology at the University of Alabama in charge of the project. He created a Human Rights Committee composed of Alabama citizens and later an Implementation Committee to supervise the reforms. Members of the Committees periodically visited the institutions and wrote reports to the court outlining Alabama's progress in implementing his orders. As new developments occurred during the implementation period, primarily related to overcrowding, the court issued additional orders to address them. Judge Varner, who succeeded Judge Johnson when Johnson was appointed to the Fifth Circuit, finally dismissed the case in 1988 after concluding that the reforms had been implemented.

FURTHER EXPANSION OF THE EIGHTH AMENDMENT

When Judge Johnson interpreted the cruel and unusual punishment clause as grounds for ordering Alabama to institute extensive prison reform, he was charting a new course for the Eighth Amendment. Other courts, including the Supreme Court in *Hutto v. Finney* (1978) had also moved in this direction, but it took a series of Supreme Court cases to clarify further the amendment's role.

The first of this line of cases did not involve prison conditions; rather it was a case about medical care, *Estelle v. Gamble* (1976). Inmate Gamble was injured when a bale of cotton fell on him while he unloaded a truck. Over a period of several months, he saw the medical staff over seventeen times, was prescribed pain pills and blood pressure medications, and relieved of his work duties. Eventually he was released to return to light duty, but he refused to work because he claimed he was in too much pain. He was disciplined for his refusal. When he complained of chest pains, he was placed on medication and moved to administrative segregation. When he complained of chest pains again, doctors administered an electrocardiogram and placed him on medication for an irregular heart beat. He filed a lawsuit against prison officials claiming they violated his Eighth Amendment rights when they failed to provide him adequate and timely medical care.

Gamble's case rested on a unique interpretation of the cruel and unusual punishment clause. He was not complaining about the nature of the punishment the sentencing court imposed on him. He did not allege that officials were actively torturing or brutalizing him. With the exception of the adequacy of his medical care, he was not complaining about the conditions under which he was living. How does inadequate medical care amount to cruel and unusual punishment in violation of the U.S. Constitution? There was no dispute that Gamble could have filed a lawsuit in state court that alleged medical malpractice, but his lawsuit was filed in federal court, alleging a violation of his constitutional rights.

In a decision that dramatically changed the interpretation of the cruel and unusual punishment clause, the majority opinion written by Justice Thurgood Marshall set the standard for courts to use in evaluating prisoners' civil rights claims that allege inadequate medical treatment. Justice Marshall began the analysis with *Trop v. Dulles* (1958), which held that punishments incompatible with "evolving standards of decency that mark the progress of a maturing society" violate the Constitution. In *Gregg v. Georgia* (1972), the Court built on the *Trop* decision by finding that punishments involving the unnecessary and wanton infliction of pain also violate the Constitution. With these two cases as a platform, Marshall noted that it is the government's obligation to provide medical care to the people it incarcerates, and a failure to do so means an inmate's medical needs cannot be met. In the worst case, this could lead to a lingering and painful death. In a less serious case, it could lead to pain and suffering that serves no penological purpose. Because the infliction of unnecessary suffering is inconsistent with contemporary standards of decency, Justice Marshall's majority opinion concluded that deliberate indifference to serious medical needs constitutes the unnecessary and wanton infliction of pain that is prohibited by the Eighth Amendment. The indifference is unconstitutional whether it comes from medical personnel or from officials who intentionally deny or delay access to medical care. Not every claim of inadequate care, however, can be based on the Eighth Amendment. The majority held that the lack of care has to be intentional or deliberate, not based on accident or negligence, and the indifference must be to serious medical needs. Interestingly, after applying its standard to Gamble's situation, the Supreme Court concluded that Gamble's case was at most medical malpractice and not of constitutional proportions. Gamble claimed he should have been given an x-ray and additional diagnostic tests. The Court concluded that decisions to order tests or provide treatment are matters of medical judgment. Without a finding of deliberate indifference, the failure to provide them can lead at the most to medical malpractice and not a claim of cruel and unusual punishment Gamble lost his battle, but his case initiated a major shift in constitutional doctrine. The Supreme Court actively shaped an expanded role for the cruel and unusual punishment clause. The Court ruled that the clause applied to deprivations suffered during imprisonment that were not specifically a part of the court-imposed sentence.

LATER TOTALITY OF CONDITIONS CASES AND THE EIGHTH AMENDMENT

We saw lower federal courts apply the cruel and unusual punishment clause to living conditions in *Holt v. Sarver* (1970) and *Pugh v. Locke* (1976). In *Hutto v. Finney* (1978), the Supreme Court upheld a lower court that applied the Eighth Amendment to conditions in punitive segregation. *Rhodes v. Chapman* (1981), however, was the Supreme Court's first opportunity to consider an Eighth Amendment challenge to the totality of prison conditions. The Court had decided *Estelle v. Gamble* (1976) several years earlier, but the facts of that case were limited to the amendment's application to medical treatment. Justice Powell wrote in the *Rhodes* majority opinion,

> Until this case, we have not considered a disputed contention that the conditions of confinement at a particular prison constituted cruel and unusual punishment. Nor have we had an occasion to consider specifically the principles relevant to assessing the claims that conditions of confinement violate the Eighth Amendment.

In *Rhodes*, prisoners in the Southern Ohio Correctional Facility alleged that housing inmates two to a cell violated the Eighth Amendment. The cells were approximately 63 square feet. The Federal District Court agreed that double-celling resulted in cells that were too small and that double-celling had become a standard practice as opposed to a temporary measure. The district court reach this conclusion based in part on experts who testified about the standards for cell sizes set by the American Correctional Association (ACA) and other profes-sional organizations. According to the experts, the facility exceeded its design capacity by 38% and each inmate had less than the recommended 50-55 square feet of living space. The Supreme Court, however, disagreed with the district court. Justice Powell noted that harsh and restrictive prison conditions are not necessarily unconstitutional. The majority of the Supreme Court Justices determined there was no evidence that double-celling inflicted unnecessary or wanton pain on prisoners or was disproportionate to the crimes for which they were incarcerated. Rejecting the argument that standards set by correctional associations should define constitutional requirements, the Court concluded that double-celling may not be an ideal environment but "the Constitution does not mandate comfortable prisons".

The focus of the *Rhodes* decision was on the type or amount of pain imposed by the practice of double-celling. The Court simply concluded there was insufficient evidence to find that double-celled inmates in the Ohio facility were suffering from unnecessary pain. The Court emphasized that the district court considered the Ohio facility top-flight and there was no evidence of additional violence as a result of double-celling and job assignments had not suffered. Inmates had access to dayrooms adjacent to the cell blocks for 6:30 a.m. to 9:30 p.m. The Justices did not attempt to examine the intent or motives of the prison officials who implemented the policy. The cells were well equipped and most prisoners had ample opportunities to spend large blocks of time outside of their cells during the day. To many prison activists and inmate litigators *Rhodes* signaled an important shift in the prisoner's rights movement. Even today, some scholars see this case as the beginning of the resurrection of the hands-off doctrine. Until *Rhodes*, the Court had ruled in favor of prisoner's claims more often than not. Now in its first case involving prison conditions and the Eighth Amendment, the Supreme Court ruled against prisoners. It refused to base constitutional minimum requirements on standards set by professional organizations with expertise in corrections. Many had hoped the *Rhodes* Court would either end the practice of putting two prisoners in a cell or result in providing inmates much larger living quarters. In the 1980s, double-celling was a common response to burgeoning prisoner populations in the states. Building enough prisons to accommodate all of the growth was cost prohibitive; double-celling was far less expensive. A finding that under certain circumstances double-celling was a constitutional violation would have had major policy implications for the future of corrections.

Concerned that *Rhodes* might send the wrong message to federal judges nationwide, Justices Brennan, Blackmun, and Stevens wrote a concurring opinion in the case that encouraged federal judges to remain active and not retreat from judicial scrutiny of prison conditions. The three Justices agreed with the majority that there was no constitutional violation as a result of double-celling at the Southern Ohio facility, but they wrote to emphasize that judicial intervention is indispensable if the Constitution is to be enforced in America's prisons. Courts take up the slack created by public apathy and the political powerlessness of inmates.

It was over a decade before the Supreme Court decided a second case alleging that living conditions in a prison were unconstitutional under the Eighth Amendment. In *Wilson v. Seiter* (1991), the Supreme Court was presented with a lawsuit filed by Pearly Wilson, incarcerated at the Hocking Correctional Facility in Nelsonville, Ohio. He alleged that the institution was overcrowded, excessively noisy, insufficiently ventilated, had unsanitary restroom, dining, and food preparation areas, and inadequate housing for mentally and physically ill prisoners. The Court began a step-by-step analysis beginning with *Estelle v. Gamble* (1976), highlighting that in *Estelle* the emphasis was on the unnecessary and *wanton* infliction of pain or *deliberate* indifference. The holding in *Rhodes v. Chapman* (1981) on the other hand, rested on the objective component of the Eighth Amendment: was the deprivation itself serious enough to violate the Constitution. That decision did not consider the officials' subjective intent. Instead of concluding that *Rhodes v. Chapman* eliminated the subjective component in Eighth Amendment analysis, the *Wilson* Court turned to its earlier decision in *Whitley v. Albers* (1986). *Whitley* was the Eighth Amendment case about official use of force against inmates during a riot, discussed in Chapter 6. The Court in *Whitley* held there must be a finding that officials acted with maliciousness and wantonness in order to establish a violation of the cruel and unusual punishment clause, which requires an analysis of their subjective intent. Justice Scalia wrote for the majority in the *Wilson v. Seiter* opinion:

> Petitioner, and the United States [government] as *amicus curiae* in support of petitioner, suggests that we draw a distinction between "short-term" or "one-time" conditions (in which a state of mind requirement would apply) and "continuing" or "systemic" conditions (where official state of mind would be irrelevant). We perceive neither a logical nor a practical basis for that distinction. The source of the intent requirement is not the predilections of this Court, but the Eighth Amendment itself, which bans only cruel and unusual *punishment*. If the pain inflicted is not formally meted out as *punishment* by the statute or the sentencing judge, some mental element must be attributed to the inflicting officer before it can qualify.

After *Wilson*, in order to establish a case that living conditions are unconstitutional, a prisoner must establish: 1) the conditions are inhumane and 2) officials acted with deliberate indifference in allowing the conditions to occur or in refusing to take steps to rectify them. The inmate carries the burden of introducing sufficient evidence addressing the motives and thought processes of officials. The Court concluded that conditions of confinement are not "punishment" formally assessed by the sentencing authority. According to the majority opinion, for prison conditions to be considered "punishment" that can be evaluated under the Eighth Amendment, officials must have intended to impose or allow inhumane conditions to develop in order to punish inmates. The same standard used to prove medical care is unconstitutionally inadequate also applies to conditions cases. If officials acted in good faith to obtain the funding necessary to eliminate or prevent the problems, or in some manner the conditions were beyond their control, the cruel and unusual punishment clause is not violated. Justice Scalia also addressed another important aspect of prison condition lawsuits. The inmates argued that each living condition must be considered as a part of the overall condition under challenge. Scalia wrote that although some conditions in combination can result in a deprivation of a single, identifiable human need, it is very different to allege that the overall living conditions violate the Eighth Amendment. Prisoners must be able to establish that a specific living condition or set of conditions have created a specific deprivation.

Four Supreme Court Justices, White, Marshall, Blackmun, and Stevens, concurred that the prisoners should not prevail in this case, but they strongly disagreed with the legal standard the majority fashioned because they believed it misrepresented the Court's previous decisions. According to the concurring opinion, conditions of confinement alone, without reference to official motive or intent, can violate the Constitution. These four Justices emphasized that *Estelle v. Gamble* (1976) and *Whitley v. Albers* (1986) were not conditions lawsuits. The Court has never made intent an element to be proved in lawsuits that challenged living conditions. In addition, according to the concurring opinion, conditions of incarceration are must be considered a part of the punishment that prisoners experience and should be subject to Eighth Amendment standards. The concurring Justices warned that requiring prisoners to prove officials' intent will make it extremely difficult for inmates to establish a constitutional violation. Unconstitutional living conditions happen over time, resulting from the actions and decisions of numerous officials, both inside and outside the institution. Concluded these four Judges, "In truth, intent simply is not very meaningful when considering a challenge to an institution, such as a prison system." They concluded that the intent requirement will insulate inhumane living conditions from constitutional challenge.

In 1993, the Supreme Court had its most recent opportunity to rule on the applicability of the Eighth Amendment to a conditions-related lawsuit. In *Helling v.McKinney* (1993), a Nevada prisoner filed a lawsuit after being assigned to a cell with another inmate who chained smoked cigarettes. The non-smoking prisoner-plaintiff alleged that exposure to second-hand smoke was harmful to his health and violated the cruel and unusual punishment clause. The inmate did not allege that his health had already been compromised from the exposure. The Court accepted that there is sufficient scientific evidence establishing the harmfulness of second-hand smoke. With that acknowledged, the Court next considered whether the Eighth Amendment required evidence that the inmate was currently suffering from disease or illness as a result of the exposure. The Court concluded that the Eighth Amendment protects against future harm. Justice White for the majority wrote, "It would be odd to deny an injunction to inmates who plainly proved an unsafe, life-threatening condition in their prison on the ground that nothing yet had happened to them…". In large response to this case, many prison and jail systems have since banned smoking inside the facilities and often in the surrounding outside grounds as well. The Court applied the "deliberate indifference" standard, namely, it asked whether prison officials were deliberately indifferent to McKinney's serious medical needs and remanded the case to the lower court for reconsideration.

The *Helling v. McKinney* case is interesting for several reasons. Two years after *Wilson v. Seiter* (1991), the Court issued a pro-prisoner decision establishing the important precedent that the cruel and unusual punishment clause applies to future harm. Officials cannot afford to be indifferent to conditions that are possibility dangerous to prisoners in the future. *Helling* also reiterated that the only indifference that rises to a constitutional violation must be deliberate, keeping the decision within the line of cases beginning with *Estelle v. Gamble* (1976) through to *Wilson v. Seiter* (1991). In the decision, we can also see how the Court responds to advances in medical and scientific knowledge. Society's standards of decency evolve with those advances and so must the law.

Helling is also interesting because the dissenting opinion authored by Justice Thomas and joined by Justice Scalia presents a bold opposition to the interpretation of the cruel and unusual punishment clause that has been evolving since the early 1970s. According to the dissenters, there are no circumstances under which the Eighth Amendment can be applied to deprivations that prisoners suffer while incarcerated because the deprivations are not a part of their criminal sentence. Thomas points out that when the amendment was ratified, the term "punishment" referred to the sentence, not the harm or losses that might occur while incarcerated. There are no historical grounds for assuming that the framers of the Constitution considered interpreting the amendment to apply to harsh prison conditions. Not until *Estelle v. Gamble* in 1976, did the Supreme Court rule that the Eighth Amendment can be applied to situations within the prison living environment. For Justices Thomas and Scalia, the amendment only proscribes inhumane prison deprivations that have been specifically inflicted as a part of a sentence meted out by a judge or jury. The dissenting opinion suggested that if given the correct case where the issue was squarely presented, Justices Thomas and Scalia would vote to overrule *Estelle*.

THE CONTROVERSY SURROUNDING TOTALITY OF CONDITIONS LAWSUITS

Pugh v. Locke was one of the earliest lawsuits in which a federal court evaluated the constitutionality of living conditions in state prisons. Although a scattering of prior state court cases had addressed conditions in a few state prisons, until the 1970s, federal judges relied on the hands-off doctrine to refuse to entertain conditions cases. As that doctrine began to dissolve in the mid-1960s, conditions cases started to make their way through the federal court system. Federal courts started to consider not only legal challenges to specific prison rules and regulations, condition cases introduced judges to issues of quality of life: sanitation, health care, food, overcrowding, recreation, etc.

It is not by accident that the earliest conditions lawsuits were filed against prison officials operating institutions in the southern United States. Early southern prisons were agricultural and ranching operations. Institutions were surrounded by thousands of acres of land that were farmed and ranched in large part by inmate labor. Inmates grew the system's food, raised the animals that provided meat, and farmed the cotton that was used to make the clothing, bedding, and linens. In prison manufacturing plants, they made the items needed to build and maintain the facilities. Some of the prison plantations were so productive they not only helped make the prisons self-sufficient, they also turned a profit for the state correctional agency, which sold the produce and products to other state agencies. Unfortunately, however, the prisoners in the southern institutions were routinely subjected to extremely harsh working conditions: long days, little time off, and unsafe environments. From the mid-1800s through the early Twentieth Century, southern prisons also engaged in leasing prisoners to private businesses. These leasing arrangements were quite lucrative for both states and the businesses that contracted for the inmate labor. The scandalous working and living conditions provided to inmates under contract leasing arrangements eventually led to widespread public scandal. Gradually, state legislatures outlawed the practice in response (Oshinsky 1996). Several southern state prison systems have a history of using prisoners to guard and supervise other inmates. It was not uncommon for these "guards" to carry weapons and have special privileges. Using inmate guards, called "trusties," significantly reduced the cost of the southern institutions but it generally resulted in a violent and brutal atmosphere where powerful, aggressive inmates ruled the weak and had substantial control of the staff that relied on their services. The few professional officers that were employed were usually untrained and underpaid.

As a result of this unique history, legislatures did not have to allocate large amounts of state funds to operate prison systems in the southern states, and southern prisons developed a long and entrenched legacy of being under funded and understaffed, where inmates lived in violent and harsh environments. Lawsuits like *Pugh v. Locke* presented facts about prison conditions that were often horrifying. It was difficult for federal judges to ignore the facts behind the cases because they were so egregious. According to Feeley and Hanson (1990) the early lawsuits filed by southern inmates challenged the premises upon which the southern institutions were built and rejected the plantation model they created. In their decisions based on the cruel and unusual punishment clause, federal judges in these cases rejected the legitimacy of the southern prison.

Although prisoners in the south filed the first conditions lawsuits, legal challenges to living conditions have not remain restricted to that region of the country. As Feeley and Rubin (1999, p.39) note, once the cases began, "There followed a dramatic proliferation of prison decisions." By 1999, they report that federal courts had declared at least one institution in forty-eight prison systems in the U.S. unconstitutional and subject to court ordered reform. In addition to state prisons, numerous local jails are also under federal court orders to reform. The scope of the court decisions has varied considerably. In some states, only one of several facilities has been found in violation. In other states, more than one is under court order. Some decisions encompass many aspects of institutional operations; others are less general and focus on a limited set of conditions. Comprehensive orders involving the entire prison system were issued against six southern states: Alabama, Arkansas, Mississippi, South Carolina, Tennessee, and Texas. Comprehensive orders involving the main maximum-security institution and several smaller units were issued in Georgia and Louisiana. The entire Florida prison system and most of the North Carolina system have been under court orders that address overcrowding and other specified conditions. Only four non-southern states have had comprehensive orders against their entire prisons systems – Alaska, Delaware, New Mexico, and Rhode Island.

Once a judge finds that certain living conditions in a facility or an entire prison system violate the cruel and unusual punishment clause, the difficult, lengthy, and expensive process of reform begins. Judges are frequently called upon in civil lawsuits to order legal "remedies" to fix a violation of the law. They order a company that has broken the Clean Air Act to take immediate steps to end the practices that caused it to pollute the environment. They order an individual who fails to pay his bills to make payment or have his wages garnished or property seized and liquidated. Legal remedies are designed to correct a wrong. Many remedies are set by statute; others have been outlined in a contractual agreement. When living conditions in a state prison violate the Constitution, the remedial process becomes quite complex. There is no contract or statute that defines exactly how the process is to proceed. Each case is different and the remedies must be tailored to the specific constitutional violations the judge has found to exist. Judge Johnson provided a list of very detailed changes that needed to be made and appointed a Human Rights Committee and later an Implementation Committee to oversee the reform. In *Ruiz v. Estelle*, 503 F.Supp.1265 (S.D. Tx. 1980), which brought comprehensive reform to the Texas system, Federal Judge William Wayne Justice appointed an Office of the Special Master under the Federal Rules of Civil Procedure to monitor the implementation of a series of detailed settlement agreements and court orders. The remedies in the *Ruiz* case were especially comprehensive.

They addressed overcrowding, staffing deployment, delivery of medical care, recreation space and activities, conditions in punitive and administrative segregation and death row, prisoner classification, law libraries, the disciplinary process, and heating and ventilation. There was little that was not subject to judicial intervention. To remedy the types of constitutional violations found in many conditions lawsuits requires taxpayer money that must first be appropriated by a state legislature. Indeed, many violations occur when correctional systems are forced to operate without sufficient funding from the state. Combine under funding with prison overcrowding and the recipe for constitutional violations is apparent. Many state legislatures have had to respond to totality of conditions lawsuits by allocating large amounts of additional funds to their prison systems.

What has been the impact of totality of conditions lawsuits? Have conditions in America's jails and prisons improved because of them? There is little debate that conditions lawsuits have had a significant and long-term impact. Feeley and Hanson (1990) hypothesis that perhaps the greatest impact has been on the southern prisons where institutional reform litigation ended the prison plantation model that had been so oppressive and brutal. Others argue that the lawsuits have had just as great an impact on institutions that were not even under court order. Corrections agencies and their attorneys followed the reform movement as it wound through the courts and responded frequently by instituting reform before it was required. They built "reform" into their operations and facilities as they came on line. In some jurisdictions, state legislatures appropriated funds to correctional agencies in hopes of avoiding litigation. Litigation also helped professionalize corrections. Courts often turned to the professional standards set by such groups as the American Correctional Association (ACA) in crafting their remedial orders. Other professional groups began to develop standards for prisons – the American Bar Association and the American Medical Association. The ACA developed a system of accreditation of state prisons. In order to achieve accreditation, facilities are inspected by the ACA to make certain they meet a long list of detailed standards in terms of living conditions and operations. Courts also ended the practice of using inmates to guard other inmates. Many courts mandated that states provide additional correctional officer training, leading to a more professional and better-educated line staff. Prison officials began to develop written policies and standardized practices. Relatively quickly, prison management adopted a more professional and bureaucratic approach.

Correctional budgets have grown dramatically in the last two decades. Although it is difficult to determine how much growth is due to the impact of institutional reform litigation and how much to population growth, experts agree that the remedial phase of a conditions case generally requires states to appropriate additional funds. States have had to build new institutions to deal with overcrowding and renovate old institutions to meet plumbing and ventilation requirements and provide more space. They have had to hire more correctional staff and provide better and additional training opportunities. They have hired more health care providers and upgraded prison medical facilities. A study by Harriman and Straussman (1983) of fourteen states under federal court order through the 1970s, found that expenditures in state corrections increased after court decisions, and corrections as a percentage of the total state budgets increased as well.

Not all experts agree that the overall impact of totality of conditions cases has benefited corrections. Critics maintain that these cases have often undermined institutional authority by preventing officials from acting decisively. Courts undermine the authority of correctional officials in the eyes of the inmates. Critics charge that this has led to reduced staff morale, greater rates of staff turnover, and increased violence in the institutions. Several studies have documented an increase in prison violence in the aftermath of court orders (Feeley and Hanson 1990). Prisoners have become more politicized and militant, resulting in a shift in who controls the institutions. Court ordered reform created a vacuum of control in some states that was filled by prison gangs. One of the most cited instances of where this happened is in Texas where the federal judge dismantled the inmate-guard system, ordering the state to increase its correctional staff in a short period of time. A wave of violence swept the Texas prisons during the transition. While the power vacuum was eventually reduced, prison gangs gained significant power during that time and remain a major problem in Texas.

Conditions lawsuits are also very expensive for a state to defend. Filed under section 1983, if the prisoner-plaintiffs are successful, the defendant state is ordered to pay the plaintiffs' attorney fees under 42 U.S.C. section 1988 (see Chapter 11). This means the state is not only paying the salaries of the state attorneys who are employed to defend the inmate lawsuits, they are ordered to pay the plaintiffs' fees as well. If the court appoints a Special Master or uses another mechanism to enforce court orders or consent decrees, the state will pay those fees. There are generally expert witness fees to be paid. Conditions cases take a long time to prepare and a long time to try. The remedial phase can last for years during which time all of the attorneys, for the state and the prisoner-plaintiffs, continue their involvement. It adds up to a costly venture that is paid out of the state budget.

Perhaps the greatest concern of critics of conditions cases is the expansive role the federal judiciary plays in these lawsuits. Not only does a conditions lawsuit involve a federal court intervening in the daily operations of an agency that belongs to the state executive branch, that involvement is generally extensive and lasts many years, in some instances several decades. Judges craft extremely detailed orders mandating reform or their decisions force the opposing parties to craft extremely detailed settlement agreements that the court must then approve. In either case, those same judges retain the case on their dockets for as long as they think necessary in order to oversee the implementation of their orders or agreements. Institutional reform is a long process that depends on many factors often external to the correctional agency itself. The state governor and legislature, the media, and public opinion may all exert influence on how quickly and smoothly reform efforts proceed. Some jurisdictions embrace reform and see court intervention as an opportunity to move forward and accomplish changes that are not politically popular but are necessary. Other jurisdictions have resisted court intervention, seeing the federal court as usurping their authority and threatening the balance of federal/state relations. Through all of this, federal courts retain their jurisdiction of the case and judges implement their orders. That may include finding state officials in contempt of court for not implementing certain reforms by a given date and assessing a civil fine against the state government. It may include appointing court officials like Special Masters, giving them extensive authority to negotiate consent agreements with the opposing parties, and to oversee the implementation of those agreements, reporting to the court periodically and bringing important matters to the court's attention. Critics allege that judges in conditions cases become part-time administrators, interfering too far into the day-to-day management of prisons. One of the most vocal critics, John DiIulio, Jr. (1987) has observed that judicial intervention has increased the complexity of work correctional officers do and in many cases has been a severe detriment to effective prison management.

Underlying the critic's argument is the more philosophical question of what is the appropriate role of the judicial system in a democracy. Federal judges are not elected and have lifetime appointments. Is it their job to determine how a state should operate its prison system or how a state should appropriate taxpayer money? Critics maintain that these issues are the proper sphere of elected representatives. Voters elect the Governor who then appoints or recommends to the legislature a commissioner of corrections. That commissioner is accountable to the people through his or her accountability to the Governor and legislature. The elected legislature is responsible for deciding how the taxpayers' money is allocated. Federal judicial intervention disrupts the balance of power between the federal and state governments and also among the three branches of government. Opponents argue that it weakens the democratic process (Feeley & Hanson 1990).

In response, supporters of judicial activism in prison cases argue that prisons deteriorated to the point of unconstitutional conditions precisely because the elected representatives rejected their responsibilities. Prisoners have never been politically popular. In many states convicted felons are disenfranchised. Families of prisoners are commonly members of this country's economic underclass. Federal judges took on the task of prison reform because elected representatives chose to ignore the problems. Courts had to force these public institutions to meet their constitutional obligations. In a real sense, federal judges facilitated the democratic process by giving a voice and protection to a population that has been traditionally ignored. Advocates of judicial activism argue that institutional reform cases are not typical lawsuits, and judges must respond differently if the Constitution is to be upheld.

It is precisely this debate about the proper role of the federal judiciary that prompted Congress to take action in 1996. The Prison Litigation Reform Act (PLRA) was enacted in that year. Since then, four U.S. Supreme Court cases have upheld the constitutionality of several of the PLRA provisions and struck down none. The PLRA responds to two of Congress's concerns: 1) inmates who were perceived as clogging up the courts, costing taxpayers large amounts of money with frivolous litigation, and 2) federal judges who intervened in the operation of state prison systems, ordered extensive and costly reforms and monitored compliance with court orders.

The PLRA seeks to address what many consider the federal courts' overreaching micromanagement of state prison operations. Many prison administrators entered into consent decrees rather than litigate and agreed to wide-ranging changes that went beyond what was constitutionally required in order to avoid expensive and time-consuming litigation and the possibility of losing. Especially in the earliest reform lawsuits, prison officials realized there were constitutional violations and the decrees would force states to appropriate the funds needed to address the problems (Herman, 1998). In other circumstances, administrators entered into consent decrees after a court found a constitutional violation. The decree gave the state the opportunity to participate in fashioning appropriate and practical relief. There were also situations where prison officials did not move their agencies into compliance with consent decree provisions and others that openly obstructed compliance and disobeyed court orders (Crouch & Marquart 1989; Yackle 1989). Whatever the circumstances, the courts remained active during the remedial phase of the lawsuits, monitoring the prisons' implementation of the various provisions. When the PLRA was enacted, many state prisons had been under consent decrees and court orders monitored by the federal courts for twenty years or longer. As discussed in greater length in Chapter 11, the PLRA attempts to limit the authority of federal courts in prison reform lawsuits. Among other significant restrictions, any relief ordered by a court must extend no further than what is required to correct the constitutional violation. No longer can federal judges approve consent decrees that provide for more reform than is absolutely necessary to fix the constitutional violation. Preliminary injunctions are limited in how long they are in effect, and court orders in prison cases terminate after two years unless the court makes additional findings to justify continuing the court's involvement.

Living Conditions on Death Row

Each state that has the death penalty provides its own living arrangements for prisoners who are sentenced to death; however, most states have created separate cell blocks or living areas for condemned prisoners. On many death rows, prisoners are totally segregated from the rest of the inmate population in terms of not only housing but also work opportunities, correctional programming, and recreation. In many states, death row inmates are held in a high security status, are not permitted to work, are fed in their cells, and cannot recreate in large groups. Some states do not allow them to attend group religious services or have contact visitation, regardless of their institutional behavior.

The majority of death sentenced inmates live under these restrictive conditions for many years. Because of the extensive due process protections available to death sentenced prisoners, the average length of stay on death row is over ten years (Bohm 2007). The isolated living environment combined with the uncertainty of execution can be agonizing and cause serious mental anxiety. Psychologists have argued that the protracted length of stay on death row can cause some inmates to become delusional and suicidal, what they term the death row syndrome or death row phenomenon. In 1989, the European Court of Human Rights decided the interesting case involving Jens Soering, a young German citizen living in England whose extradition was sought by officials in Virginia where he faced murder charges for a crime he allegedly committed in that state when he was 18 years old. His lawyers fought extradition. They took the case to the European Court, which blocked his extradition, noting specifically that if extradited to Virginia, Soering would face the extreme living conditions known as the "death row phenomenon". The Court concluded it could not approve sending him to such a degrading and inhumane environment. As a result of the ruling, England obtained assurances from Virginia that prosecutors would not seek the death penalty in his case. He was eventually extradited, tried and convicted, and sentenced to life in prison. (Wilson 2003).

Because there are so few women sentenced to death (51 as of December 31, 2007), they often face unique issues. The American Civil Liberties Union and the American Friends Service Committee (2004) examined the forgotten population of women sentenced to death, and found that seven state death rows each house only one woman. All death rows house very few women. As a result they are even more isolated than men on death row. Compared to their male counterparts who are sentenced to die, they generally have less interaction with other inmates and staff.

To date the Supreme Court has not addressed the constitutionality of the long delays between sentencing and execution, nor has it set forth any specific or special constitutional requirements for conditions on death row. In 2009, the Court declined to hear a case involving a condemned inmate in Florida facing execution after spending 32 years on death row, however, three Justice expressed serious concerns about this issue.

Living Conditions on Death Row (cont.)

Death row inmates have successfully challenged their living conditions under the Eighth Amendment, using the same arguments available to all prisoners who allege that their living conditions violate the Constitution. Under *Wilson v. Seiter* (1991), they must show that the conditions are objectively in violation of the cruel and unusual punishment clause, causing substantial risk of serious harm to inmates, and that prison officials acted with deliberate indifference in allowing the conditions to develop or persist.

Death row inmates in Mississippi challenged their living conditions in *Gates v. Cook*, 376 F. 3d 323 (5th Cir. 2004). The district court found that inmates were living in filthy, poorly lit cells with chipped peeling paint, dried fecal matter and food encrusted on the walls, and toilets that flooded. Officials failed to provide inmates with adequate cleaning supplies. The court also found that the ventilation was inadequate for the summer months in the un-air-conditioned cells, increasing the probability of heat-related illnesses. Inadequate screening on the cell windows created a problem with mosquitoes. Health care for mentally ill death row inmates was consistently inadequate. The district court issued extensive injunctive relief to remedy the situation. In a partial victory for the death row inmates, the Fifth Circuit Court of Appeals affirmed some of the district court's injunctive orders and vacated others. In particular, the Court of Appeals upheld those injunctions addressing sanitation issues and providing better mental health care.

Death row inmates in the Union Correctional Institution in Florida alleged that the high temperature in their cells during the hot and humid summer months amounted to cruel and unusual punishment. In *Chandler v. Crosby*, 379 F.3d 1278 (11th Cir. 2004), the court found that the cells on death row were not air conditioned, there were no circulating fans, and the exhaust vents were not designed to cool the air. Florida death row inmates spent considerable time in their cells and were permitted to leave them to recreate twice a week for two hours each time, to shower three times a week, attorney and media visits, personal visits, use of the law library, and medical appointments. Nonetheless, the appeals court agreed with the district court that the death-sentenced inmates had failed to establish a constitutional violation. Although the Eighth Amendment applies to claims of inadequate cooling and ventilation, the prisoners' discomfort was not severe and did not result from heat that was unconstitutionally excessive. The court emphasized there was a ventilation system that effectively circulated the air, the cells were not subject to direct sunlight, inmates were not required to wear clothes in their cells, every cell had running hot and cold water, and while in their cells the inmates were sedentary. In both *Gates v. Cook* and *Chandler v. Crosby*, death row inmates did not raise constitutional challenges specific to being housed on death row.

Living Conditions on Death Row (cont.)

In recent years, several states have made attempts to reform the isolated living conditions on their death rows. In 1986, Texas initiated a plan that allowed some well-behaved death row inmates to work in a special garment factory for only death row inmates. The working inmates also had increased out-of-cell privileges, although they remained segregated from the general population prisoners. Unfortunately, an escape attempt in 1998 by death row inmates assigned to the work program caused officials to terminate the program. Death row was relocated to a newer, more secure facility and all death row inmates now live in their cells 23 hours a day, are not allowed to work and have limited out-of-cell activities. Tennessee also instituted an incentive program for condemned prisoners, to award good behavior. The program allows inmates to earn an opportunity to work and for increased recreation time. The Tennessee program is still in operation (Johnson 2003).

RETURNING TO CORRECTIONAL HEATH CARE AND THE LAW

The Supreme Court later used its interpretation of the cruel and unusual punishment clause in *Estelle v. Gamble* (1976) to analyze how the Eighth Amendment applies to prison condition lawsuits. Before Chapter 8 wraps up, we return to where we left *Estelle* and examine more closely several of the legal issues surrounding the delivery of health care in prisons and jails. The Supreme Court has decided very few cases directly involving prisoner health care. *Estelle v. Gamble* set the standard: a constitutional violation is implicated if evidence establishes that the inmate suffered from *deliberate* indifference to *serious* medical needs. In *West v. Atkins* (1988), the Supreme Court ruled that the Eighth Amendment applies to private health care providers who contract their services with the state prison system. When such a private contractor treats an inmate they are acting under color of law and can be sued in federal court for constitutional violations if they have been deliberately indifferent to a prisoner's serious medical needs. It is not relevant that they were not state employees. This is an especially important clarification as more and more prison systems move to privatize their medical services.

Washington v. Harper (1990) involved a prisoner who needed drug therapy for serious mental health problems. Harper had been incarcerated in the Washington State Penitentiary in the early 1980s, during which time he was assigned to a psychiatric center and consented to being treated with antipsychotic drugs. After having his parole revoked for attacking two nurses in a psychiatric ward where he was civilly committed, he returned to prison and was placed in a center for inmates with severe mental disorders. At first he consented to drug treatment, however, after several months Harper refused to continue with the antipsychotic medications. Antipsychotic drugs often have serious side effects that range from uncomfortable to dangerous. Harper's physician and prison officials initiated the process provided by prison policy to approve treating him against his will. Their request was granted, at which point Harper filed a lawsuit alleging he had not been afforded adequate due process in violation of the Fourteenth Amendment. The U.S. Supreme Court examined Washington State's prison policy for the involuntary treatment of severely mentally ill inmates and concluded that the policy provided adequate due process protection. The Court ruled that before a prisoner can be treated without his or her consent, the state must first establish that the inmate is dangerous to himself or others, or is seriously disruptive to the environment and that drug treatment is in the inmate's best *medical* interest. To make these determinations, the state must first conduct a hearing with the inmate having the right to attend and present and cross-examine witnesses. The decision maker at the hearing does not have to be a judge. *Washington v. Harper* sets limits on the prison staff by requiring that prisoners can be treated against their will only if the state can prove: 1) they are dangerous or disruptive to the environment, and 2) it can be shown that the medication benefits the inmate medically. The medical benefit requirement is intended to prevent officials from treating inmates with drugs solely as a management tool. On the other hand, officials have a significant amount of flexibility and control because a judicial hearing is not constitutionally required.

In *Pennsylvania Department of Corrections v. Yeskey* (1998), the Supreme Court ruled that the provisions of the Americans with Disabilities Act of 1990 (ADA) apply to prisoners. The facts of this case involved a first-time offender who was sentenced to a Pennsylvania prison for 18-36 months, but recommended by the judge for a six-month boot camp. Correctional agency officials rejected the recommendation because Yeskey suffered from hypertension, and they were concerned about his health in a boot camp program that required rigorous physical activity. Yeskey sued under the ADA, which prohibits a public entity from discriminating against a qualified individual with a disability because of that disability. In a unanimous decision, the Court ruled that the Pennsylvania correctional system was a public entity under the Act, providing services, programs, activities, and benefits that bring it squarely within the intent of the legislation. This case makes clear that state officials must follow the ADA when developing and operating programs and facilities for prisoners. This includes making certain there are appropriate physical facilities for inmates with disabilities and that programs and other activities are available to them. It is no defense that such accommodations may be costly or time-consuming.

The lower federal courts have had to decide the vast majority of legal issues involving prisoner health care. There are unique challenges to delivering health care in the correctional setting, and federal judges and juries have addressed a multitude of prisoner lawsuits alleging such constitutional violations as poor access to care, including insufficient numbers of physicians and other providers, access controlled by nonmedical personnel, poor quality of care, and inadequately equipped care facilities. Although the facts of individual cases are determinative in those lawsuits, there are some settled legal questions. The lower federal courts have held that prisoners are entitled to reasonable or adequate medical care, not state of the art care; ordinary and normal health care needs are the criteria (the Constitution does not require a correctional system to provide a sex change operation); prisoners are constitutionally entitled to dental and psychiatric care as well as medically necessary equipment, such as eye glasses, canes, crutches, and wheel chairs; just like any other person, a competent prisoner can refuse medical treatment; and prisoners can be required to pay nominal fees to offset the expense of providing health care, although care cannot be denied because an inmate cannot afford the fees (Palmer & Palmer 2004). Not to be forgotten in any lawsuit involving prisoner health care is that negligent care is not a constitutional violation. A prisoner must prove that the poor care he or she was provided resulted from deliberate, intentional indifference.

HIV raised many legal issues in correctional health care in the 1980s. The states developed their own sets of policies with many differences across the jurisdictions. Inmates challenged policies that required mandatory HIV testing, while other inmates filed lawsuits demanding mandatory testing in states that had not adopted such a policy. Litigation ensued over policies that segregated HIV inmates from the general population and, at the same time, litigation in other states sought segregated housing for HIV infected prisoners. Lawsuits were filed alleging that officials failed to protect prisoners and staff from HIV infection. Lawsuits questioned the constitutionality of policies that both failed to keep an inmate's HIV infection status confidential, and other lawsuits claimed it was unconstitutional to keep such information confidential. As it currently stands, courts have supported most HIV policies in correctional institutions if they are based on legitimate needs and are rationally related to those needs. Mandatory testing has been upheld, as is a policy not to require testing. Segregating HIV inmates has been upheld, as has placing infected inmates in the general population if it will not compromise their health care and their conduct does not threaten other inmates or staff with infection. Confidentiality has become a more difficult issue. Not keeping a prisoner's medical condition confidential can place him or her in danger of being mistreated by other inmates and even staff. Legal precedent has developed in favor of a constitutional requirement to honor the confidentiality of an inmates HIV infected status as long as keeping that information secret does not place some one else in harm's way (Belbot & del Carmen 1991). As new medical protocols develop for treating HIV and other infectious diseases common in prison, such as hepatitis C, legal battles will continue over the constitutionally required quality of care. Behind those battles will be the rising price tag of health care.

Conditions in Supermax Prisons

As of 2004, 44 states had supermax prisons, housing approximately 25,000 prisoners, and designed to hold the most violent, disruptive inmates in single-cells for generally 23 hours a day. Inmates do not work and have little correctional programming activities available to them. They eat meals in their cells. They are escorted outside of their cells in handcuffs and sometimes leg chains. Twenty years ago supermax prisons were rare in the U.S. They are costly to build, staff, and operate. Supermax prisons can be stand-alone units or be a part of another correctional facility. By isolating the most violent, disruptive inmates in secure supermax units, officials hope to increase the safety, order, and control throughout the prison. In some states, inmates can be held in supermax units for an indefinite length of time. States use different terminology to describe their supermax facilities, such as special housing unit, intensive management unit, and administrative segregation. Common to all supermax facilities is that inmates have minimal contact with other inmates and staff (Mears 2006).

The strict rules and restricted living conditions under which super max inmates live has raised a lot of controversy. Their living conditions are often similar to the segregated and isolated conditions under which condemned inmates live on many death rows. Inmates in supermax prisons have filed lawsuits that challenge their extreme living conditions. Ohio supermax inmates filed a class-action lawsuit that living conditions in Ohio's supermax prison, the Ohio State Penitentiary (ORP), violated the Eighth Amendment's prohibition against cruel and unusual punishment. Specifically, the inmates complained about isolation in a 7-by-14–foot cell for 23 hours a day, fluorescent lights on in the cell at all times and punishment if inmates tried to cover their eyes, shackling and strip searches when prisoners were taken out of their cells, no contact visitation, outdoor recreation for only one hour each day in an unheated cell with a screened window, mental health interviews conducted through cell doors, psychotherapy sessions with prisoners chained to a pole, and discipline that included taking away inmates' bedding and clothing and serving food loaf bricks for meals. The lawsuit contended that the severe conditions led to prisoner suicides, increased prisoners aggression and mental illness. In 2001, the federal district court judge prohibited Ohio from assigning mentally ill inmates to the ORP. In *Austin v. Wilkinson*, 2002 U.S. Dist. LEXIS 27439 (N. D. Ohio 2002), the district court approved a settlement agreement between the inmates and the state correctional agency regarding psychiatric and medical health care, the application of physical restraints, and outdoor activity.

In *Madrid v. Gomez*, 889 F. Supp. 1146 (N.D. Calif. 1995), inmates incarcerated in the Special Housing Unit (SHU) in the Pelican Bay State Prison in California challenged the constitutionality of a broad range of practices and conditions, including excessive use of force, inadequate medical and mental health care, and inhumane living conditions. The court found serious constitutional deficiencies in the medical and mental health care provided to inmates to which officials had been deliberately indifferent. The court found that the extreme isolation imposed on SHU inmates did not violate the Eighth

> **Conditions in Supermax Prisons (cont.)**
>
> Amendment because there was no evidence that that the degree of mental injury suffered by the inmates was sufficiently serious to violate the Eighth Amendment. However, in an important finding, the court concluded that certain groups of inmates who are at high risk for suffering serious injury to their mental health as a result of being incarcerated in an isolated environment, should not be assigned to the SHU. Officials were ordered to take steps to identify those inmates and make certain they would not be so assigned.

SUMMARY

The meaning of the Eighth Amendment has evolved significantly. Beginning with the Supreme Court's decision in *Estelle v. Gamble* (1976), the amendment's reach was extended to include issues beyond the scope of the court-ordered sentence imposed on offenders. After *Estelle*, the health care provided to prisoners was also to be evaluated under a standard that the Court determined was required by the Eighth Amendment. Through a series of subsequent Supreme Court cases, the amendment's reach was extended even further to include the conditions under which prisoners live. It is a fascinating example of how law evolves over time to respond to changes in our appreciation and understanding of society and matters of justice. It is not an evolution without its critics, as expressed by Supreme Court Justices Thomas and Scalia in their dissent in *Helling v. McKinney* (1993).

It is also an evolution that has opened up new legal questions. How poor must the prisoners' living conditions be in order to trigger Eighth Amendment protection? Must there also be evidence that prison officials deliberately permitted the conditions to develop before prisoners are protected by the cruel and unusual punishment clause? The Court had to address these matters as well, and wrote opinions that were decidedly favorable to prison administrators. Although there is no bright line that separates conditions that amount in seriousness to constitutional violations from those that do not, it is clear that not all "bad" conditions create a constitutional problem. Most importantly, it is also clear that even if the living conditions are arguably below the constitutional minimum, prisoners must provide evidence that administrators were deliberately indifferent to allowing the conditions to exist.

Studying the evolution of the Eighth Amendment in prisoners' rights cases is a "case study" in how law and society interact to shape our social institutions.

DISCUSSION QUESTIONS

1. Do you agree that the Eighth Amendment should be applied to prison condition cases? Give the advantages and disadvantages of interpreting the amendment to include prison conditions.

2. What are the arguments for and against federal judicial intervention in prison condition cases?

3. List the reasons why providing health care inside correctional institutions is more difficult than providing it in the outside world. What are some of the special issues that occur in a prison health care, including such relatively "basic" things as inmates actually getting to the prison clinic and prescribing prescription drugs. How can some of these difficulties add to or complicate lawsuits regarding inadequate health care.

4. How has the subjective "deliberate indifference" standard evolved since it was first enunciated in *Estelle v. Gamble* (1976)?

5. Have conditions lawsuits helped reform prisons in the U.S.?

SUGGESTED READINGS AND REFERENCES

American Civil Liberties Union & American Friends Service Committee (2004). The *Forgotten Population: A Look at Death Row in the United States Through the Experiences of Women.* Retrieved May 1, 2008 from http://www.aclu.org/womensrights/crimjustice/13270pub20050120.html

Belbot, Barbara A. and Rolando V. del Carmen (1991) "AIDS in Prison - Legal Issues." *Crime and Delinquency*, 37 (January): 135-152.

Bohm, Robert M. (2007) *DeathQuest III.* Newark, N.J.: LexisNexis Group.

Conrad, John P. (1989), "From barbarism toward decency: Alabama's long road to prison reform," *Journal of Research in Crime and Delinquency* 26(4): 307-328.

Crouch, Ben M. and James W. Marquart (1989). *An Appeal to Justice: Litigated Reform of Texas Prisons.* Austin: University of Texas Press.

DiIulio Jr., John J. (1987). *Governing Prisons: A Comparative Study of Correctional Management.* New York: The Free Press.

Feeley, Malcolm M. and Roger A. Hanson (1990). "The impact of judicial intervention on prisons and jails: a framework for analysis and a review of the literature." In John DiIulio Jr. (Ed.) *Courts, Corrections, and the Constitution.* New York and Oxford: Oxford University Press.

Feeley, Malcolm M. and Edward Rubin (1999). *Judicial Policy Making and the Modern State: How the Courts Reformed America's Prisons.* Cambridge: Cambridge University Press.

Harriman, Linda and Jeffrey D. Straussman (1983). "Do judges determine budget decisions? Federal court decisions in prison reform and state spending for corrections." *Public Administration Review* 43:343-51.

Herman, Susan (1998). "Slashing and Burning Prisoners' Rights: Congress and the Supreme Court in Dialogue," 77 Oregon Law Review 1229.

Johnson, Robert (2003). "Life and the sentence of death: historical and contemporary perspectives." In James R. Acker, Robert M. Bohm, & Charles S. Lanier (Eds.) *America's Experiment with Capital Punishment.* Durham, N.C.: Carolina Academic Press.

Mears, Daniel P. (2006). *Evaluating the effectiveness of supermax prisons.* Washington, D.C.: Urban Institute Justice Policy Center . Retrieved May 28, 2008, from http://www.urban.org/url.cfm?ID=411326.

Oshinsky, David M. (1996). *Worse Than Slavery: Parchman Farm and the Ordeal of Jim Crow Justice.* New York: The Free Press.

Smith, Christopher E. (2000). "The governance of corrections: implications of the changing interface of courts and corrections." In Boundary Changes in Criminal Justice organizations. Vol. 2. 113-166. Office of Justice Programs or the NIJ.

Wilson, Robert J. (2003). "The influence of international law and practice on the death penalty in the United States." In James R. Acker, Robert M. Bohm, & Charles S. Lanier (Eds.) *America's Experiment with Capital Punishment.* Durham, N.C.: Carolina Academic Press.

Yackle, Larry W. (1989). *Reform and Regret: The Story of Federal Judicial Involvement in the American Penal System.* New York and Oxford: Oxford University Press.

Jails and Prisoner Litigation and Reform

INTRODUCTION

The Bureau of Justice Statistics reports that at midyear 2007, local jails in the United States held 780,581 persons, not including offenders assigned to community based sentences such as weekend reporting, work release, electronic monitoring, and other alternative programs, which accounted for an additional 68,245 offenders under jail supervision. The jail population in the U.S. increased from 226 jail inmates per 100,000 residents in 2000 to 259 per 100,000 residents in 2007. Jails range from facilities that house four or five persons to the largest jail in the U.S. in Los Angeles County, California that housed 21,364 persons at the BJS mid-year count in 2007. New York City had the second largest population at 19,686 (Sabol & Minton 2008). There are over 3300 local jails operated by city and county governments in the United States and nearly 13 million people are admitted into these jails over a year's time (Mumola 2005). Some of those individuals are admitted for only a few hours; others are admitted for several months to a year.

Jails perform a very different function in the criminal justice system than prisons, in part because they confine a mix of people for a variety of reasons. They house people who have not been convicted of crimes and are waiting for arraignment and trial. They also house people who have been convicted of crimes but are waiting to be sentenced by the court. On June 30, 2007, 62% of the inmates in U.S. jails were awaiting court action on a current charge (Sabol & Minton 2008). Jails are also used to confine probation, parole, and bail bond violators and absconders. Juveniles are often detained temporarily in jails before they are transferred to juvenile authorities. Increasingly jails are being used as alternatives to inadequate community mental health care facilities (Steadman & Veysey, 1997). There are jail inmates waiting to be transferred to federal, state or other authorities. Due to overcrowding in federal and state prisons, it is not unusual for jails to house federal and state convicts until beds open up and the inmates can be transferred. Finally jails confine people who have been sentenced to short periods of incarceration, generally less than one year.

The county government operates and funds jails in most jurisdictions. In others the county and city governments partner to operate the local jail. In many jurisdictions, county or city officials delegate jail operations to a local law enforcement agency, often the county sheriff's department. Law enforcement agencies have not always been the best jail administrators. They often lack the expertise and interest needed to operate such complex correctional facilities. Jails are expensive items in a county's budget and some smaller communities have joined forces to operate regional jails that serve several counties.

Jails have multiple missions, made more difficult because there is a significant overcrowding problem in many jurisdictions with the largest jail populations. In mid-year 2007, nationwide 96% of local jail capacity was occupied. Jurisdictions with smaller jails generally had a lower occupancy rate than jails in larger jurisdictions (Sabol & Minton 2008). When jail populations reach such high capacity levels, administrators have little flexibility to make the best classification decisions and housing assignments that help keep a facility safe. It is more difficult to separate violent and nonviolent offenders and to protect inmates with mental health problems. Classifying jail inmates is more difficult in jails than in prisons because officials often have limited information about inmates. Although jail staff interviews them, it takes time to confirm the information that inmates provide. For inmates who are there for a short time, it is difficult to perform thorough medical and mental health assessments. Although jails may have separate cells for predatory inmates, dormitory style group housing dominates jail design.

THE SUPREME COURT AND THE RIGHTS OF JAIL INMATES

Many issues about constitutional rights are common to both jail and prison inmates, but there are some issues that are peculiar to jails and their role in the criminal justice system. In 1979, the U.S. Supreme Court decided its most important case concerning the rights of jail inmates, *Bell v. Wolfish*. In that case, inmates housed at the federal Metropolitan Correctional Center in New York

City filed a class action challenging a number of policies and practices. Most of the inmates at the MCC were pretrial detainees. The facility had no barred cells. Inmates were housed in dormitory style rooms. Inmates complained about the practice of housing two inmates to a room originally designed for single occupancy and body cavity searches conducted after contact visits. They also complained about the rule that required inmates to remain outside their cells during routine searches and regulations that prohibited them from receiving hard-back books not sent directly by a bookstore or publisher, as well as food and personal items sent from outside the institution. The pretrial detainees argued that these policies amounted to punishment and violated their due process rights. Since they had not been convicted of crimes and were still presumed to be innocent, such restrictions deprived them of liberty in violation of the Constitution. The federal district court and the appeals court agreed with the inmates and enjoined the practices and policies the inmates had challenged.

Obviously this was an important case and an opportunity for the Supreme Court to consider the constitutional rights of individuals who are confined prior to trial and are cloaked with the presumption of innocence. The Court had to decide whether the fact that they had not been convicted impacted the extent of their constitutional protections. Some of these inmates would eventually be found or plead guilty, but others would be found innocent, and still others would be released after having their charges dismissed. Nonetheless, they were all confined, and jail officials had to take reasonable measures to provide a safe and secure living environment. Officials contended that body cavity searches after visits (without the need to establish individualized suspicion) and regulations prohibiting certain items being sent to inmates from the outside were standard and basic security practices. Double bunking was an unfortunate necessity occasioned by rising jail admission rates.

The Supreme Court decided that when the issue involves evaluating the constitutionality of restrictions on pretrial detainees or their living conditions, courts must determine whether the restrictions amount to punishment. According to the majority opinion, unless inmates can show that officials expressly intended to punish the detainees, if the restriction or condition is reasonably related to a legitimate nonpunitive government purpose, it is not punishment. On the other hand, if the restriction or condition is arbitrary or serves no legitimate purpose, a court could infer that the purpose is punishment and, therefore, unconstitutional when imposed on pretrial detainees.

The Court then applied the standard it had devised to the specific practices and conditions inmates complained about at the Metropolitan Correctional Center. One by one, the Court concluded that there was a legitimate and reasonable government purpose served and that officials never intended to punish the detainees. Officials need the tools to manage a detention facility and keep order and discipline. That may require imposing restrictions on detainees. Double bunking was a practice that did not amount to punishment, the Court concluded, because the living conditions at the facility still met constitutional standards. The average length of stay for pretrial detainees was only 60 days. They spent significant portions of their days outside of their rooms and had opportunities for outside room activities. Although conditions were crowded, other essential services had not been compromised. The publisher-only rule was designed to help officials prevent smuggling of contraband in books sent from outside the institution. The rule was neutral and not targeted to any particular book, and there were alternative ways for inmates to get reading materials. Restrictions on packages were also a rational attempt to reduce opportunities for smuggling in contraband. The room search rule did not violate the Fourth Amendment because it helped officials conduct safer and more effective searches. Permitting inmates to be present during a search might result in friction between officers and inmates. The body cavity searches after visiting did not violate the Constitution. The Court emphasized that loss of freedom of choice and privacy are part of confinement. Detention interferes with a detainee's desire to live with as few restraints as possible; however, that desire does not convert those restrictions into punishment.

In analyzing the rights of pretrial detainees, the Supreme Court did not rely on the Eighth Amendment's cruel and unusual punishment clause because that clause only protects individuals who have been convicted of crimes. Its focus is cruel and unusual "punishment" and, although they are confined, pretrial detainees are not being punished. Their detention does not remove their presumed innocence in our justice system. Instead, in *Bell v. Wolfish* (1979), the Court based its legal analysis on the due process clause. Because the inmates at the Metropolitan Correctional Center were detained by the federal government, the Court was guided by the Fifth Amendment's due process clause. The Fourteenth Amendment's due process clause protects detainees confined in state or local detention facilities. In this context, both due process clauses have been interpreted the same way. Under both clauses, the question is whether, as the result of jail regulations, practices, or conditions, a detainee's life, liberty, or property were deprived without due process of law. How does a court decide if there's been a due process deprivation? According to the Supreme Court, a lower court must decide if the regulations or conditions punished the detainees as opposed to being rational responses to the legitimate need to provide a safe, secure, and orderly environment. The decision in *Bell v. Wolfish* makes it very difficult for detainees to show that jail restrictions or conditions deprive them of life, liberty, or property. In that case inmates argued they had lost their liberty to be free of intrusive and embarrassing body cavity searches and to be present during room searches to make sure officials did not wreck or steal their property. They argued they had lost their liberty to be confined more comfortably and securely in a room designed for only one inmate. The losses occurred without due process because the detainees had not been convicted of crimes. In response to each challenge the Court articulated a legitimate administrative need and found the restriction or condition was not intended to be punishment and served the government's needs.

There was a vocal dissent in the *Bell v. Wolfish* case. Justice Marshall argued that unconvicted detainees should have greater constitutional protections. Many detainees are in jail is because they were too poor to post bail. He concluded that when a restriction impinges on the constitutional rights of a detainee, the government must establish that the restriction is substantially necessary to administer the jail. If it impinges on a fundamental interest or causes significant injury, the government must show a compelling governmental necessity. He characterized body cavity searches as "one of the most grievous offenses against personal and common decency." Inmates wear one-piece jump suits and contact visits occur in a glass-enclosed room and are monitored by officials. The searches do not meet the compelling necessity test, according to Marshall. Justice Stevens, joined by Justice Brennan, wrote in a dissenting opinion that the blanket application of the publisher-only rule inflicted punishment and, therefore, violated inmates' due process rights.

Of course, along with pretrial detainees, jails house convicted offenders who are serving time in jail as punishment and are protected by the Eighth Amendment. In a strange twist, their complaints about jail conditions are analyzed under the cruel and unusual punishment clause, while detainees' complaints are analyzed under the due process clauses. People living under the same conditions and restrictions must rely on different constitutional amendments in the event they file lawsuits. Yet, quite likely, convicted offenders and pretrial detainees are living side by side. The unique role jails play in the justice system has required courts to examine the Constitution carefully. In deciding the Eighth Amendment only addresses conditions of punishment, the Supreme Court was bound by established legal precedent and history. Although it eventually determined that none of the practices at issue in *Bell v. Wolfish* violated the Constitution, it recognized that pretrial detainees do have constitutional protections under the due process clauses. Lower federal courts that have decided cases involving pretrial detainees, have interpreted the due process clauses to provide the same types of protection provided to convicted offenders under the Eighth Amendment.

In addition to *Bell v. Wolfish*, the Supreme Court addressed the rights of jail inmates in *Block v. Rutherford* (1984). Relying on the due process protections provided by the Fourteenth Amendment, inmates in the Los Angeles County Jail challenged a blanket prohibition on contact visits and the jail's practice of scheduling cell searches when inmates were not in or around their cells. Although they acknowledged that jail officials had legitimate security concerns with both visitation and cell searches, the inmates argued that the policies were unreasonable and were exaggerated responses to those concerns.

Block v. Rutherford (1984) was an important case because it required the Court to apply its holding in *Bell v. Wolfish*, decided only five years earlier. In

Block, the Court was able to demonstrate more specifically at what point an administrative policy or practice, however well-intentioned, crosses over the line and becomes punitive. In a 6-3 decision, the majority supported the constitutionality of both the regulation that prohibited all contact visits and the practice of searching inmates' cells out of their presence. The majority held that prohibiting contact visits is not excessive given the security risks involved. Contact visits increase the risk of drugs, weapons, and other contraband making their way into the jail. Many pretrial detainees are awaiting trial for violent crimes or have violent criminal histories, and there was no reason to believe that pretrial inmates were any less violent or posed any less risk than post-conviction inmates. The Court reasoned that for everyone's safety officials should be allowed to take measures to reduce the risks related to contact visitation. It is not reasonable to require jail officials to develop a program to identify which inmates are good risks versus which are bad. With respect to cell searches, the Court supported the need to conduct searches randomly, without a schedule and without the inmate's presence. The Supreme Court reaffirmed what it had emphasized in *Bell v. Wolfish*. Judges should pay deference to the experience and expertise of correctional authorities who must make difficult decisions that reconcile inmates' claims, the security of the institution, and the safety of all who work and live there. Correctional officials are not constitutionally required to use the least restrictive means available to accomplish legitimate goals. Since *Block v. Rutherford*, it is clear that jail administrators have significant discretion to impose regulations they deem necessary on all of the inmates in their facilities.

LOWER COURTS AND THE RIGHTS OF JAIL INMATES

Although the Supreme Court has decided only a few cases involving jails, the lower federal courts have decided many lawsuits filed by jail inmates involving a wide range of issues, such as the availability of medical care, access to courts, freedom of religion, and overall living conditions. Courts analyze the claims using the same legal tests and standards developed in prison cases (except that the Eighth Amendment does not protect pretrial detainees) however, the differences between prisons and jails may result in different obligations being imposed on jail officials. The average length of stay for a jail inmate is significantly less than for a prison inmate. That difference will impact the range of health services jails are required to provide or the extent of legal materials in jail law libraries. In *Strickler v. Waters*, 989 F.2d 1375 (4th Cir. 1993), the Court of Appeals for the Fourth Circuit held that the legal materials provided in the local jail's library were sufficient despite the fact that they were less extensive than what is typically provided in a state prison. Responses to a survey of jail and prison systems conducted by Margo Schlanger (2003) confirmed what most courts have experienced: jail officials reported that far fewer lawsuits are filed against them in a year's time compared to the number filed against prison officials. That same survey found that lawsuits concerning medical care are by far the most frequently filed cases, followed by cases with use of force issues. Experts agree that jail inmates file fewer lawsuits because they are detained for relatively short periods of time - not because jail conditions are less likely to violate the Constitution than conditions in the nation's prisons.

JAIL SUICIDE CASES

One of the most important issues for jail administrators is preventing inmate suicide. When individuals are admitted into the jail, they are often at their weakest point emotionally and physically – frightened, confused, angry, or despondent. They may be intoxicated or drugged. Officials regularly screen inmates when they enter a jail facility to try to determine their suicide risk. The good news is that according to a study conducted by the Bureau of Justice Statistics, jail suicides declined steadily from 1983 to 2002. In 1983, suicide was the most common cause of deaths in jail, accounting for 56% of all deaths, but by 2002, the most common cause was natural causes, with suicides accounting for only 32% of jail deaths. Nearly half of all jail suicides occur within the first week in custody. Historically, state prison suicide death rates have been much lower than those of jails. In 2002, the suicide rate in jails was three times the rate in state prisons (Mumola, 2005).

One reason jail officials have become proactive in this area is because an inmate suicide often leads to a lawsuit. Family members of the suicide victim can file a civil rights lawsuit alleging that officials were deliberately indifferent to the safety of their loved one, which they often combine with a wrongful death claim under state tort law. Lawsuits involving inmate suicide are not uncommon and can be very costly for local governments. In 2004, the City of Philadelphia settled for $3.5 million to be paid to the guardian of Charles Foster who suffered irreversible brain damage when he tried to hang himself in his holding cell at the Philadelphia Police Department. When he was arrested he threatened suicide and was put on suicide precautions at the police department lockup. When he was transferred to the main building, however, the officers were not informed, and Foster tried to hang himself with his shirt (Jail Suicide/Mental Health Update, Winter 2004).

In *Farmer v. Brennan* (1994), the Supreme Court ruled that a correctional official can be held liable for injury to an inmate if they knew he or she faced a substantial risk of serious harm and disregarded that risk by failing to take measures to lessen it. Such official behavior amounts to deliberate indifference, a phrase we see often in correctional law. Although the *Farmer* case involved a state prison inmate who had been sexually assaulted by other prisoners, the legal principle also applies in a situation where officials know a jail inmate is a suicide risk but they fail to take reasonable steps to protect him from harming himself. If the inmate is a convicted offender, the Eighth Amendment's cruel and unusual punishment clause is the legal basis for such a claim. If the inmate is a pretrial detainee, the Fifth or Fourteenth Amendment's due process clause provides the legal basis. Jail and prison officials are liable only if there is evidence they were actually aware of specific facts that indicated an inmate was at substantial risk and then deliberately failed to take reasonable steps to avoid it.

Many jail suicide lawsuits involve allegations that jail personnel received inadequate training on suicide prevention, which contributed to an inmate's serious injuries or death. That evidence involves identifying not only the specific training that could have been but was not provided, but also showing that the training would have reduced the risk of harm, making officials' failure to provide it obvious deliberate indifference. Of course, adequate training rests first on having an adequate suicide prevention program in place. Chapter 11 explains that state agencies cannot be sued under section 1983 and state officials can be sued only in their individual capacities. Unlike states, however, county and city governmental agencies and their officials can be sued under section 1983 for a failure to have an adequate program in place to protect inmates from harm as well as adequate training and supervision of the agency's personnel. *Wever v. Lincoln County*, 388 F.3d 601 (2004) provides a good example of a jail suicide case. In 2001, Lincoln County police in Nebraska responded to a 911 call from a depressed and weeping Dennis Wever. He agreed to go to a hospital but was arrested instead when he became combative and volatile. He was forcibly handcuffed and suffered a few cuts during the process. He became combative during the ride to the police station and had to be physically subdued, after which officers took him to a hospital where he was treated in the squad car for his physical injuries. Up until his arrest, Wever told police he was not suicidal, however, once he was arrested he told police he would commit suicide if he was jailed. Despite his suicide threats, Wever was placed in an isolation cell in the jail. When he requested a blanket, a jailor, who had been advised about Wever's suicide threats, provided a blanket to him, asking that he use the blanket for covering himself. Within half an hour of receiving the blanket, however, Wever hung himself with the blanket. One of the legal issues the court considered in the Wever case was whether the county sheriff, who took no part in the arrest and was not present during the suicide was immune from liability for Wever's death. Wever's family sued the police department and its chief, Lincoln County, the county sheriff, and several officers. The sheriff maintained he had an adequate suicide prevention policy in place at the jail at the time of Wever's death. The court refused to rule that the sheriff had good faith immunity from liability. The evidence showed that three inmates had died of suicide in the Lincoln County jail, one as recently as 1996 and the other in 1999, putting the sheriff on notice of problems in his facility. While a single incident may not provide notice of a deficient policy or poor training, the court concluded there was sufficient evidence in this case that the sheriff was not entitled to qualified immunity (See Chapter 11 for a complete discussion of qualified immunity). The court also found there was insufficient evidence addressing what kind of policy was in place when Wever died.

To help jails address suicide prevention, the National Commission on Correctional Health Care (NCCHC) provides a comprehensive set of standards. According to the NCCHC standards, key components of an adequate suicide prevention program include: identification mechanisms to screen inmates as potential suicide risks during admission, training staff to recognize verbal and behavioral clues that indicate an inmate is a suicide risk, assessment procedures for mental health professionals to assess risk, monitoring procedures for inmates who are at risk that require regular, documented cell visits, housing that does not isolate an inmate at risk, referral procedures to mental health facilities when needed, communication avenues between health care and correctional personnel regarding an inmate's status, specific procedures for how to intervene in a suicide in progress, procedures for notifying administrators, authorities, and family members of suicide attempts, reporting procedures for documenting suicide attempts, and review procedures if a suicide or an attempt occurs. Having a suicide prevention program in place that meets standards like those promulgated by the NCCHC helps local agencies and jail officials avoid lawsuits. Most importantly, the standards help prevent inmate suicides. When a suicide does occur, having an adequate program in place with a properly trained staff reduces the possibility that a jail agency or official being held legally liable for the inmate's death.

SUMMARY

Jails are a very different correctional environment than prisons because they do more; they also function as facilities that detain people who have not been convicted of crimes. Their multiple roles have raised important and hotly debated legal issues. Although the Supreme Court ruled in *Bell v. Wolfish* (1979) and *Block v. Rutherford* (1984) that pretrial detainees can be subjected to the same restrictions as convicted offenders, think about the large number of people processed through America's jails each year and how many of them are never charged with a crime, the charges are dropped, or they are acquitted. Furthermore, many are detained prior to trial because they could not afford to post bond. For all intents and purposes, their experience while detained mirrors the experience of convicted offenders. From a system's perspective, large numbers of detainees dramatically increase the size and cost of a community's jail population. It is an interesting and pressing problem that few people outside of the criminal justice system think about, that is until their spouse/child/sibling/parent is arrested.

Because jails detain people immediately after they are arrested, the population is less stable than the prison population, and jail officials know less about the individuals they house. Classification is less precise. Detainees and convicted offenders often live together. Jails are operated and funded by local governments. Struggling counties and regions find it difficult to appropriate the funds needed to build, staff, and maintain their jails. Jail officials have some of the toughest jobs in the criminal justice system. Like prison officials, jail officials face lawsuits on a regular basis, although research demonstrates they are sued considerably less often. In large part that is because the average length of stay in jail is considerably shorter than in prison. It is certainly not because jails face fewer problems or less demands than prisons. Like prisons, jail conditions require constant vigilance and comprehensive accountability programs. Unfortunately, jails must remedy their legal problems with far fewer resources than are available to state institutions. Jails are generally not the subject of Hollywood movies, television shows, or even documentaries about crime and punishment. When the public turns its attention to incarceration, the focus is usually on the prison system. In reality, however, many more Americans are affected by what happens in our local jails than in our prisons, making it important to understand and appreciate the complexity of the task assigned to jail officials.

DISCUSSION QUESTIONS

1. How do jails differ from prisons and how do those differences impact liability issues under section 1983?

2. Explain why pretrial detainees are not protected by the Eighth Amendment and what constitutional protections they are afforded instead.

3. Discuss the Supreme Court's decisions in *Bell v. Wolfish* and *Block v. Rutherford*. Do you agree with the Supreme Court in those cases, or should pretrial detainees be given greater protections than persons convicted of crimes? Explain your position.

4. An inmate commits suicide in the local jail and his parents consult an attorney about the possibility of suing jail officials for a violation of the Fourteenth Amendment's due process clause. Discuss what type of fact issues an attorney would explore about this case to determine if officials should be held liable.

5. What steps can jail officials take to prevent inmate suicide?

SUGGESTED READINGS AND REFERENCES

Mahoney, B. & Smith, W. (2005). Pretrial release and detention in Harris County: Assessment and recommendations. Denver: The Justice Management Institute.

Mumola, C. (2005). Bureau of Justice Statistics special report: Suicide and homicide in state and local jails. Washington D.C.: Department of Justice.

National Center on Institutions and Alternatives & the National Institute of Corrections (2004, Winter). National standards for jail suicide prevention. Jail Suicide/Mental Health Update 13(3) 5-6.

Sabol, W. & Minton, T. (2008) Bureau of Justice Statistics Bulletin: Prison and jail inmates in midyear 2007. Washington, D.C.: Department of Justice.

Schlanger, M. (2003). Inmate litigation: Results of a national survey. LJN Exchange 2003, 1-12.

Steadman, H. J. & Veysey, B. M. (1997). National Institute of Justice research in brief: Providing services for jail inmates with mental disorders. Washington, D.C.: DOJ.

CHAPTER 10:

Probation and Parole

INTRODUCTION

The growing United States prison population has been the subject of much debate and discussion by the public and criminal justice practitioners. While the number of people incarcerated has risen dramatically during the past three decades, the number of people on probation or parole (community supervision) has been increasing at an even faster rate. Between 1995 and 2006, the number of people on community supervision increased by over one million offenders. As of 2006, there were over five million individuals on probation or parole in the United States (Glaze & Bonczar 2007).

Although the United States Supreme Court decides several prison law cases every term, it hears very few cases involving probation and parole. It is unfortunate that so little attention is paid to probation and parole law, for decisions in this area impact significant numbers of offenders and criminal justice personnel. In this chapter we provide an overview of the important legal issues in probation and parole.

An offender may be released into the community either on probation or parole. Probation is a substitute for incarceration of convicted criminals. The offender is released into the community under the supervision of a probation officer in lieu of incarceration. Probation has the twin goals of maximizing the liberty of the offender while still protecting the public. It is less costly, and generally more rehabilitative in nature than incarceration. Probation is typically controlled by the judge. An offender who is charged with violating his or her probation is brought back before the judge who decides whether the offender should be allowed to remain on probation (often with additional conditions) or be incarcerated.

According to the Supreme Court, the purpose of probation is "to provide an individualized program offering a young or unhardened offender an opportunity to rehabilitate himself without institutional confinement under the tutelage of a probation officer and under the continuing power of the court to impose institutional punishment for his original offense in the event that he abuse the opportunity" (*Roberts v. United States*, 1943).

Parole is the early, conditional release of a prisoner who has served part of the term for which he was sentenced to prison, under supervision of a parole officer. It is the extension of incarceration. Parole has the goal of reintegrating the offender into the community while maintaining some degree of supervision over the parolee's conduct, thus protecting the public. Typically parole is controlled by the state Department of Corrections, as the agency charged with supervising persons who have been sentenced to incarceration.

CONDITIONS OF PROBATION AND PAROLE

Courts and parole boards have broad authority to impose probation and parole conditions. There are general and specific conditions. General conditions are those that apply to all probationers or parolees, and are usually specified by statute. They include not associating with known criminals, consenting to searches by law enforcement personnel or caseworkers, not using drugs or alcohol, making periodic reports to a probation or parole officer, notifying the officer about changes in employment or residence, obtaining permission for out-of-state travel, not possessing a firearm, and obeying the law. Specific conditions are those that apply to individual offenders, and are imposed by the sentencing judge or the parole authority. It is not uncommon for judges or parole boards to impose special conditions in an attempt to tailor the terms of probation or parole to the individual's crime and circumstances, including such things as counseling, psychotherapy, or drug and alcohol treatment. The general rule is that the authority to impose special conditions cannot be delegated to probation or parole officers, although officers are often permitted to determine the precise mode of how a condition will be implemented.

How Conditions Are Imposed

Probation and parole conditions are imposed either by the judge at sentencing, or by a parole board at the parole hearing. While most state laws suggest conditions to be imposed, the judge or board generally has complete discretion to accept, modify, or reject these conditions.

Surprisingly few state statutes specify the goals to be served by probation and parole conditions, but courts have focused on the twin goals of rehabilitation and community protection. These interests are seen by courts as of sufficient importance to meet the "compelling state interest" required for abridgement of "fundamental" constitutional rights.

While rehabilitation and public safety are the most frequently cited goals of probation and parole, defining these terms with precision is difficult. Rehabilitation generally encompasses conditions which involve treatment, education and reintegration of the offender; public safety involves conditions such as a ban on association with criminals, possession of weapons, and a requirement to obey the law.

Legal Limitations on Conditions

Generally, there are no limits on what conditions can be imposed on probationers and parolees as long as they are reasonably related to the offender's crime or to the offender's rehabilitation, and that the conditions are do-able. Many conditions impinge on fundamental constitutional rights, but courts have upheld these conditions under the rationale that a probationer or parolee loses some of the full complement of rights upon conviction--a variation on the concept of civil death. Generally, a probation or parole condition will be upheld so long as it is reasonably related to protection of the public, rehabilitation of the offender, or the offense committed. While judges and parole boards are given tremendous latitude in establishing conditions, in reality many use a list of previously adopted standard conditions for every individual.

The validity of such conditions is based on (1) whether they are too harsh, in violation of the Eighth Amendment's ban on cruel and unusual punishment, and (2) whether there is a relationship between the offense and the prescribed treatment. Additionally, courts have indicated that revocation is not permitted if an offender fails to undergo a prescribed treatment because they are indigent.

Considering how many individuals today are on either probation or parole, the amount of litigation concerning the legality of conditions is relatively small. This is likely because the probationer/parolee has agreed to the conditions and is aware of the practical consequences of challenging them. When conditions are challenged, a variety of claims are frequently raised. These include invalid consent, vagueness, unequal enforcement of the law, and infringement upon a fundamental right.

Individuals may waive their rights as long as the waiver is freely and voluntarily given. Courts have held that some constitutional rights may not be waived, particularly if the only alternative to waiver is incarceration. This is often seen as coercive.

The Due Process clause of the Fourteenth Amendment prohibits the enforcement of vague laws because a person cannot conform his or her conduct if they do not know precisely what is expected of them. Probation and parole conditions are often challenged on the grounds of vagueness, as offenders assert they did not understand the meaning of particular terms. Some conditions are expressed in a very general way, such as "avoid disreputable places" or "do not associate with undesirable individuals." Courts have generally held probation and parole conditions to a lesser standard of clarity than statutory provisions, inquiring only as to whether the phrase in question is of common, everyday English usage.

Unequal enforcement of conditions can be the basis for liability under the Equal Protection clause of the Fourteenth Amendment. Under this provision, unreasonable distinctions between individuals or classes of individuals are prohibited. The actions of probation and parole officers are sometimes challenged on the grounds of unequal enforcement—the probationer/parolee asserts that he or she has been singled out for harassment by the officer. Courts generally require clear evidence of officer misconduct in these cases.

In general, probation and parole conditions are valid, as long as they: (1) do not violate the Constitution, (2) are reasonable, (3) are unambiguous, and (4) are intended to promote the rehabilitation of the offender and/or the protection of society. When a "fundamental right" is abridged, however, the courts will examine the condition more closely, using what is referred to as "strict scrutiny" review. Under this standard of review, a probation or parole condition is valid only if there is a showing of both (1) a compelling state interest and (2) no less restrictive means of accomplishing the purpose. Rights deemed fundamental by the Supreme Court are found largely in the protections afforded citizens in the Bill of Rights. The First Amendment guarantees of freedom of speech, assembly, and religion are prime examples.

Nonassociation Conditions

A notion as old as crime itself is that hanging out with the "wrong crowd" will get a person in trouble. There is support in criminology research for this belief, and it serves as the basis for one of the most common probation and parole conditions, the limitation on association. This condition forbids the offender from having contact with certain persons or types of persons.

This limitation is justified on the ground that association with criminals or other "shady" characters will both interfere with the rehabilitation of the offender and reduce public safety. This limitation may apply to a category of persons, such as those with a criminal record, or those who are not "law-abiding" or are of "disreputable or harmful character;" it may also apply to specific, named persons. Nonassociation provisions are authorized by statute in some jurisdictions, and by case law in others.

Nonassociation conditions are frequently challenged as unconstitutional. These challenges fall into one of four categories: (1) the condition is unrelated to the purpose of probation/parole, (2) the condition violates the right of privacy, (3) the language of the condition is too vague, and (4) the condition violates the First Amendment.

Claims that a nonassociation condition is unrelated to the traditional purposes of parole (protection of the public and rehabilitation of the offender) are rarely successful. Courts generally accept without question the assertion that prohibiting contact with criminals and other unsavory types is conducive to public safety and rehabilitation.

Claims that a nonassociation condition violates the right of privacy are also rarely successful. While the right of privacy is not expressly provided in the Constitution, the Supreme Court has held that a limited right of privacy does exist. Areas of conduct in which this right has been held to exist include family and marital relations. These are "fundamental rights" and any limitation on them is subject to "strict scrutiny" review by the courts. This means the limitation on the right will be upheld only if it both promotes a "compelling state interest" and is "narrowly tailored" to promote that interest. Nonassociation conditions have usually been upheld under this standard of review, except in some limited circumstances where the nonassociation condition infringed on specific familial rights such as prohibiting a spouse from living with their spouse.

Claims that a nonassociation condition is void because it is vague are sometimes successful. Due process requires that probation and parole conditions are stated clearly enough so that the average person can understand them and know what conduct is and is not permitted. Successful challenges have focused on the language of conditions which prohibit association with all criminals, without regard for whether the probationer/parolee was aware that the person with whom he or she was associating had a criminal record.

Claims that a nonassociation condition violates the First Amendment are the most likely to succeed. The First Amendment expressly includes the right of freedom of association, and a nonassociation condition infringes on this right. Probationers and parolees, however, enjoy only conditional freedom from confinement, and this freedom comes at the expense of some rights. Courts have long upheld conditions which restrict even "fundamental" rights, such as the freedom of association, so long as the condition is related to a compelling state interest, such as protecting the public or promoting rehabilitation.

The Supreme Court has decided only one case involving the constitutionality of a nonassociation condition. In *Arciniega v. Freeman* (1971) the Court interpreted the meaning of a parole condition which prohibited "association" with other ex-convicts, holding that such a provision did not apply to "incidental" contact.

Arciniega v. Freeman (1971)

Raymond Arciniega was paroled in 1967, after serving seven years of a ten year sentence for drug distribution. One of the conditions of his parole was a prohibition on associating with persons having criminal records. In 1969, the California Parole Board revoked his parole on the ground that he had violated the non-association provision by working in a restaurant where two other ex-convicts worked.

Arciniega filed a writ of habeas corpus, asserting there was no evidence that he had actually associated with his ex-convict co-workers. The federal district court upheld the Parole Board. The Court of Appeals sustained the parole revocation on the ground that Arciniega worked at the same place as other ex-convicts, a sufficient basis for the Parole Board to conclude that he had "associated" with ex-convicts.

The Supreme Court reversed the lower courts. Although the Court admitted that the Parole Board "has wide authority to set conditions," including the authority to prohibit association with ex-convicts, it held there must be "satisfactory evidence" of a parole violation to justify parole revocation. The Court examined the record of the case to determine whether such "satisfactory evidence" existed in this case. The Court determined that "the parole condition restricting association was (not) intended to apply to incidental contacts between ex-convicts in the course of work on a legitimate job." Since the record indicated that parole was revoked solely on this ground, the Court reversed the revocation of parole.

Unresolved by the Court's decision in *Arciniega* was the question of exactly what constitutes "incidental" contact in other situations, as well as the applicability of the holding to similar situations such as probation revocation hearings. There are several areas which pose potential problems regarding limitations on association with other parolees. Often parolees participate in programs composed of individuals with special needs, such as educational programs, vocational training, alcohol and drug treatment, and psychological counseling. Restrictions on association with other parolees presents an obvious problem for these programs. For example, participation in Alcoholics Anonymous by parolees is not uncommon. In this program members are required to have a sponsor who has similar experiences and maintains a close relationship with the individual. Accordingly, an ex-convict may request another ex-convict to be his or her sponsor. Should this type of association be restricted? If it is not, how would courts differentiate between legitimate self-help organizations and sham organizations created to avoid the restriction on association?

Another area of concern is Intensive Supervision Probation (ISP). ISP has become increasingly popular because it can be used to divert offenders from prison, is not as lenient as regular probation, increases control over marginal offenders, and is less costly than incarceration. ISP programs provide for offenders to perform community work, work at lawful employment, and hopefully become responsible members of the community. Because offenders are out in the community when involved in ISP programs, their chances of "incidental contact" with other offenders increase, and with the increased level of supervision involved in ISP probation officers are more likely to become aware of any prohibited association. This could lead to an increase in the number of probation revocations. With numerous offenders involved in ISP programs the Court may have to reevaluate its definition of "incidental contact" as well as clarify the meaning of "association."

Arciniega v. Freeman is a relatively obscure case in the annals of probation and parole law, but it is nonetheless important, because it is the only Supreme Court pronouncement thus far concerning a parole condition. In the twenty years since the decision lower courts have not strayed far from the Supreme Court's definition of "association." In *Arciniega* the Court held that "incidental contact" did not constitute "satisfactory evidence" of association. But the Court did not specify how much contact is too much, or how much evidence of association is required. The lower court cases interpreting *Arciniega* have failed to clarify this issue.

Travel Conditions

Probation and parole conditions are often categorized into two groups: reform and control. Reform conditions are intended to facilitate the rehabilitation of the offender, while control conditions are intended to facilitate the supervision of the offender. A common probation and parole condition is one which limits in some way the offender's right to travel. This sort of condition is imposed in at least seventy-five percent of jurisdictions in this country, and comes in a variety of forms. Such a limitation is an example of a control condition.

The right to travel is an ancient one, recognized in English law as early as the Magna Carta (1215). While a right to travel is not specifically mentioned in the Constitution, courts have recognized a constitutional right to interstate travel derived from Article IV, Section Two, of the Constitution, which states that "the citizens of each state shall be entitled to all Privileges and Immunities of Citizens in the several States." The right to travel is a fundamental right, meaning courts will examine any attempt to restrict it very closely, applying the "strict scrutiny" test, which requires a showing of a "compelling state interest" and that there is no less means of accomplishing the purpose.

There are no United States Supreme Court decisions regarding the constitutionality of probation and parole conditions limiting the right to travel. There have been a number of lower federal court decisions and state court decisions, however, involving challenges to such conditions. Although the right to travel is fundamental, and a probation or parole condition limiting freedom of movement infringes on the right, the restriction is not necessarily invalid. Courts have long upheld conditions which restrict even "fundamental" rights, such as the right of travel, so long as the condition is related to a compelling state interest, such as protecting the public or promoting rehabilitation. Probation and parole conditions which impose reasonable restrictions on the ability of the offender to travel or move about are usually upheld, on the ground that they are appropriate means of both fostering rehabilitation and protecting the public.

Conditions prohibiting the offender from traveling may require that the offender stay within the city, county, state or country which has jurisdiction over the case. Conditions prohibiting the offender from being at a particular place may refer to places where criminal activity is known to occur, or where the offender's presence is likely to lead to trouble or criminal involvement, such as a bar, or the residence of the victim of the offender. Conditions requiring the offender to be somewhere include those which require the offender to live in a particular residence or halfway house, and those which require the offender to be present at treatment or counseling sessions.

Perhaps the most common probation and parole condition is one which requires the offender to remain within a certain geographical area, such as the state or county. Such conditions are generally upheld by the courts. The rationale for upholding such restrictions on the ability to travel include protection of the public and promotion of offender rehabilitation. The public is protected because it is easier to supervise the offender if he or she remains within a limited area. Rehabilitation is fostered because it keeps the offender from going to areas where he or she might be more likely to engage in criminal conduct and because it makes it easier for the probation/parole officer to supervise the offender and help reintegrate the offender into society.

A common condition affecting the freedom of movement is one which requires the offender to be at a particular place at a particular time, such as one in which the offender is required to remain at home during the evening hours.

This is a form of curfew. While general curfews for adults are frequently declared unconstitutional by the courts, probation and parole conditions involving a curfew for the offender are often upheld. The justification for upholding a curfew condition is usually that it will protect the public and promote the rehabilitation of the offender by keeping him or her away from places where they are more likely to engage in inappropriate and/or illegal behavior.

Probation and parole conditions prohibiting an offender from being in a particular place are not uncommon. For example, an offender might be prohibited from being in a bar, the residence of the victim of his offense, or a school. Courts have struck down such limitations when the state was unable to demonstrate that there is a relationship between the offense and the place prohibited. When the state is able to establish such a relationship, however, courts are likely to uphold the prohibition as fostering rehabilitation and protecting the public.

A condition which bars the offender from a large area, such as a city, county, or state, is likely to be voided by the courts. Excluding the offender from such a large area is a form of banishment. Banishment as punishment has a long history in other countries, including England. Banishment has not enjoyed a favored position in this country, however, and it is prohibited by several state constitutions. It is considered bad public policy because it is not related to the offense, and permits a jurisdiction to rid itself of its "criminal element" by dumping unwanted individuals on another jurisdiction. Additionally, banishment has been held to serve no valid rehabilitative purpose. However, a limitation on travel within a state or city may survive if the limitation is clearly linked to valid goal(s) of probation and parole. Furthermore, use of the Interstate Compact for the supervision of parolees and probationers does not constitute banishment.

First Amendment Freedom of Speech

Individual rights protected under the First Amendment include freedom of speech, assembly, association, and religion. Freedom of speech is one of the most cherished of individual rights, and courts look closely at any probation or parole condition which infringes on this right. Freedom of assembly is closely related to the freedom of speech, as is the freedom of association. These are sometimes described as "political rights," because they are essential to the promotion of political discourse and debate. While the freedom of speech is highly treasured, it is not absolute. Thus the government may impose some restrictions on the exercise of the right, such as prohibiting the yelling of "fire" in a crowded movie theater or inciting people to immediate, violent overthrow of the government.

While First Amendment rights are fundamental rights, this does not necessarily mean that any condition restricting an offender's First Amendment rights is invalid. Probationers and parolees both enjoy only conditional freedom from confinement, and this freedom comes at the expense of some rights. Courts will uphold conditions which restrict even fundamental rights, so long as the condition is related to a compelling state interest, such as protecting the public or promoting rehabilitation.

Probation and parole conditions limiting speech are relatively rare, and most involve probationers who committed crimes while engaged in political demonstrations. Typical conditions bar the making of speeches, distribution of printed materials, and public demonstrations or picketing. Such conditions were not uncommon during the Vietnam War, when political protests occurred with some regularity. Courts have seen a recurrence of such conditions in recent years, largely as a result of antiabortion protests. Some conditions have barred nonpolitical speech. These conditions often are intended to limit the ability of offenders to profit from the publication of materials documenting their criminal exploits.

Courts, recognizing the importance of the freedom of speech, tend to examine restrictions on the right very closely. In general, those cases upholding conditions have focused on the relationship between the condition and the goals of rehabilitation and protection of the public. Cases striking such conditions have generally done so on the ground that they are overbroad, and restrict more speech than is necessary.

First Amendment Religious Freedom

Freedom of religion is another highly valued right. The Free Exercise Clause of the First Amendment allows individuals to conduct their religious life largely free of government interference. As discussed in Chapter 4, the reach of this clause has even been extended to many prison religious activities. Under this clause, the government is prohibited from infringing on the free exercise of an individual's religious beliefs, and is also prohibited from promoting one religious belief over another.

Cases involving conditions limiting an offender's freedom of religion are even rarer than those involving freedom of speech. Often these cases involve a probation or parole condition requiring an offender to attend church. Courts have consistently held that probation and parole conditions either requiring or preventing attendance at church are unlawful.

Conditions Mandating Education and Employment Training

A common probation and parole condition is the requirement that the offender attend school or an educational program of some kind. The frequency with which this condition is applied is not surprising, given the high value placed on education in American society and the relatively low education level of most offenders. The type of education required depends on the offender. He or she may be required to attend high school, college or vocational school, or to participate in programs aimed at allowing the participant to achieve the high school equivalency degree, or GED. Juvenile offenders may be required to attend school; adult offenders are generally required to attend some form of adult education program. Other, offense-related educational programs may also be required, such as attendance at an alcohol and drug awareness class, or driver safety class.

The authority to require the offender to participate in educational programs may be found in specific statutes, or under the court and parole board's general authority to impose any condition which is reasonably related to the primary goals of probation and parole—rehabilitation and protection of the public. While the evidence regarding the rehabilitative effects of education programs on recidivism is mixed, historically there has been strong support for such programs. The assumption is that an offender with a basic education is less likely to recidivate and more likely to see themselves as members of law-abiding society.

Similar to the condition requiring participation in educational programming is the condition mandating participation in job training. Offenders who have either completed basic educational programs or are in need of a marketable job skill are often required to obtain some form of job training. The justification for such a condition is also similar to the justification for mandatory education—rehabilitation and protection of the public. The assumption is that an offender with a job skill is less likely to return to their criminal ways as they will develop a legitimate means of obtaining money.

Conditions Mandating Medical Treatment

Conditions mandating medical treatment can take several forms, including surgical procedures, psychological treatment, or some type of counseling. Conditions requiring an offender to undergo some type of surgical procedure are relatively rare, although there have been calls in recent years for greater use of such conditions, at least in regards to sexual offenders. More commonly, the offender is required to obtain some form of counseling. Challenges to conditions mandating medical treatment are based in several different provisions of the Constitution, including the First and Eighth Amendments, and the general right to privacy. These challenges are relatively rare, no doubt in large part because such conditions are themselves rare. Generally, courts have taken the position that a condition requiring medical treatment is not per se unconstitutional, so long as the treatment is reasonably related to the goal of rehabilitation. Additionally, courts have noted that the offender always has the option of rejecting such a condition.

Conditions Mandating Therapy

Conditions mandating some form of therapy or counseling are much more common than those requiring the offender to undergo a medical procedure. Primarily because these conditions are less physically invasive, they are also much more likely to be upheld by the courts. Additionally, it is often easier to establish a connection between the mandated therapy and the goals of probation and parole.

Conditions requiring the offender to receive some form of therapy or counseling may be authorized by a state statute, or by parole authority regulations. This authorization is frequently vague, merely authorizing "psychological or psychiatric treatment" without providing more specifics. A number of states now provide specific authorization for counseling for sex offenders. Conditions mandating therapy or counseling are quite popular, as there is widespread sentiment that most offenders can benefit from professional attention.

There have been very few challenges to probation and parole conditions mandating therapy or counseling. Courts have routinely rejected such challenges, so long as the treatment is in reasonably related to the needs of the offender. Courts have also made it clear that offenders are only required to make reasonable efforts to comply with the treatment condition. Requiring an offender to obtain expensive treatment that he or she clearly cannot afford may be invalidated by the courts.

Conditions Mandating Restitution

A common probation and parole condition requires the offender make restitution to the victim. Restitution is different from victim compensation, where compensation is given to the victim by the state. It is also different from a fine, which is money paid by the offender to the state and is not treated as compensation. Restitution serves both as an act of atonement by the offender and rehabilitation of the victim.

Restitution is ancient. It is mentioned in the Bible as well as the Code of Hammurabi, and received the enthusiastic support of the eighteenth century reformer Jeremy Bentham. Restitution gained prominence as a sentencing option in the modern era in Alameda County, California in 1966. Every jurisdiction allows for the imposition of restitution as a probation condition, and in a third of the states, courts are required by law to order restitution absent extraordinary circumstances (U.S. Department of Justice 2002). Victim restitution forces the offender to acknowledge the consequences of his or her actions, which will hopefully foster a sense of greater responsibility. It is important to note that restitution may only be imposed by judges, acting either pursuant to a statutory mandate or within the scope of their authority to impose reasonable probation conditions. Probation officers are charged with the responsibility of overseeing the collection of the restitution, which can include both payments to the victim and community service in lieu of payment. Restitution is often victim initiated— if the victim does not inform the court of losses suffered, restitution may not be ordered.

Restitution serves a number of purposes. These include (1) providing redress for victims of crime; (2) fostering rehabilitation of the offender; (3)

providing accountability for the offender; (4) deterrence of further criminal activity; (5) an intermediate sanction that is less severe on the offender; (6) reduces demands on the criminal justice system; (7) reduces the need for vengeance. The sanction is most often used for crimes involving damage to property or economic crimes; it is used much less frequently for violent crimes, as it is difficult to determine the appropriate compensation for such injuries, and it is not seen as an appropriate sanction for such serious offenses.

The authority to require an offender to make restitution has been repeatedly upheld by the courts. Ordinarily, there must be a finding or plea of guilty before restitution can be ordered, although this does not apply to cases involving restitution ordered during the pretrial diversion process. Courts may specify the amount, method of payment, and other conditions relating to restitution.

Several issues involving restitution arise. Perhaps most importantly, the United States Supreme Court ruled in *Bearden v. Georgia* (1985) that probation cannot be revoked because of an offender's inability to pay restitution as a condition of probation when the failure to pay is a result of indigence and not a mere refusal to pay. In this case Bearden was ordered to pay a $500 fine and $200 in restitution, but was unable to find employment and consequently failed to pay either the fine or thee restitution. His probation was revoked and he was incarcerated. He argued, and the Supreme Court agreed, that the Equal Protection Clause of the Fourteenth Amendment barred the revocation of probation for a no-willful failure to pay restitution. The Court determined that revocation was proper only if the failure to pay was intentional and the offender did not make a good faith effort to obtain the means to pay. One result of this ruling has been that some offenders may have completed all their probation conditions except restitution, and thus have their probation extended to allow them time to pay.

The specific restitution amount must be set by the judge. Some states set the restitution amount by statute for a specific offense by statute. Most courts require payment of a fixed amount, rather than a general requirement to "compensate the victim for all losses suffered" or some such language. The judge's duty to set the amount of restitution may not be delegated to the probation officer. Instead the judge must set the amount. While the amount cannot be delegated to the probation officer, the court may ask for a recommendation, and may delegate the mode of payment.

The general rule is that restitution can be required only for crimes for which the offender has been convicted. Thus if a person is convicted of one burglary but is suspected in several others, restitution can be required only for the conviction. Restitution may be required, however, in the absence of a conviction, if the offender admits responsibility for the other crimes.

PROTECTION FROM UNREASONABLE SEARCHES AND SEIZURES

Individuals convicted of crime, whether incarcerated or on probation or parole, do not retain the privacy rights enjoyed by the average citizen. Indeed, prisoners have no reasonable expectation of privacy and are subject to warrantless searches based on less than probable cause. This limitation is also evident in regards to probation and parole conditions that impinge on the Fourth Amendment right to be free from "unreasonable" searches and seizures. What may be an unreasonable search when the target is an ordinary citizen may be reasonable when the target is a probationer or parolee. Courts frequently base this distinction on the rationale that a probationer or parolee has a lessened expectation of privacy than the ordinary citizen. There are several policy reasons which support allowing searches of probationers and parolees. These include protection of the public, reducing recidivism through deterrence of criminal conduct by the client, and promoting alternatives to incarceration and, hopefully, rehabilitation through reintegration in the community.

Consent to search is one of the most common conditions of probation and parole. The condition generally covers searches conducted by probation or parole officers, and often allows searches by police officers as well. The scope of the search usually includes the offender's person and property. The terms of the condition may include blanket permission to be searched by caseworkers or law enforcement personnel, or may be limited to searches conducted by the caseworker. While this condition is widespread, it is rarely specifically authorized by statute. Instead, the condition is usually justified under the broad discretionary authority of the sentencing court (for probation) or the parole agency (for parole). While this condition is almost always upheld, some courts have struck it down in specific instances where consent to search was not appropriately related to the offense and background of the offender.

The Fourth Amendment controls all searches and seizures conducted by state actors, be they police or probation officers. All searches and seizures must be conducted either (1) based on a warrant, issued upon a showing of "probable cause," or (2) without a warrant, so long as the search is not "unreasonable"--meaning there must be a showing of probable cause and an exigent circumstance or exception which justifies failure to obtain a warrant. Exigent circumstances include such situations as danger to public safety and hot pursuit. Exceptions to the warrant requirement include inventory searches, plain view searches, search incident to arrest and others. The two exceptions relevant to caseworkers are consent and special needs of law enforcement.

Consent is a voluntary waiver of a person's Fourth Amendment rights. It may be given expressly, by implication, or by a prior agreement (such as a condition of probation or parole). An interesting, and common, situation is the one in which the terms of probation or parole include a waiver of the right to be free from unreasonable searches and seizures. There are a number of exceptions to the warrant requirement, one of which is consent. So long as consent is freely given, it constitutes a valid waiver of one's Fourth Amendment rights. This waiver need not be informed, or knowing--that is, law enforcement personnel are not required to advise a person that he or she has the right to refuse to consent to a warrantless search. The sole requirement is voluntariness, the absence of coercion or duress. Some of the factors the Court considers in determining whether consent is voluntary include intelligence and age.

Another exception to the warrant requirement that comes into play in probation and parole situations is the "special needs of law enforcement" exception. Under this exception, courts have determined that in certain situations a warrant is counterproductive because it interferes with the government's objective. Courts must balance the degree of intrusion into an individual's right to privacy with the burden on the government. The Court has upheld searches in schools and drug-testing in certain occupations under this exception. In *Griffin v. Wisconsin* (1987), the Court held that a state regulation allowing "reasonable" searches of probationers by a probation officer was constitutionally valid, on the grounds that the warrant and probable cause requirement would unduly hamper the state's probation system. The Court did not find it necessary to address the issue of the validity of the probationers' consent, since the regulation was upheld under the "special needs" exception. In *United States v.Knights* (2001), the high court expanded its decision in *Griffin* when it held that a police officer can search a probationer without a warrant if the officer has reasonable suspicion that the probationer is engaged in criminal activity.

In 2006, the Court decided *Samson v. California* involving the suspicionless search of a parolee by law enforcement officials. When Samson was paroled by the State of California, he was required to sign an agreement that he could be searched by a parole officer or a police officer at any time of day or night, without a search warrant and with or without cause. Sampson was stopped by a police officer who recognized him. Although the officer confirmed that Samson did not have an outstanding warrant, the officer searched Samson pursuant to the agreement the parolee signed when he was released, consenting to suspicionless searches. The officer admitted that at the time of the search, he had no reasonable suspicion that Samson was involved in criminal activity. During the search the officer discovered methamphetamine. The Court ruled that the Fourth Amendment did not prohibit the officer's suspicionless search because Samson's status as a parolee diminished his reasonable expectations of privacy. Samson agreed to suspicionless searches as a condition of his parole; California had a substantial interest in using such searches to enhance its ability to supervise its parolees effectively.

PRIVILEGE AGAINST SELF-INCRIMINATION

The Supreme Court has accorded criminal suspects the right to be apprised of their Fifth and Sixth Amendment rights, such as the right to counsel and the privilege against self-incrimination, prior to custodial interrogation. The Court created the *Miranda* warnings because it felt that they were necessary to effectively secure a criminal suspect's privilege against self-incrimination. Prior to *Miranda v. Arizona* (1966), the Court focused on whether a statement was voluntary--that is, not coerced by the police. The Court determined in *Miranda* that voluntariness alone was not enough--because an incriminating statement was potentially devastating to a defendant, such statements should be admitted only if they were made freely and with full knowledge of one's constitutional rights.

The Court, however, has refused to extend the *Miranda* warnings to interrogation of probationers or parolees by their caseworkers. While the Supreme Court has not directly addressed the issue, most lower courts have held that the *Miranda* warnings are not required before a caseworker speaks with a client, primarily on the rationale that to require the warnings would do serious damage to the relationship between the caseworker and client, creating a law enforcement/interrogation type of atmosphere rather than a counseling type of atmosphere.

While caseworkers are not required to Mirandize their clients before engaging in a routine office visit, a different situation arises when the probation or parole officer has placed the client under arrest. *Miranda* warnings are required whenever someone is in custody and interrogation is about to commence. An ordinary conversation between client and caseworker does not fall into this category. But once a caseworker has begun investigating a possible crime, and has arrested the client, then *Miranda* warnings are required. The same is true if the caseworker is questioning a client who has been arrested by the police and brought to the caseworker for questioning.

PRIVILEGED COMMUNICATIONS

Courts have long recognized that certain communications should remain confidential, regardless of their probative value in court. Every state has case law and statutes according the privilege of confidentiality to certain relationships, such as doctor-patient, husband-wife, lawyer-client, and clergy-parishioner. Confidentiality is not a constitutional right but an evidentiary privilege. This means that the person who enjoys the privilege must exercise it to keep a communication confidential. In other words, the person must assert the privilege--it will not be extended to him unless he specifically requests it.

The importance of privileged communications for criminal justice caseworkers involves their designation, in some states, as counselors. This designation suggests the caseworker-client relationship may be akin to the doctor-patient relationship and that therefore communications between caseworker and client may be privileged. But most courts have not taken this view. There are exceptions to the doctor-patient privilege, and courts have declined to extend the common law evidentiary privilege of confidentiality to the caseworker-offender relationship, regardless whether the caseworker is a probation officer or a parole officer. Thus, conversations between a parolee and his or her caseworker are not treated as confidential. The rationale most often proffered for this distinction is that a criminal justice counselor is not a private counselor, but a counselor and a law enforcement agent (*Fare v. Michael C.*, 1979).

Parole Release Decisions

In *Greenholtz v. Inmates of Nebraska Penal and Correctional Complex* (1979), the Supreme Court considered a challenge to the Nebraska parole statutes, specifically the due process rights of inmates being considered for parole release. The Court reviewed the two stage process in Nebraska, which consisted of an informal hearing where the parole board reviewed inmates applying for parole to make an initial decision, followed by a second, formal hearing where the inmate could call witnesses and be represented by counsel. The Supreme Court began by noting that inmates do not have the inherent right to be released conditionally before the end of their prison term. Because they do not have a constitutional right to parole, they have no rights that mandate a certain type of hearing with specific procedures that must be followed under the Fourteenth Amendment's due process clause. States are not even required to establish a parole system. Parole is a discretionary decision that involves a subjective decision about whether a prisoner is ready to be released to the community.

In the case of Nebraska's statutes, however, the Supreme Court decided that under state law, prisoners were entitled to some procedural protections because the state had created a liberty interest for inmates in a parole system. The Court went on to decide that the procedures Nebraska had in place were sufficient to protect that liberty interest.

A few years later, the Supreme Court decided another case involving parole eligibility. In *Connecticut Board of Pardons v. Dumscat* (1981), the Court ruled that Dumschat did not have a right to a hearing before his application for a commuted sentence was denied even though the vast majority of inmates who applied for commutation received it. In its ruling, the Court noted that state law gave complete discretion to the parole board, and that he had no due process rights to be heard.

The Court's decisions have consistently held that parole boards have discretion in making parole release decisions and inmates have limited due process rights in the process. Parole decisions require a subjective evaluation of an inmate's readiness for release. It is a multi-dimensional decision that involves much more than reviewing a set of facts and deciding what facts are true and which are not; nor is it an adversarial process.

In *Jaffee v. Redmond* (1996), the Supreme Court held that there is a psychotherapist-patient privilege with respect to confidential communications. Furthermore, this privilege extends to communications between licensed social workers and patients as well. While this decision was in accord with the rule in most states, it is potentially significant in that it may open the door for extension of the privilege to other relationships that involves medical/psychological counseling. This could include criminal justice caseworkers. Courts have not yet taken this step, however, and since most criminal justice counselors are not licensed therapists, courts may distinguish them from social workers and psychotherapists on this basis.

APPLICATION OF THE EXCLUSIONARY RULE TO PROBATION AND PAROLE

The Supreme Court created the exclusionary rule primarily as a means of deterring unlawful conduct by law enforcement officers. According to the rule, evidence obtained unlawfully by law enforcement personnel may be excluded from trial. This extends to physical evidence as well as testimonial evidence. The Court embraced the exclusionary rule somewhat reluctantly, as a last resort.

In 1998, in the case *Pennsylvania Board of Probation and Parole v. Scott*, the Court ruled that the exclusionary rule does not apply to parole revocation hearings. When Scott was released on parole, he was prohibited from possessing a firearm. He was arrested on a warrant based on evidence that he had a firearm, consumed alcohol, and assaulted a coworker. Before he was transferred to jail, he gave the parole officers who arrested him the keys to his home which was owned by his mother. The officers entered the home but waited until Scott's mother returned to conduct a search of his bedroom. They did not request her consent. Although they found nothing incriminating in Scott's room, they found forearms in an adjacent room. Scott's parole was revoked by a parole hearing officer, despite Scott's objections that the search violated the Fourth Amendment and the firearms should be excluded from evidence during the revocation hearing.

RIGHT TO DUE PROCESS IN PROBATION/PAROLE REVOCATION HEARINGS

While those convicted of a crime clearly do not retain all of their rights, the Supreme Court has made it clear that the Fifth Amendment's Due Process clause does apply, not only during incarceration but also at probation and parole revocation hearings. This is a significant change from prior practice.

In *Morrissey v. Brewer* (1972) the Court held that due process required, at a minimum, that parole revocation procedures include: (1) written notice of the claimed parole violation; (2) disclosure to the parolee of the evidence against him or her; (3) an opportunity for the parolee to present evidence and witnesses, and to be heard; (4) the right of the parolee to confront and examine witnesses; (5) a neutral and detached hearing committee; and (6) a written statement by the parole board of the evidence and reasons for revoking parole. Parolees have a right to a preliminary hearing to be held soon after their arrest to determine if probable cause or reasonable grounds exist that they violated their parole conditions. The parolee can appear at the hearing and present evidence to the hearing officer. Parolees are entitled to a second hearing to be held within a reasonable time (the Court suggested two months would be reasonable) after the parolee was taken into custody. This second stage of the process is the actual revocation hearing. It leads to the final decision on revocation. The parolee has a right to attend and present evidence.

In *Gagnon v. Scarpelli* (1973) the Court held that the requirements for a probation revocation hearing are identical to the requirements for a parole revocation hearing. While the Court admitted that parole and probation are not identical, revocation of probation where sentence has been imposed previously is fundamentally indistinguishable form revocation of parole. Both probationers and parolees face a significant and grievous loss of liberty when they face revocation.

The right to have counsel during a revocation proceeding is a bit more complicated. In *Mempa v. Rhay* (1967), the Court held that the Sixth Amendment right to counsel applies to a combined probation revocation and sentencing hearing, on the grounds that the right to counsel attaches at any stage in a criminal proceeding where substantial rights of a criminal defendant are involved. Counsel should be provided at a hearing where a probationer is faced with having his or her probation revoked and the possibility of being sentenced to prison. The Court, however, did not rule that offenders have the right to counsel at probation revocation hearings involving offenders who have already been sentenced to prison but whose imprisonment was deferred while they completed a probation sentence.

In *Gagnon v. Scarpelli*, the Court discussed the right to counsel in greater detail. Although the case involved a probationer, the Court ruled on the Sixth Amendment right to counsel for both parolees and probationers who had deferred prison sentences. The Court observed that because revocation hearings for these offenders are more informal than what happens in courtrooms, the introduction of attorneys would alter the nature of the proceedings. Hearing committees are charged with making discretionary decisions based on predicting an offender's future conduct, which involves more than fact finding. Counsel would prolong the process, make it more expensive because the state would also have to be represented by counsel, and change the proceeding into an adversarial matter. For these reasons, the Supreme Court ruled that the right to counsel should be considered on a case-by-case basis. Although counsel would not be required in many revocation hearings, indigent probationers or parolees may be entitled to counsel if they request counsel and make a reasonable claim that they did not violate a condition of their conditional release or that there are substantial reasons which justified or mitigated the violation and make revocation inappropriate under those circumstances. The committee must also consider the offender's ability to articulate their case. If the committee refuses a request for counsel, it must state the reasons for its decision in writing.

SEX OFFENDERS

In the last ten to fifteen years, states have enacted a range of laws concerning sex offenders. While registration was once a common probation or parole condition for sex offenders, today registration, notification, and commitment proceedings are dealt with by statute. These more recent requirements have had a major impact on the workload and job requirements of probation and parole officers.

Spurred by media accounts of horrible child sexual assault cases, Congress and the state legislatures have passed a variety of laws affecting the rights of convicted sex offenders. These laws vary in the details, but focus on three primary objectives: (1) requiring sex offenders to register with local authorities; (2) requiring local law enforcement to notify the community about the presence of sex offenders living in the community; and (3) permitting the state to pursue civil commitment of sex offenders after they have served a period of incarceration. Each of these objectives presents potential legal issues.

While these laws are obviously popular, they are not without controversy. Social scientists have pointed out that there is little empirical proof that such laws reduce recidivism, while legal scholars have suggested the laws may violate any number of constitutional rights, including the ban on ex post facto laws, the prohibition on double jeopardy, and the right of privacy (Sims & Reynolds 2007).

Sex Offender Registration

The Jacob Wetterling Crimes Against Children and Sexually Violent Registration Act, passed by the U.S. Congress in 1994, established a national sex offender and child abuse registry, and required states to pass similar registration and tracking systems or face a loss of federal monies. Today all fifty states require that convicted sex offenders register with local authorities. States vary with regard to who is required to register. In some states only those convicted of a sex offense after passage of the registration requirement must comply, while in other states the registration requirement is applied retroactively. Some states require anyone convicted of a sexual offense to register; others also require those convicted of a violent crime against a child to register.

Typical registration requirements include requiring a released offender to register with the local law enforcement agency in the jurisdiction where they are living, to verify their address annually, and to do so for a period of years—often between twenty and thirty years. Failure to comply is a felony, punishable as a new offense.

The Wetterling Act has been amended several times since 1994, to impose additional registration requirements for repeat offenders and those whose acts were especially heinous, sexually violent offenders, federal and military offenders, and offenders who are nonresident workers and students. Registered sex offenders are also required to report their registration to any institution of higher education where they are employed or enrolled as students.

Community Notification

In 1989, Washington was the first state to pass a sex offender notification statute. The notification movement gained national attention and tremendous momentum with the passage of New Jersey's notification statute in 1994. In 1995, the U.S. Congress enacted Megan's Law, named after Megan Kanka, a seven year old girl from New Jersey who was sexually abused and murdered by a twice-convicted sex offender who lived across the street. Megan's law requires communities to establish notification systems when a sex offender is released from prison. Many consider notification statutes as a necessary supplement to registration laws because they believe registration alone fails to protect the public adequately. Every state has enacted laws addressing notifying communities where sex offenders live in their neighborhoods. Some states authorize local law enforcement officials to decide whether to release information about sex offenders, the manner of notification, and the amount of information to be released. Other state laws require members of the public to request information about convicted sex offenders in their communities from a central registry maintained by the state. In Louisiana, paroled sex offenders are required to identify themselves as sex offenders to members of the community where they live (Samuels 2000).

Civil Commitment

The United States Supreme Court upheld civil commitment of sex offenders in *Kansas v. Hendricks* (1997). Kansas passed legislation in 1994 establishing procedures for the civil commitment of persons who were deemed likely to engage in "predatory acts of sexual violence" due to either a "mental abnormality" or "personality disorder." The statute was applied to Hendricks, after he finished serving a term of imprisonment for child molestation, and he was ordered civilly committed. Hendricks had a history of sexually molesting children and had received treatment in the past but it had not proved to be effective. Hendricks challenged his commitment on double jeopardy, ex post facto, and due process grounds. In a narrow 5-4 decision, the Supreme Court upheld the Kansas civil commitment statute. The high court reasoned that neither the Double Jeopardy nor Ex Post Facto clauses applied, because civil commitment is not punitive but regulatory, and these clauses apply only to punishment. Hendrick's civil commitment was designed not as punishment for his past crimes, but rather to keep and monitor him until such time as he is no longer a threat to society. Even if Hendricks never responds favorably to treatment, the Court noted that it has upheld civil commitment in the past when an individual is believed to be a danger to society. The Supreme Court found no due process violation because civil commitment for a mental abnormality does not violate the concept of "ordered liberty."

The Court had a second opportunity to review a sex offender commitment statute in *Seling v. Young* (2001). Seling was also a repeat violent sex offender, and under the Washington state statute, he was civilly committed as a sexually violent predator to a facility when he was released from prison. He appealed, urging many of the same arguments raised in the Kansas case. In Selig's case, there was also evidence that the conditions of his civil commitment were very punitive. The facility was located within the department of corrections and relied on the department for essential services. Selig was placed under restrictions that he claimed were nonpunitive. The facility did not have a certified sex offender treatment counselor, and the failure to participate in therapy resulted in a loss of privileges. The Supreme Court was unconvinced by Selig's arguments. The Court ruled that a statute which is a civil law cannot be deemed "punitive" as it is applied in an individual case. The nature of the Washington law is civil confinement. Unless the evidence is clear that the law is punitive in either its purpose or its effect, so much so as to negate what the statute was originally intended to accomplish, a person cannot argue that "as-applied" he should be entitled to release. The Court commented that there will be much variety in how states implement sex offender commitment statutes, and it was not willing to get involved in evaluating which approaches could be considered nonpunitive. The Court noted that Selig could file a lawsuit in state court if Washington was not abiding by the law's requirements.

In its third opinion about sex offender civil commitment statutes, the Supreme Court considered another challenge to the Kansas statute. Crane, who had previously been convicted of a sex offense, was civilly committed after exposing himself to a woman and ordering her to perform oral sex. Crane challenged his civil commitment on the grounds that state needed but failed to show that he lacked total control of his behavior. In *Kansas v. Crane* (2002), the Supreme Court disagreed with Crane and ruled that the Kansas Sexually Violent predator Act does not require a showing that the offender has total or complete lack of control of his conduct. It is sufficient if there is proof the offender has serious difficulty in controlling his or her behavior.

Controversy Surrounding Sex Offender Legislation

A great deal of controversy surrounds sex offender legislation. Opponents of the legislation argue that registration and notification requirements, while popular, suffer from a number of legal flaws, and are simply bad public policy. They maintain that registration and notification lull the public into a false sense of safety. Further, registration and notification requirements are unconstitutional because offenders have already paid their debt to society through incarceration, and that registration and notification amount to further punishment, in violation of the Double Jeopardy clause. Supporters of sex offender legislation insist that registration and notification are not punishment, and that any punishment that occurs in the process of providing civil protection is simply an unavoidable side effect.

Opponents argue that registration and notification requirements violate the Constitution's prohibition on ex post facto laws. Ex post facto laws are laws enacted after a person engages in certain behavior and which retroactively impose punishment for that behavior. The Supreme Court resolved the ex post facto issue in *Smith v. Doe* (2003), when it considered the retroactive application of Alaska's sex offender registration and notification requirements to offenders convicted of aggravated sex offenses and who had been released from prison and completed sex offender rehabilitation programs. They were convicted before the Alaska legislature enacted the statutes in question and argued the ex post facto clause prohibited applying the requirements to them. The Court rejected their argument on the grounds that registration and notification requirements are not punitive but civil in nature. Because they do not involve punishment, imposing them retroactively does not trigger the ex post facto clause. Given the Court's reasoning in *Smith v. Doe*, it seems doubtful that a court would find sex offender registration and notification laws in violation of the Double Jeopardy Clause.

In 2003, the Supreme Court decided a case that challenged Connecticut's sex offender registration and notification laws, arguing that the disclosure of an offender's name and other information provided on the state's registry violated the due process clause. The offender was not afforded a hearing before the disclosure of the information to determine if he was likely to be "currently dangerous." In *Connecticut Department of Public Safety v. Doe* (2003), the Court ruled that the offender's due process rights were not violated because the law's requirements depend solely on whether the offender was convicted. The offender has no procedural right to a hearing about his current or future dangerousness to the community.

For opponents, sex offender laws violate the offender's right to privacy. That loss of privacy results in harassment and vigilantism against offenders, which will harm them and their ability to reintegrate and rehabilitate, and lead to increased financial costs (specialized case loads, additional duties for probation and parole officers and local law enforcement in maintaining lists and notifying the public). In response, supporters counter that registration is constitutional because it involves a minimal intrusion on the privacy of offenders, and the intrusion is clearly justified when balanced against the interests of society. Supporters point out that vigilantism can be controlled through prosecution.

THE COLLATERAL CONSEQUENCES OF CONVICTION

Individuals convicted of crime, whether incarcerated or under some form of community supervision, do not enjoy the same rights as the average citizen. In addition to receiving a sentence, offenders lose some of their rights. The sentence an individual receives upon conviction is sometimes referred to as a direct sanction. Rights lost as a result of conviction are referred to as collateral consequences. These collateral consequences include a variety of items, including the restriction of certain civil rights, such as the right to vote, and other disabilities, such as limitations on the ability to own a firearm. Reintegration is difficult for offenders because a criminal conviction carries with it a stigma. No matter what the offender does, from here on out they will thought of primarily as an "ex-con." Many employers will be reluctant to hire them, while others in the community will shun them. These sorts of barriers to successful reintegration are informal in nature. More formal barriers to successful reintegration come in the form of collateral consequences of conviction.

Civil Death and Disabilities

A civil right is a right that belongs to a person by virtue of citizenship. Civil rights are sometimes referred to as rights of citizenship. In *Trop v. Dulles*, decided in 1958, the United States Supreme Court held that depriving someone of their national citizenship as punishment for desertion from the military during wartime violated the Eighth Amendment's prohibition on cruel and unusual punishment, because it left the individual entirely outside of civilized society. This was a major shift from the early common law, when a person could be declared outside the protection of the law (literally an "outlaw") and suffer loss of all his civil rights and the forfeiture of his property to the sovereign. Such laws were known as Bills of Attainder, and were so disliked by the Founding Fathers that they were specifically barred in the Constitution, one of only three individual rights mentioned in the text of the Constitution.

Based on the Court's decision in *Trop*, a court would not uphold the stripping of a person's citizenship upon conviction of a crime. Courts have routinely upheld, however, the stripping of some civil rights as a consequence of conviction. Civil rights which are commonly lost by offenders include the right to vote, the right to hold office, and the right to serve on a jury. Rights such as these, related as they are to participation in democratic government, are sometimes referred to as political rights. These rights are generally lost automatically upon conviction.

Several recent studies have examined the status of civil disabilities today. Unlike in years past, when persons convicted of a crime became literal "slaves of the state" and suffered a total and permanent loss of rights, or "civil death," states today generally restrict only some rights, and often allow those who have lost their rights to petition for their return. Only four states still have a civil death statute on the books, and this punishment is limited, in three states, to offenders sentenced to life imprisonment.

Restrictions on civil/political rights vary among the states. Currently, forty-seven states restrict the right to vote. Fourteen states permanently deprive convicted felons of the right to vote, while eighteen states suspend the right until the offender has completed the imposed sentence, including any term of probation or parole. Thirteen states restrict voting rights only during incarceration.

Limitations on the ability of offenders to hold office are also commonplace. Twenty-five states impose some sort of restriction on holding public office after a conviction. Six states permanently restrict this right, while nineteen others return the right after discharge from probation or parole.

While many in contemporary society may view it as a burden, jury service is considered an important part of a democratic society and a valued right. Thirty-one states permanently restrict the right to serve on a jury for convicted felons. Another ten states restrict this right only during the sentence; four other states restrict the right during the sentence and for an additional fixed term of years beyond.

There are a number of disabilities that accompany conviction but do not affect rights related to the ability to participate in political activity. These disabilities are also considered collateral consequences of conviction. Some of these consequences are really more criminal than civil in nature. Examples include restrictions on the possession of firearms, restrictions on or revocation of driving privileges, and the requirement that the offender register with local authorities. Other consequences include the denial of pension and workers' compensation benefits, control of one's children, and marriage.

Among the most frequent disabilities imposed is the restriction on the possession and/or use of firearms. Federal law prohibits all convicted felons from possessing firearms. In addition, twenty-eight states permanently deprive felons of this right, while five more states deprive felons for a period of years after completion of the sentence. The remaining seventeen states limit the restriction to felons convicted of a crime of violence.

The disability that has seen the greatest increase in use by the states since 1986 is the requirement that offenders register with local law enforcement authorities. While in 1986 only eight states required any offenders to register, by 1996 forty-six states had such a requirement. Of these forty-five states also require registration for sex offenders. This development is no doubt a response to recent Congressional legislation which has encouraged the passage of such state legislation.

A number of states impose restrictions on the family rights of offenders, including matters such as marriage and parental rights. Currently twenty-nine states provide that a felony conviction is grounds for divorce; of these nineteen states require a conviction and imprisonment while ten require a conviction alone. A number of states provide that while a conviction is not per se grounds for divorce, it may be used in support of a petition for divorce. Nineteen states permit the termination of parental rights of convicted felons. Some states require that the felony demonstrate that the parent is "unfit," while other states permit termination of parental rights after any felony conviction.

Finally, there are a variety of disabilities imposed on offenders either informally or through operation of an administrative or licensing requirement. Examples include the social stigmatization suffered by "ex-cons," the reluctance of many employers to hire convicted felons, and the exclusion of persons of "poor moral character" from many occupations which require licensing by the state. A criminal conviction is generally considered evidence of poor moral character and acts to bar an offender from becoming licensed in a variety of trades.

Civil disabilities related to participation in political life have traditionally been justified on the grounds that (1) a loss of such rights is an appropriate form of punishment for a criminal offense, and (2) it is inappropriate to allow someone who has violated the laws of society from participating in the public affairs of society. Other disabilities, particularly those adversely affecting the ability of the offender in the community from achieving rehabilitation and reintegration (such as limits on employment), are harder to justify as serving a rational purpose.

Civil disabilities have been challenged on a number of grounds, including the denial of due process and equal protection of the laws, and being overbroad. Opponents have also argued that such disabilities interfere with the rehabilitation of the offender. Despite these criticisms, civil disabilities remain a prominent component of the criminal sentence.

RESTORATION OF THE CIVIL RIGHTS OF OFFENDERS

While the direct consequences of a conviction end with the completion of the sentence, the collateral effects of a conviction often continue until there is some affirmative action taken to eliminate them. Civil disabilities may be removed and civil rights restored in a variety of ways, including pardon, sentence expungement, and sealing of a criminal record. Not all actions restoring civil rights completely eliminate the disabilities associated with a conviction, however.

Pardon

The power to pardon originally belonged to the sovereign or king and has existed since the early common law. In twenty-two states the power now resides with the governor; in eleven states the power rests with the Parole Board, and in another sixteen states the power is shared by the governor and the Parole Board. A pardon is meant to be a forgiveness of crime, and has been used both when it is determined that an innocent person was wrongly convicted, and to reduce an unduly harsh sentence on a guilty person. This is also known as sentence commutation.

A full pardon completely eliminates the legal consequences of a conviction. The authorities are mixed on whether it wipes out the crime as though it never happened or whether it simply eliminates the consequences of the conviction. This later view is the majority view, and has been endorsed by the United States Supreme Court.

A pardon generally restores those civil rights lost upon conviction. It does not, however remove licensing disqualifications such as the requirement of "good moral character." Consequently, ex-offenders may still be barred from employment in occupations which have such licensing requirements. While these licensing restrictions vary widely by state, examples of occupations with such requirements include barbers, contractors, plumbers, and, of course, lawyers.

Expungement

Offenders may also seek to have their criminal record expunged. Expungement allows the offender to say he or she has never been convicted. Expungement does not automatically restore the offender's rights, however. Only twenty-seven states restore rights through expungement, and not all offenders are eligible for expungement. This is often restricted to those convicted of less serious offenses or juvenile offenders. A number of states require the passage of a period of time before the ex-offender is eligible to apply for expungement. Similarly, many states allow probationers to apply for expungement of their record if they successfully complete their probation and after a period of years. This approach has been endorsed by the American Bar Association as conducive to the goal of rehabilitation of the offender.

Sealing of Records

Sealing is similar to expungement, but goes one step further by actually concealing the record. Where an expunged record may still be examined by certain individuals, a sealed record may not be legally examined by anyone. Typically sealing is reserved for juvenile offenders.

Automatic Restoration of Rights

Restoration of rights may also occur automatically, upon completion of the sentence. This is generally provided for by statute. Courts generally treat automatic restoration similar to a pardon, in holding that civil rights are fully restored, but that there is no effect on collateral consequences such as the occupational licensing disqualification.

A number of states provide for the automatic restoration of rights. Forty-two states currently have some provision for the automatic restoration of rights: twenty states provide for the automatic restoration of all civil rights upon completion of a sentence, while twenty-two restore some of the rights lost.

SUMMARY

As we have seen, there are many more people in the Unites States on conditional release on any given day than there are in prison and jail, however, the Supreme Court and lower courts have decided fewer cases about the rights of probationers and parolees than they have about the rights of incarcerated offenders. That makes sense, considering that probationers and parolees have much more freedom than prisoners. They have also agreed to certain restrictions on their rights in exchange for release. The types of legal issues that have concerned the courts involve restrictions on travel and the First Amendment rights of association, speech, and religion. Other cases have looked at conditions that have mandated probationers and parolees to engage in education programs, medical treatment, and therapy. It is clear that if the conditions are reasonably related to the offender's rehabilitation, are achievable and serve a legitimate government interest, they will be upheld.

Probationers and parolees have far fewer protections than the average person under the Fourth Amendment. The Supreme Court has decided several cases recognizing the limited nature of their right to be protected from unreasonable searches and seizures. In *Samson v. California* (2006), the Court upheld a warrantless, suspicionless search based on a parolee's agreement signed agreement to allow such searches in exchange for release. Under the Fifth Amendment right against self-incrimination, lower courts have ruled that caseworkers are not required to Mirandize probationers and parolees before routine office visits. Lower courts have refused to extend the privilege of confidentiality to the caseworker-offender relationship. The exclusionary rule does not apply to parole revocation hearings. It is clear that conditional release includes significant restrictions on offenders' constitutional rights. The courts justify the restrictions as necessary to protect the public's safety as well as to aid the goals of rehabilitation. In the past 15 years, states have enacted even greater restrictions on convicted sex offenders, including registration and notification laws. So far, the Supreme Court has upheld the constitutionality of these statutes, including laws that allow for the civil commitment of predatory sex offenders after they have been released from prison.

To complete the picture, convicted offenders who have served their time live with significant civil disabilities involving the right to vote, serve in public office or on a jury, be licensed by the state to work in certain professions, carry a weapon, and may even face restrictions on their parental rights. It is clear that a criminal sentence includes significant ramifications in addition to spending time incarcerated in a prison or jail. For many offenders it is a lifetime penalty, even as they go to work everyday, socialize with friends and family, and make plans for their futures.

DISCUSSION QUESTIONS

1. Discuss the long-term consequences of a criminal conviction, both in terms of restrictions on constitutional rights and civil disabilities. Do we make it too difficult for offenders to succeed once they have been released from prison or while they are on probation?

2. Outline the due process protections afforded probationers and parolees who face revocation. What are the differences between these protections and the protections afforded to a person facing a trial on guilt or innocence?

3. Sex offenders face significant legal requirements. Discuss those requirements and evaluate their short-term and long-term consequences. Review your state's requirements. Check a state website that includes information notifying the public of the names and whereabouts of sex offenders in that state. Detail the kind of information that can be gleaned from those websites.

SUGGESTED READINGS AND REFERENCES

Glaze, L. & Bonczar, T. (2007). Bureau of Justice Statistics Bulletin: Probation and Parole in the United States, 2006. Washington, D.C.: Department of Justice.

Sims, B. & Reynolds, M. (2007) "Sex Offender Registration, Notification, and Civil Commitment Statutes" in *Current Legal Issues in Criminal Justice* (Ed. Hemmens, C.). Los Angeles: Roxbury Publishing Company.

Office for Victims of Crime (2002, updated 2007). "Status of the Law: Right to Restitution – Legal Series Bulletin #6." Washington, D.C.: U.S. Department of Justice.

Zevitz, R. G. & Farkas, M. A. (2000). Research in Brief - Sex Offender Community Notification: Assessing the Impact in Wisconsin. Washington, D.C.: National Institute of Justice.

CHAPTER 11:
Civil Liability

INTRODUCTION

Imagine being incarcerated in the Arkansas prison system in 1959. Most of the time you are guarded by another inmate who has been issued a gun or a club by prison officials and given the authority to keep your cellblock quiet. The inmate was chosen because he is strong, authoritative, and willing to use force. You are required to work in the fields ten hours a day, six, sometimes seven days a week. White and African-American prisoners are segregated into separate housing blocks and assigned to different prison jobs. It is apparent that white prisoners have the choicest job assignments. Inmates who get into trouble disappear for weeks, even months at a time, sent to solitary confinement where they live in darkness, are served bread and water, and have no running water. They relieve themselves in a bucket that is occasionally switched out.

You and your fellow prisoners never even consider filing a lawsuit because the courts have made it clear that they are unwilling to get involved. There is no internal grievance system. If you did complain, you would surely be sent to solitary or be whipped with a five-foot long, four inches wide leather strap. In fact, you have heard about a prisoner who tried to file a lawsuit. He disappeared after the judge in whose court it was filed called the warden to let him know about it.

Students have already learned that today's prisoners are no longer compelled to endure such serious and dangerous deprivations at the hands of corrections officials. Although statistics show that prisoners are busy filing appeals and petitions for writs of habeas corpus, the largest percentage of prisoner cases complain about the conditions under which prisoners live or specific institutional regulations they believe are unfair. Chapters 1 through 10 examine the constitutional rights of prisoners, probationers, and parolees As demonstrated in those chapters, lawsuits about prison conditions have attacked the adequacy of medical care, alleged that facilities are unsanitary, demanded better food and more recreation time, complained about second-hand cigarette smoke, and charged officials with creating an unsafe living environment. Lawsuits about prison regulations have challenged prison disciplinary rules, the ability of inmates to access the courts, and the process by which troublesome prisoners are assigned to administrative segregation. Often times, prisoners combine several different types of complaints in a single lawsuit. Prisoners litigate as single individuals, as individuals in a group of other prisoners, and as part of class action lawsuits. They file cases in both state and federal courts. Obviously, today's prisoners live in a very different legal environment than the prisoners who were incarcerated in 1959.

Chapter 11 examines the legal basis for prisoner rights lawsuits. It looks at the legal mechanisms by which prisoners can bring their complaints to the attention of authorities. It is not sufficient for an inmate to send a letter to a judge and complain that his or her rights have been violated. Prisoners, like all plaintiffs to a lawsuit, must plead their case in certain way, following certain rules. They must sue the appropriate defendants. The law, under certain circumstances, protects defendants from liability even though the plaintiff can prove a constitutional violation.

Chapter 11 focuses primarily on a federal law, 42 U.S.C. section 1983, which provides the grounds for the majority of civil rights cases, and also looks at how corrections officials can defend themselves against this type of lawsuit. The body of case law that interprets section 1983 is quite complex. The chapter introduces students to the basic foundations of a lawsuit filed under that statute. For every court opinion that attempts to clarify section 1983, there are others that recognize exceptions to the clarification. Although section 1983 provides inmates access to federal courts, the law's complexity creates a road to those courts with many difficult twists and turns. Chapter 11 also examines the Prison Litigation Reform Act and prisoner grievance systems. It concludes with a look at how prisoners can use state personal injury law to their advantage and under what circumstances officials can be held criminally liable for violating an inmate's rights.

SECTION 1983

Interpreting Section 1983

Congress enacted the federal statute 42 U.S.C. section 1983, also known as the Civil Rights Act, in 1871 in response to arbitrary and capricious enforcement of the laws against the freed slaves by state and local officials in the South. Officials abused their positions as elected and appointed officeholders to deny freedmen and women their rights, privileges, and immunities under the federal Constitution and statutes. They refused to use their authority to protect the freed slaves and at times actively participated in violating their rights. When the states refused to take action, the federal legislature enacted section 1983. The Civil Rights Act of 1871 has also been called the Klu Klux Klan Act because many southern government officials were also members of the Klan. Although section 1983 has been law since 1871, until the civil rights movement began in the late 1950s and early 1960s, it was seldom used. When attorneys took the battle for equal rights into the courtroom, they rediscovered section 1983. For that reason, judicial opinions interpreting the statute are relatively recent, dating back to the 1960s.

The text of section 1983 is brief:

Every person who, under color of any statute, ordinance, regulation, custom, or usage, of any state or territory, subjects, or causes to be subject, any citizen of the United States or other person within the jurisdiction thereof to the deprivation of rights, privileges, or immunities secured by the Constitution and laws, shall be liable to the party injured in an action at law, suit in equity, or other proper proceeding for redress.

The federal judges who have had to interpret the statute in literally thousands of court cases have hammered out much of the meaning of section 1983. Because it remains a frequently used statute, however, courts continue to interpret its meaning as new circumstances arise that require legal judgment concerning its application. The Supreme Court's interpretations bind the lower courts and extend nationwide, however, the high court cannot consider every petition for *certiorari* that concerns section 1983. The Supreme Court's section 1983 opinions often leave unresolved issues that later surface, eventually to be settled by the federal courts of appeal.

Requirements for Filing a Section 1983 Civil Rights Lawsuit

- Lawsuit must be against a "person"
- Who acted under color of the law of any state, territory, or District of Columbia (federal officials must be sued in a *Bivens* actions)
- And caused a violation of a federal constitutional right or right under federal law
- That resulted in injury

Who is Considered a Section 1983 "person"?

One of the most important things the courts have had to do is define who or what should be considered a "person" under section 1983. In addition to meaning a natural person, over the last couple centuries American courts have recognized that there are also legal persons, which can include corporations and governmental entities. Based on what the Supreme Court decided is the language of section 1983 and its legislative history, the Court ruled in *Will v. Michigan Department of State Police* (1989) that a state is not considered a person within the meaning of the statute. The Court also ruled that state officials acting in their official capacities are not section 1983 "persons" because litigation seeking damages against them in their official capacity would really be litigation against the state. The official would be sued as a representative of the state, making the state the actual defendant, and any damages would have to be paid from the state treasury. Under section 1983, state officials must be sued in their individual capacities. Prisoners' section 1983 lawsuits must be directed at individual correctional superintendents, wardens, correctional officers and other staff.

As defendants in their individual capacities, state officials are personally liable for any monetary damages that may be awarded against them. Most states have passed legislation that directs the state attorney's office to represent state prison officials who are sued as individuals, and pays any damages awarded against them. Such an arrangement, called indemnification, helps state governments attract people to enter and remain in the correctional field. It is also intended to free officials to make tough decisions without fear of financial ruin if they become defendants in a legal case. Municipal and county officers found personally liable are also usually indemnified according to local statutes. Most indemnification statutes do not authorize damages to be paid for official actions that were malicious or outrageous.

With all of that said, and to make it even more confusing, state officials can be sued in their official capacities under section 1983 for injunctive relief. Injunctions require officials to take or stop taking specific actions in the future.

A lawsuit seeking an injunction is not considered directed against the state, even though complying with the injunction may involve a state expenditure.

In contrast to what happens when a prisoner sues a state agency or department, section 1983 lawsuits against local governmental entities are not considered lawsuits against the state. Prisoners can initiate lawsuits against local jail officials in their official capacities under section 1983. In *Monell v. Department of Social Services* (1978), the Supreme Court ruled that Congress did not intend to exclude cities and other local governments from section 1983 lawsuits. In *City of Canton v. Harris* (1989), the Court further clarified that such lawsuits require evidence that the local governmental unit's customs, practices, or policies were responsible for the constitutional violation. Those policies, practices, and customs can include such things as failure to train or supervise officers, as well as failure to terminate employment when appropriate. As a result of the *Canton* decision, even though municipalities and counties can be sued under section 1983, they cannot be held liable for all of the unauthorized acts of their employees. In a case where the plaintiff alleges that a city or county violated his civil rights, he must also establish that the local government unit ratified or somehow adopted those actions. The local government's liability under section 1983 is restricted to actions for which the government unit itself can be held responsible. For instance, an allegation that a local correctional agency failed to properly train its officers, causing harm to an inmate, is not sufficient by itself to establish a section 1983 claim. The plaintiff must also show that the failure to train amounted to a policy, a deliberate decision on the part of government officials. Perhaps the need for additional training is known within the department, as is the possibility of harm that might result from inadequate training. A case can be made that the city policymakers were indifferent and the failure to provide more training amounted to a policy for which the city is liable.

Indeed, the doctrine of *respondeat superior* cannot be applied to any section 1983 lawsuit. *Respondeat superior* allows supervisors to be held liable for the torts committed by their subordinate employees whether or not the supervisor had actual knowledge of the actions at the time they occurred. Under this doctrine, employers are generally liable for the torts of their employees that were committed while the employees were acting within the scope of their employment. If a prisoner sues a higher-level prison official based on a claim against a correctional officer, he must be able to prove that the higher level official actually knew about the guard's conduct, or that he should have known. If a supervisor works closely with his or her subordinates, a case can be made that it is logical to assume the supervisor knew or should have known, especially if the guard's conduct is part of a pattern of conduct. Supervisors who fail to take action on prior complaints or devise policies to avoid foreseeable violations are also at risk under section 1983.

The text of 42 U.S.C. section 1983 states specifically that civil rights lawsuits can be brought against a person who "under color of any statute, ordinance, regulation, custom, or usage, of any State or Territory or the District of Columbia". Violations under federal law are not included on that list. In *Bivens v. Six Unknown Federal Narcotics Agents* (1971), the Supreme Court ruled that a plaintiff is able to sue federal officers for violations of their constitutional rights in a lawsuit very much like a section 1983 claim. Known as *Bivens* actions, the lawsuits hold federal officers accountable in the same way that section 1983 holds state officers accountable. Just as in section 1983 lawsuits, a federal prisoner must bring his or her action against a federal officer in their individual capacities, not in their official capacities.

A recent development in the corrections industry that has challenged the courts is the growth of private prisons, jails, halfway houses, detention facilities, and community-based residences. Although corrections industry has been in the process of privatizing for a couple of decades, the pace has increased rapidly since the mid-1990s. There is an ongoing debate about whether privatization can produce the cost savings it has promised and whether the facilities can provide the amount and quality of services needed. Privatization has also raised new legal questions under the Civil Rights Act. As you will read later in this chapter, in 1997 the Supreme Court ruled in *Richardson v. McKnight* that correctional officers in private facilities do not enjoy the same amount of protection from section 1983 lawsuits as do officers in public facilities.

In 2001, the Court ruled in *Correctional Services Corp. v. Malesko* that a prisoner housed in a community correctional center under contract with the Federal Bureau of Prisons could not sue the Correctional Services Corporation under section 1983. Malesko had a heart condition that limited his ability to climb stairs. He had permission to use the elevator; however when an employee of the corporation forbade him to use it, he climbed the stairs and suffered a heart attack. In a 5-4 split decision, the Supreme Court ruled that a *Bivens* type lawsuit requesting damages for an Eighth Amendment violation can only be filed against an individual, not a private corporate entity. The majority held that the definition of "persons" should not be extended to include private entities. The Court reasoned that *Bivens* actions do not permit prisoners in the custody of the federal government to sue the Federal Bureau of Prisons. They must sue the officer responsible for the violation in their individual capacity. *Bivens* purpose was to deter individual federal officers from constitutional violations. To allow federal civil rights lawsuits against private corporations would impose asymmetrical liability costs on private prisons.

Who Is Considered a "Person" under Section 1983?	
Local government entities and agencies	YES
Local government official in their official capacity	YES
State official in their individual capacity	YES
The state, state agency, or state official acting in their official capacity	NO

What Conduct is Included "under color of law"?

In addition to defining the word "person," courts have also had to address the meaning of the phrase "under color of any statute, ordinance, regulation, custom, or usage," which is generally shortened to "under color of law." If a government official is acting in the course of his or her employment, they are generally considered acting under color of law. Wearing a government uniform, using government equipment to carry out a task, working on government property, holding oneself out as a government official, providing services generally provided by a government are the types of factors a court considers in reaching an under "color of law" decision. In *Monroe v. Pape* (1961), the Supreme Court considered a section 1983 action against several Chicago police officers who entered the plaintiff's home without a warrant and forced them to stand nude during the search. Even though the officers' conduct clearly violated state law and department policy, the Court ruled the officers had acted under color of law because their abuse of power in what was possible in that they were clothed in the authority of state law. It does not matter under section 1983 if the officers' actions were in direct conflict with the legal standards by which they were supposed to abide.

Private persons who contract with a state correctional agency to provide services can be considered acting under color of law, even if they do not work exclusively for the state or were not on the state payroll. In *West v. Atkins* (1988), the Supreme Court considered a case involving a private physician who contracted with the North Carolina corrections department to provide medical services to prisoners two days a week. The doctor was not on the state's regular payroll or considered an employee of the state. He was sued by an inmate under section 1983 who alleged he violated the Eighth Amendment when he was indifferent to the inmate's serious medical needs. The Court ruled unanimously that the physician had acted under color of law. The salient point was not the terms of his employment, but his function within the state system.

Deprivation of Federal Rights

Finally, section 1983 requires that the person who is sued under color of law be responsible for causing a deprivation of federal constitutional rights or of federal law. A violation of a state law or a state constitutional provision does not provide the necessary foundation for a section 1983 lawsuit. That does not mean a prisoner has no way to remedy the situation. It means that section 1983 is not available to help the prisoner, and he or she has to look elsewhere to state law to find the basis for their claim.

An example of a federal statute that could provide the basis for a section 1983 lawsuit is the Americans With Disabilities Act (ADA) , passed by Congress in 1990. The ADA protects persons with disabilities against discrimination from participating in government programs. The language of the ADA does not exclude prisoners from its coverage. In *Pennsylvania Department of Corrections v. Yeskey* (1998), the Supreme Court faced this issue when Ronald Yeskey filed a section 1983 lawsuit alleging that state officials violated his right under the ADA to be placed in a boot camp for first-time offenders. The court that sentenced Yeskey recommended that he be placed in the boot camp, which could have lead to his release on parole in just six months. Yeskey, however, suffered from hypertension and the state refused to admit him into that program. The Supreme Court ruled unanimously that the ADA does apply to prisoners. As a result of that opinion, correctional agencies must consider how the ADA affects cell construction, modification of inmate assignments, and the scheduling of programs and activities.

Section 1983 provides inmates with a key to unlock the doors of the courthouse and seek relief. It is obviously complicated. It is easy to understand why inmates, who generally are acting *pro se*, interpreting section 1983 on their own, make many mistakes. Even with prison law libraries and special prisoner's rights manuals to help, pleading a case under the statute can be daunting.

Legal Remedies under Section 1983

Inmates can sue for and courts can award damages to prisoners who are successful in their civil rights claims. Compensatory damages are meant to compensate a plaintiff for the violation of their civil rights. Compensation is only available if the prisoner proves that he or she suffered actual harm from the deprivation. Under the Prison Litigation Reform Act (PLRA), discussed in more detail in this chapter, prisoners are prohibited from filing lawsuits in federal court requesting damages for emotional or mental injuries unless they can also establish that they suffered physical injury. Nominal damages are sometimes awarded if there is sufficient evidence of a constitutional violation, but the inmate did not suffer any actual damages or the damage was minimal. Punitive damages can also be awarded under section 1983. They are intended to "punish" the defendant for intentional or malicious constitutional deprivations. A reckless or callous disregard for an inmate's constitutional rights can also serve as a basis for punitive damages. If punitive damages are awarded, they must be paid by the state official in their individual capacity.

Although prisoners often request monetary damages in their civil rights lawsuits, they are generally much more successful in obtaining injunctive relief. A declaratory injunction is a court ruling, before a prisoner's rights have been violated, that a particular law, regulation, policy, or practice is illegal. It is designed for situations where prisoners have advance notice that a particular action is going to be taken or a regulation is going to be implemented. A mandatory injunction is a court order directing a defendant to take a particular action or to cease engaging in a particular action. For example, a prisoner who alleges her right to exercise her religion has been violated because a regulation prohibits special diets for inmates with religious dietary restrictions might request a mandatory injunction compelling officials to take specific steps to accommodate her First Amendment rights. Prisoners complaining about the unsanitary conditions of their housing areas may request that officials clean the cellblocks and maintain their cleanliness at a certain level.

Injunctions can become very detailed because judges try to compose them in such a way that it is clear what action must be taken and by which date it must be completed. In prisoner's rights cases, judges have issued extremely detailed injunctions that have mandated specific steps the defendant must take. For example, an injunction that orders a correctional agency to offer better health care might include details about how that is to be accomplished: hiring more doctors and nurses, even specifying an actual number; building more infirmaries, actually specifying which prison units need infirmaries; or purchasing newer, more modern medical equipment, specifying what particular pieces of equipment are needed. Concern about how federal courts have used injunctions extensively to intervene in the operation of correctional facilities, spurred Congress to impose limitations on federal judges in the Prison Litigation Reform Act, discussed later in this chapter.

Attorney's Fees under Section 1983

In the American legal system, unless there is a law or a contract that specifies otherwise, litigants to a lawsuit pay their own attorney's fees. The Civil Rights Attorney's Fees Award Act of 1976, 42 U.S.C. Section 1988, was passed by Congress to allow the court to award attorney's fees to the prevailing party in any Section 1983 action and certain other lawsuits that enforce federal statutes. The purpose of the act is to encourage attorneys to take on difficult civil rights cases even if the plaintiff is unable to pay for the legal services. Since many civil rights cases do not result in large money awards, it is unlikely that attorneys would take such cases on a contingency fee. Congress reasoned that without the ability to have their fees awarded if they were successful, few attorneys would take on civil rights litigation.

A prevailing party must have succeeded on any significant claim and have been awarded some relief. At the very least, the prevailing party must show that the resolution of the lawsuit materially changed the relationship of the parties and they achieved some of the benefit they were seeking when they sued. Attorney's fees can also be awarded as part of a consent decree, which is an agreement between the parties as to how to settle a lawsuit. The Supreme Court held in *Hughes v. Rowe* (1980), that prevailing defendants in a section 1983 lawsuit should not normally recover their attorney's fees from a plaintiff because awarding the fees would discourage plaintiffs from bringing claims to court, undermining section 1983's ability to encourage private persons to enforce civil rights laws. The amount of fees to be awarded to a prevailing party depends on the number of hours the attorney spent on the litigation and the reasonable hourly rate paid to attorneys in the community where the fee is awarded. Just as the PLRA has imposed limits in other areas of prisoner litigation, the Act placed a cap on the hourly rate that can be charged when an inmate seeks attorney's fees.

The Advantages of a Section 1983 Lawsuit

Prisoners can file lawsuits in state court alleging violations under state law and the state constitution. Because state courts have broader jurisdiction than federal courts, they can also file lawsuits in state courts that allege violations of the federal Constitution or a federal law. It is common for prisoners to combine allegations that claim violations of both federal and state laws and constitutions in the same lawsuit. Those combined claims can be filed in a state or federal court.

Although prisoners have a choice of going to federal or state court, prisoner's rights lawsuits are generally filed in federal courts. Prisoners prefer the federal judiciary for several reasons. Federal judges are appointed for life. They are not subject to the type of political pressure that state court judges face. The state judiciary is elected in many states. In others, state judges are appointed initially but must be voted into office after their first term in an uncontested election. Federal judges are free to make difficult or unpopular decisions without concern for their jobs. They are free to interpret the federal Constitution to protect the rights of people the general public may not like. When prisoners began to file section 1983 lawsuits after *Cooper v. Pate* was decided in 1964, it was not long before federal district and appellate courts rendered important decisions that upheld the prisoners' claims. The U.S. Supreme Court got in the business of writing landmark opinions that significantly impacted correctional institutions throughout the entire United States. Students have been introduced to those opinions in Chapters 1 through 10 of this book. Prisoners naturally gravitated to the judicial forum that promised them more protection. Although federal judges no longer provide the same sympathetic ear to prisoners they once did, inmates still generally prefer litigating in the federal system. Federal judges have more experience interpreting section 1983 and the federal Constitution than do state judges and, despite their increasingly more conservative approach to inmate claims, they remain more sensitive to issues of individual rights. Federal courts try to facilitate prisoner *pro se* lawsuits by providing instructions on how to file a civil rights lawsuit by publishing and making available a model section

1983 Complaint form. Federal courts are required to liberally construe prisoners' *pro se* Complaints.

Because federal judges have been rendering fewer decisions in favor of inmates in recent years, however, some state prisoners are taking their complaints to state courts. State constitutions and statutes can sometimes protect rights not protected under federal law. The U.S. Constitution only sets the minimum level of protection required, leaving states free to expand those rights through statute or their own constitutions. A good example is the case *Cooper v. Morin*, 49 N.Y.2d 69 (1979). The New York court concluded under that state's constitution female pretrial detainees had a right to contact visits with their families, even though the U.S. Constitution did not guarantee such a right.

Whether an inmate lawsuit is filed in state or federal court, section 1983 permits a court to award attorneys' fees to the prevailing party. As this chapter discusses, there are other legal claims available to inmates in addition to section 1983; however, none of them offer an award of attorney's fees to the prevailing party. In a state tort case, the attorney will receive a percentage of the monetary damages. Monetary damage awards in prisoner's cases are often quite small. There may even be legal blocks that make it impossible for an inmate to sue under state law.

How Corrections Officials Defend Against Civil Rights Lawsuits

Section 1983 requires the defendant be a person, who was acting under color of law when they violated the plaintiff's rights under the U.S. Constitution or federal law. Unless all of those requirements are met, the court will dismiss the lawsuit. Although not technically considered a defense, failing to meet the statute's requirements offers the defendant an expeditious and straightforward way to end the proceeding without being found liable. As we have seen, however, whether someone can be considered a person, acting under color of law sometimes raises important and complicated legal issues that have to be litigated before liability can even be addressed. Fortunately, over the last several decades, courts have substantially defined the person and under color of law issues through numerous opinions. Municipalities and other local governmental units are considered section 1983 persons. When states, state agencies, and state officials are sued for damages, they are not. Nevertheless, novel legal questions continue to arise as correctional administrators adopt new ways to fulfill their mission.

Statutes of limitation help assure that legal claims do not grow stale, and that potential defendants are not in the position of waiting and wondering for unreasonable periods of time if they are going to be sued. Plaintiffs are forced to gather enough evidence and formulate their legal claims while issues are fresh. Section 1983 does not provide its own limitations for filing lawsuits. Courts have concluded that the statute of limitation period for civil rights lawsuits is governed by the limitation period imposed on personal injury lawsuits under the law in the state where the federal lawsuit is filed. Many states have multiple statutes of limitation on personal injury lawsuits depending on the type of action involved, such as an intentional versus negligence tort.

Perhaps the most important defense available to a defendant to a section 1983 lawsuit is found in the doctrine of personal immunity, of which there are two types: absolute and qualified. The law has long recognized that a limited number of government officials are absolutely immune from personal liability in civil rights litigation. Federal and state legislators and judges, while carrying out their official duties, cannot be sued for money damages no matter how egregious their actions or the damage they caused. They are shielded by absolute immunity so they can make important, controversial decisions without concern because someone does not agree with their exercise of discretion. In the criminal justice system, prosecutors also enjoy absolute immunity in connection with their traditional role of courtroom advocacy. Absolute immunity does not protect officials from criminal prosecution if their actions violated the criminal law. Judges can still be impeached under the state or federal statute that applies to them. If officials are engaged in an ongoing activity that violates someone's civil rights, the plaintiff is still able to seek injunctive relief.

Correctional officials, police officers, and others employed in the criminal justice system, excluding judges and prosecutors, do not enjoy absolute immunity from a civil rights lawsuit. In a series of decisions over many years, however, the U.S. Supreme Court created the doctrine of qualified immunity to protect all government officials, not just those involved in criminal justice, who do not enjoy absolute immunity. In doing so, the Court recognizes that many officials have to use discretion on a regular basis to make difficult but necessary decisions. Sometimes officials make reasonable, understandable mistakes, based on the information they have at the time. Without some protection from personal liability, these officials would be reluctant to perform their duties. Individuals would shy away from public service, afraid of being held personally liable for the decisions they made in good faith.

In *Harlow v. Fitzgerald* (1982), a case unrelated to criminal justice, the Supreme Court laid out the parameters of the doctrine of qualified immunity as it currently applies. State officials who did not disregard clearly established statutory or constitutional rights of which a reasonable person would have known enjoy qualified immunity and are shielded from civil rights personal liability lawsuits. The judge determines the law that was applicable and whether it was clearly established at the time the official took action. If it was not clearly established, it is not reasonable to expect an official to know the law prohibited his or her conduct, or to have anticipated future legal developments. On the other hand, if the law was clearly established, a competent public official should have known their actions were unlawful. By "clearly established" the Court refers to not only written statutes and regulations but also the judicial interpretations of those statutes and regulations found in court opinions.

Importantly, the official's intention when they engaged in the challenged conduct is irrelevant. The defendant's motives could have been malicious, but it would not matter if the law was not clearly established at the time. Until the issue of qualified immunity is decided, a civil rights lawsuit cannot proceed. In this way, officials are not subjected to the burden and expense of defending a lawsuit if qualified immunity protects them. Not only is the defendant spared the burden; the court's valuable time is not wasted because the case is dismissed. Qualified immunity protects federal officials sued in a *Bivens* action the same way it protects state officials. Qualified immunity only protects individuals from responsibility for monetary damages; it is not a defense against a request for an injunction.

In *Procunier v. Navarette* (1978) the Supreme Court ruled that prison officials are only entitled to qualified immunity. In *Cleavinger v. Saxner* (1985), the Court refused to extend absolute immunity to members of a prison disciplinary committee who argued they were entitled to absolute protection because they were acting like judges. The Court decided that disciplinary committee members are like judges in some respects, but not in others. They are employees of the correctional agency. In addition, disciplinary hearings differ considerably from trials on guilt or innocence. Disciplinary judges, therefore, are not afforded absolute immunity, only qualified immunity.

The Supreme Court has considered whether correctional officers employed by private prison management firms are also entitled to qualified immunity from section 1983 lawsuits. In a controversial 5-4 decision, *Richardson v. McKnight* (1997), the majority concluded that no special reasons exist, in historical precedent or otherwise, for extending the qualified immunity doctrine to persons employed by a private company that is performing the same work as state prison guards. Qualified immunity preserves the ability of government officials to serve the public good by protecting the public from officials who are too timid to do their job. The Court reasoned that the competitive marketplace puts pressure on a private prison company to make certain that its employees vigorously perform their duties. The company can reward those who do the right thing and fire those who do not without civil service restrictions. They can have employment contracts that guarantee to indemnify employees who are found liable. The dissenting Justices disagreed and emphasized that the majority's decision created two sets of correctional officers whose only difference is the source of their authority. They perform the same duties and have the same power over inmates. The dissent expressed concern that the majority decision will raise the cost of privatizing prisons and discourage states from moving in that direction.

Immunity Defenses to Section 1983 Lawsuits

Absolute Immunity: only available to judges and prosecutors in their official capacities. Not available to members of prison disciplinary committees.

Qualified Immunity: available to government officials if it can be shown they did not disregard a clearly established statutory or constitutional right of which a reasonable person would have known. Not available to persons employed by companies who operate private prisons.

THE PRISONER LITIGATION EXPLOSION

Since *Cooper v. Pate* was decided in 1964, prisoners have filed thousands of civil rights lawsuits. According to the Bureau of Justice Statistics (Scalia, 2002), forty-four percent (44%) of all the 58,257 petitions filed in the year 2000 by state and federal prisoners in federal district courts alleged that officials violated the inmates' civil rights. The balance of the prisoner petitions challenged the constitutionality of a sentence or conviction. More than half (53%) of the petitions filed by state prisoners in 2000 alleged civil rights violations. In contrast, only 9% of the petitions filed by federal inmates claimed civil rights violations. In order to handle the large number of prisoner lawsuits, federal courts have had to devise operating procedures to keep the dockets moving. Prisoners representing themselves file the majority of the cases. Many federal judges hire *pro se* law clerks assigned to review and organize lawsuits that have been filed by individuals without the assistance of counsel. *Pro se* law clerks evaluate the merits of the lawsuit on its face, determine if the inmate has properly alleged a claim under federal law or the Constitution, whether the procedural rules have been followed, and determine which lawsuits should be summarily dismissed. They make recommendations to the district court judge and prepare the court pleadings for the judge's signature required to dismiss a case.

A 1995 report by Roger Hanson and Henry Daley looked at section 1983 litigation filed by state prisoners by examining a large sample of cases filed in 1992 in nine U.S. District Courts located in Alabama, California, Florida, Indiana, Louisiana, Missouri, New York, Pennsylvania, and Texas. Researchers collected data on numerous issues including, among other things, the type(s) of complaint inmates raised, the number of issues raised in a single lawsuit, the type of correctional institutions involved, dates of key events (filing of the case, important hearings, trial, disposition of case), how the lawsuit was resolved (dismissal, trial, or other), and reasons why cases were dismissed. Hanson and Daley found that in the lawsuits they reviewed physical security, medical treatment, and due process were the most frequent issues raised. The vast number of inmates acted as their own attorney. Seventy-four percent (74%) of inmate cases were dismissed on the court's own motion; 20% were dismissed on the motion of the defendant; 4% were dismissed under stipulation. Only 2% resulted in a trial verdict. Most dismissals (38%) were the result of failing to comply with court rules (such as not responding on time to the court's request for documents), no evidence of a constitutional violation (19%), or frivolous claims (19%).

The researchers classified the outcome of the cases into three categories: win nothing, win little, and win big. They defined "win nothing" as an issue that is dismissed by the court or pursuant to the defendant's motion to dismiss. "Win little" happens when the inmate and the correctional agency settle the case before trial and agree to compensate the inmate or change a policy or practice. "Win big" means a judge or jury rendered a verdict for the prisoner. They concluded that in 94% of the cases they studied, inmates win nothing because the issues they raised were dismissed. Prisoners win little with 4% of their issues. Only 2% of the issues result in trial verdicts, and less than half of them involve a verdict favorable to the prisoner.

THE PRISON LITIGATION REFORM ACT

The Prison Litigation Reform Act (PLRA) was enacted in 1996 by the U.S. Congress to respond to two concerns: 1) inmates who many perceived were clogging up the courts with frivolous litigation, and 2) federal judges who intervened in the operation of state prison systems and ordered extensive and costly reforms. The Act includes several provisions that attempt both to reduce the number of inmate lawsuits filed under 42 U.S.C §1983 and federal court intervention.

Reducing Prisoner Lawsuits

One of the PLRA's most important provisions requires prisoners to exhaust any remedies available through their administrative inmate grievance systems before they can file a lawsuit. The requirement to exhaust administrative remedies is a common doctrine in many areas of law. If a grievant files a lawsuit without exhausting administrative remedies, the court must dismiss the suit or delay considering it until after the requirement is met. Requiring exhaustion attempts to reduce lawsuits and lighten the caseloads of overcrowded courts. Reducing the numbers and types of lawsuits that an agency has to defend in court also benefits the agency.

The exhaustion requirement was first introduced to prisoner litigation in 1980 in the Civil Rights of Institutionalized Persons Act (42 U.S.C. §1997e). In the PLRA, however, Congress strengthened the exhaustion requirement for prisoners. The Act states that "No action shall be brought with respect to prison conditions under section 1983 of this title, or any other Federal law, by a prisoner confined in any jail, prison, or other correctional facility until such administrative remedies as are available are exhausted." The new, much stronger requirement quickly raised arguments concerning the definition of "administrative remedies as are available." In 2001, the U. S. Supreme Court addressed the issue in *Booth v. Churner*. Booth filed a §1983 lawsuit alleging that Pennsylvania prison officials used excessive force against him and denied him medical attention for the injuries they caused. He requested an injunction ordering officials to take steps to reduce the potential for prisoner abuse and asked for monetary damages to compensate him for his injuries. He did not file an administrative grievance because the prisoner grievance system in Pennsylvania did not permit prisoners to receive an award of money damages. A unanimous Supreme Court ruled that Congress mandated that prisoners must go through the grievance procedure regardless of the type of relief offered, or not offered, through the process.

A year after *Booth v. Churner*, the Supreme Court decided *Porter v. Nussle* (2002). Nussle alleged that prison officials subjected him to prolonged harassment and intimidation. He filed a §1983 lawsuit without first filing a grievance. The issue revolved around defining certain phrases in the PLRA. What did Congress mean when it legislated that: "No action shall be brought with respect to prison conditions under section 1983 of this title, or any other Federal law ...."? Do "prison conditions" include isolated, single incidents directed at specific persons or only ongoing conditions of confinement that impact large numbers of prisoners? A unanimous Supreme Court concluded that the exhaustion requirement applies to all inmate lawsuits, whether they involve general conditions or particular incidents, excessive force or some other wrong.

To further underscore the broad scope of the PLRA's mandatory exhaustion requirement, the Supreme Court decided *Woodford v. Ngo* (2006), which involved a California prisoner who filed an administrative grievance complaining about prison conditions. The grievance was rejected because it was filed outside the deadline set under state law. Ngo filed a lawsuit arguing that he was not able to exhaust his administrative remedies. The Supreme Court upheld the dismissal of his lawsuit by the federal district court. The Supreme Court majority held that Ngo had failed to properly exhaust his grievance remedies because he failed to follow the procedures and timetable outlined by statute. Under the PLRA, his lawsuit must be dismissed.

The PLRA also includes a provision that "No federal civil action may be brought by a prisoner confined in a jail, prison, or other correctional facility, for mental or emotional injury suffered while in custody without a prior showing of physical injury." This means a prisoner cannot claim compensatory damages for emotional injury that resulted from officials' unconstitutional conduct, unless he or she can also show they suffered a physical injury.

Before the PLRA, federal law authorized federal courts to allow prisoners to file lawsuits *in forma pauperis* (IFP) if they filed an affidavit stating they were unable to pay the filing fee or other costs associated with a lawsuit. Most prisoner civil rights lawsuits are filed IFP. Under the PLRA, a prisoner must disclose in an affidavit that seeks IFP status all of the assets they possess and include a certified copy of their trust fund account statement for the 6-month period immediately preceding filing the lawsuit. In addition, the PLRA requires federal courts to collect some or the entire filing fee from IFP prisoners based on a percentage of the funds he or she has in their trust account. The new law forces prisoners to engage in a cost-benefit analysis before filing a lawsuit. The intent is to prevent prisoners from filing lawsuits as a diversion from the boredom of prison life or as a way to hassle officials.

The PLRA also prohibits a prisoner from proceeding IFP if he or she, while incarcerated, has on three or more occasions filed a lawsuit or an appeal that was dismissed on the grounds that it was frivolous, malicious, or failed to state a claim upon which relief could be granted. The only exception to this "three-strikes" restriction, is if prisoners can show they are under imminent danger of serious physical injury. The "three strikes" provision is designed to reduce the large number of prisoner lawsuits that allege frivolous claims.

Finally, the PLRA imposes restrictions on the attorney fees awarded under 42 U.S.C. §1988 to plaintiffs who prevail in prisoner civil rights cases. It allows the court to award fees only when they were "directly and reasonably incurred in proving an actual violation" of a prisoner's rights. The attorney's fees must now be proportionate to the amount of relief ordered by the court, regardless if the actual money judgment is modest.

Reducing Federal Court Intervention

The PLRA also addressed what critics considered federal court micromanagement of state prisons. When the PLRA was enacted in 1996, many state prisons were operating under consent decrees or court orders that had been monitored by the federal courts for twenty years or longer. Some of those decrees ordered remedies that went beyond what the Constitution mandates. The 1996 statute provides that a federal court shall not grant or approve any prospective (future) relief in a prison conditions lawsuit unless the court makes written findings that such relief is narrowly drawn, extends no further than is necessary to correct the violation, and is the least intrusive means necessary to correct it. Prospective relief is any relief other than compensatory or money damages that may be granted or approved by the court. The court must also consider any adverse impact the relief might have on public safety or the operation of the criminal justice system. The PLRA prohibits any prospective relief that does not comply with the statute's provisions, and federal judges cannot order or approve consent decrees that require reforms beyond what is required under the Constitution.

The second restriction imposed by the PLRA controls how long prospective relief can remain in effect. This provision included the many court orders that were already in force at the time the PLRA was enacted. Prospective relief should be terminated upon the motion of any party or intervener 1) two years after the date the court granted or approved the relief; 2) one year after the court entered an order denying termination of the relief under the statute; or 3) in the case of an order issued before the enactment of the PLRA, two years after the date of enactment. In this way, the PLRA imposes significant time limits on how long a federal judge can keep a case open so he or she can monitor whether state officials abide by consent decrees and court orders. Federal court intervention terminates according to the requirements of the PLRA.

The third significant change under the PLRA provides that in any prison conditions lawsuit, a defendant is entitled to immediate termination of any prospective relief if it had been granted or approved without a court finding that the relief was narrowly drawn, extends no further than is necessary to correct the violation, and is the least intrusive means necessary to correct the violation. Prospective relief should not be terminated if the court makes written findings that the relief is still necessary to correct a current and ongoing violation of a federal right, extends no further than is necessary, is narrowly drawn and the least intrusive means necessary.

A fourth important PLRA provision provides that if a party files a motion for termination, the court must issue an automatic stay of any prospective relief that begins 30 days after the filing of the motion and ending on the day the court issues a final order. In 1997, Congress amended the PLRA to permit courts to delay entering an automatic stay for not more than 60 days for good cause. The U.S. Supreme Court considered constitutional challenges to the automatic stay provisions in *Miller v. French* (2000). In that case the state of Indiana filed a motion to terminate an injunction issued by a federal district court in 1975 and modified in 1988, to remedy Eighth Amendment violations at the Pendleton Correctional Facility. The injunction addressed double-celling and over-crowding, the use of mechanical restraints, staffing, and the quality of food and medical services. The prisoners argued that the PLRA's automatic stay provision was unconstitutional. The Supreme Court disagreed and upheld the automatic stay provisions. According to the Court, the stay is mandatory and helps implement the termination provisions of the PLRA.

Finally, the PLRA places tight restrictions on prisoner release orders designed to reduce overcrowding. Release orders can only be issued by a panel of three judges that must find by clear and convincing evidence that crowding is the primary cause of the constitutional violation and no other remedy will correct it.

Scalia's research for the Bureau of Justice Statistics (2002) showed that after the PLRA went into effect, prisoners filed fewer civil rights lawsuits; in 1995, prisoners filed 41,679 versus 25,504 filed in 2000. Between 1995 and 2000, there was a decrease from 37 to 19 per 1000 inmates in the rate at which federal and state inmates filed civil rights cases.

Criticisms of the PLRA

Despite studies that suggest the PLRA has reduced the numbers of prisoner lawsuits, several key provisions of the act have generated intense criticism, in particular the exhaustion requirement. Prisoner grievance systems have their own procedural and deadline requirements. Most of them have one or two levels of review, each level with its own requirements. Critics argue that it is quite possible for prisoners who are illiterate, have limited intelligence, or are mentally ill to make mistakes and fail to comply with the grievance system's mandates. Those failures may be as simple as completing the wrong grievance form or submitting it to the wrong office. An internal grievance system deadline can pass even before the error is brought to the prisoner's attention. Yet, as the Supreme Court made clear in its 2006 decision, Woodford v. Ngo, those prisoners' lawsuits would be dismissed.

The PLRA bars a prisoner from filing as lawsuit for mental or emotional injuries that do not also result in physical injury. An example would be the case Harper v. Showers, 174 F.3d 716 (5th Cir. 1999), in which the Fifth Circuit held that a prisoner failed to meet the physical injury requirement based on allegations that officials maliciously assigned him to a cell covered with human waste and forcing him to live with the screams of psychiatric prisoners who regularly beat on the metal toilets, shorted out the power in the cellblock, flooded the cellblock, and lit fires. The case was dismissed without a decision based on what actually occurred. It was dismissed because the prisoner could not show he suffered any physical injury to accompany the emotional and mental injuries he claimed to suffer. Critics charge that the PLRA makes it possible for officials to engage in unconstitutional conduct with impunity in cases where prisoners cannot establish physical injuries.

Another criticism of the PLRA addresses the reduced attorneys' fees that can be awarded when the plaintiff-prisoner prevails. The Civil Rights Attorney's Fees Award Act provides a way to compensate attorneys who take on the difficult job of filing civil rights lawsuits, often representing clients with few resources in cases that often do not result in lucrative damage awards The PLRA attorney fee provisions now reduces the likelihood that attorneys can afford to take on prisoner cases. By limiting attorneys' fees, attorneys are reluctant to take on cases that can generate only nominal damages, even though a prisoner may have suffered a grievous violation of a constitutional right. Critics maintain that attorneys who represent prisoners should be compensated on the same basis as they are in compensated for civil rights cases involving the general public.

Critics also challenge the PLRA provision that terminates consent decrees after only two years. Termination can disrupt the progress that is being made because of the consent decree. Although prisoners can avoid termination by showing an ongoing constitutional violation still exists, that showing requires a court hearing which involves delay and expense.

Finally, the PLRA is not restricted to only incarcerated offenders in adult prisons and jails. Juveniles incarcerated or detained in juvenile facilities are also bound by the same restrictions, including having to exhaust their administrative remedies.

STATE TORT LAWSUITS

Section 1983 litigation only addresses violations of the U.S. Constitution or federal law. The Supreme Court ruled in *Daniels v. Williams* (1986) that a prison official's negligence does not amount to a violation of the Constitution and cannot be litigated under the civil rights statute. In *Daniels,* the inmate sought to recover damages for physical injuries he suffered when a correctional officer negligently left a pillow on a stairway, causing the inmate to slip and fall. The Court did not agree that the officer's actions amounted to a deprivation of the prisoner's right to be free of injury because the Civil Rights Act was intended to protect individuals from the arbitrary exercise of government power. The officer's negligence was not the type of behavior the law was meant to prohibit. In *Parratt v. Taylor* (1981), the Supreme Court decided that an inmate who ordered a hobby kit that officials lost through their own negligence did not have a constitutional claim pursuant to section 1983. The Court directed the prisoner to get relief by using the state tort claims process already available to him. The consequence of the Court's two rulings is that the appropriate remedy for an inmate injured due to the negligence of a prison official is to file a lawsuit alleging a violation of state tort law.

Suing the government or a government official in a tort lawsuit is more complicated than suing a private person or entity. Under the doctrine of sovereign immunity, citizens cannot sue the government or its agents unless the government consents. The doctrine has a long history and was intended to protect the sovereign, the King or Queen, who could do no wrong. Nowadays the doctrine is justified because it protects public monies from being used to pay successful plaintiffs in personal injury lawsuits and allows officials to perform their duties without fear of litigation. If a state has not given its permission to be sued in a state tort lawsuit, the case is dismissed. Most states, however, have passed laws that severely limit the doctrine of sovereign immunity. Sovereign immunity no longer offers a blanket defense to states and agents of the state.

In order to successfully win any tort action, the prisoner must establish four separate elements: 1) officials had a duty to the inmate; 2) they breached that duty; 3) their failure to live up to their duty was the proximate cause of the inmate's injury; and 4) the inmate suffered injury. Prison officials have many duties toward inmates, such as to provide adequate medical services, food and other necessities, to protect prisoners from being harmed by other prisoners, to provide a safe work environment, and not to use unnecessary or excessive force against prisoners. They are negligent in those duties when they fail to live up to a reasonable standard of care in performing them. Failure to live up to that standard is considered a breach of the duty. In addition to alleging negligence, if the facts warrant, prisoners can file tort lawsuits against officials for intentional injuries, such as assault and battery. This type of claim is known as an intentional tort, as opposed to a negligent tort.

Congress enacted the Federal Tort Claims Act (FTCA), which allows the federal government to be held liable for damages caused by the negligent or intentional acts of its employees committed within the scope of their employment. Prisoners in federal custody must sue the United States using the FTCA if they are alleging a personal injury claim as opposed to a section 1983 claim. In *Ali v. Federal Bureau of Prisons* (2008), prisoner Ali was transferred from the U.S. Penitentiary in Atlanta to the U.S. Penitentiary in Big Sandy Kentucky. Before leaving Atlanta, he packed two duffle bags of personal property which the Bureau inventoried and shipped to Big Sandy, however, when the bags arrived there were missing items. Ali filed an administrative claim which was denied. He then filed a lawsuit. The court dismissed his lawsuit based on a provision in the Federal Tort Claims Act which provides that the federal government is not liable for any "claim arising in respect of the assessment or collection of any tax or customs duty, or the detention of any goods, merchandise, or other property by any officer of customs or excise or any other law enforcement officer". The Supreme Court agreed. The Court held that although the FTCA allows claims against the U.S. for monetary damages caused by the negligence or wrongful acts of federal employees acting in the scope of their job, the FTCA also creates an exception for claims filed against any law enforcement officer involved in the detention of property. The exception is not limited to law enforcement officers engaged in enforcing customs or excise (tax) laws. It also applies to the Federal Bureau of Prison officers involved in the transfer of Ali's property.

Because lawsuits frequently combine several legal claims, prisoners often allege a constitutional violation under section 1983 resulting from a staff assault (as a violation of the cruel and unusual punishment clause of the Eighth Amendment) while also arguing the official is liable for the assault under the state's intentional tort statute. It is important to remember that although there may be claims under state tort laws that parallel claims alleging constitutional violations, such as an Eighth Amendment claim of excessive force, there are constitutional claims that have no parallel, such as violations under the Due Process Clause or the First Amendment. In these cases, an inmate must rely on section 1983 or a state constitutional provision that provides comparable protection. In these cases, there is no state tort law for prisoners to use as an alternative basis for their lawsuit.

Elements of a Prisoner State or Federal Tort Lawsuit

Officials had a duty to the prisoner
Officials breached that duty
The breach was the proximate cause of the prisoner's injury
The prisoner suffered injury

ADMINISTRATIVE GRIEVANCE SYSTEMS

Most prisons and jail systems have implemented administrative grievance procedures that allow prisoners to file complaints internally about polices or practices. Once a grievance is filed, officials investigate it and report back their findings to the prisoner-grievant. If a grievance is sustained by the investigator, officials must take the appropriate steps to remedy the situation. If the investigator does not sustain the grievance, the prisoner is so informed and, in most grievance systems, has the opportunity to appeal the finding to a higher administrative level. Grievance systems are designed to help reduce prisoner litigation. If problems can be resolved internally, prisoners won't find it necessary to file expensive, time-consuming lawsuits.

There are no legal requirements that force prison and jail systems to implement prisoner grievance systems and jurisdictions have the freedom to design a grievance system any way they choose. Correctional systems that have implemented grievance systems provide forms for prisoners when they file a grievance and generally set deadlines for when how long after an incident occurs, a grievance must be filed, similar to a statute of limitations. Officials have a certain amount of time to investigate a complaint and inform the prisoner of their findings. In turn, prisoners who are unhappy with the response to their grievance have a deadline after receiving the response to file an appeal. Prisoners grieve about a wide range of things. Some complaints involve a specific incident and the parties involved. Other grievances are more general, complaining about such things as the quality of the food, conditions in the cellblocks, or lack of recreation equipment. Prisoners file thousands of grievances a year, and the larger prison systems have departments whose sole responsibility is operating the inmate grievance system – all the way making the unit level where the initial investigation takes place up through the appellate levels. Most correctional grievance systems do not include prisoner participation in investigating or evaluating grievances. In those systems that do include prisoners, their role is second to the decision-making role of correctional officials.

As discussed earlier in this chapter, the Prison Litigation Reform Act (PLRA) requires that prisoners must exhaust the remedies available through the grievance system, meaning they must not only file a grievance and wait for the official response, if there is also an appeal procedure available, they must also go through that entire procedure before they can file a lawsuit. Grievance systems are not popular among prisoners who, for the most part, believe that grievance investigations, conducted by correctional officials, are heavily weighted in favor of the agency. They lack confidence in grievance systems, which are operated by the same prison system about which they are complaining.

Some prisons systems also have implemented an ombudsman program to handle and investigate complaints. In some of these programs, the ombudsperson is an independent official, housed outside of the correctional system, and better positioned to be fair and impartial, especially in comparison to the correctional officials who investigate and resolve prisoner grievances. For example, the Michigan ombudsperson reports to the state legislature and makes reports and recommendations to the legislature about prison conditions based on the complaints the office has received and investigated. Originally designed to handle prisoners' complaints, the Michigan legislature has since changed its mandate and the office is now responsible for responding to complaints from the state legislators and no longer handles complaints directly from inmates (Smith 2000). In other programs, the ombuds function is placed in the correctional system. The Texas Department of Criminal Justice Ombudsman Program is a part of that agency and responds to complaints from the general public and elected officials. Like the Michigan ombuds program, the office does not accept complaints from offenders who are directed instead to use the prisoner grievance system.

CRIMINAL SANCTIONS FOR VIOLATING A PRISONER'S CONSTITUTIONAL RIGHTS

There are also criminal remedies available for certain violations of an inmate's civil rights. Under 18 U.S.C. section 242, whoever, under color of law, willfully subjects a person to the deprivation of any rights, privileges, or immunities protected by the federal Constitution or laws shall be fined or imprisoned not more than one year, or both. If bodily injury results from the deprivation or if the acts include the use or attempted use of a dangerous weapon, explosives, or fire, the punishment increases to a fine or not more than ten years of incarceration. If death results from the deprivation or if the acts include kidnapping, attempted kidnapping, aggravated sexual abuse, attempted aggravated sexual abuse, or an attempt to kill, the criminal sanction is a fine or imprisonment for any term of years or for life, or may include death. The deprivation must be willful, which means the prosecution must establish beyond a reasonable doubt that there was specific intent to deprive a person of their federal rights. It is also criminal to conspire to injure, oppress, threaten, or intimidate any person in the free exercise of any right or privilege protected by the Constitution or federal law under 18 U.S.C. section 241. The sanction can be a fine or not more than ten years in prison.

Most states also have criminal statutes that prohibit correctional officers from mistreating prisoners. The Texas Penal Code section 39.04 states that if an employee of a correctional facility intentionally denies or impedes a person in custody in the exercise or enjoyment of any right, privilege, or immunity knowing his conduct is unlawful, he can be found guilty of a Class A misdemeanor. If the official engages in sexual intercourse with an individual in custody the punishment is a state jail felony. Failure to give notice, conduct an investigation and file a report of a prisoner's death is a Class B misdemeanor. In states without specific penal laws against official mistreatment correctional officials are subject to the general penal statutes – criminal assault and battery and homicide.

SUMMARY

The prisoners' rights movement overturned the unofficial "hands-off" doctrine that had kept inmates out of the court system since the beginning of the Republic. *Cooper v Pate* in 1964, opened the doors when the Supreme Court ruled that prisoners are able to allege violations of their federal rights by using 42 U.S.C. section 1983, the Civil Rights Act that dates back to 1871. Gradually, the Court and the lower federal courts defined the key terms in section 1983, adding flesh to the bones of a very lean statute that had not seen much use until the civil rights movement in the 1960s.

Cities and local governmental units are considered "persons" under the Act and can be sued for money damages if the plaintiff can establish that they actually participated in the constitutional violation. State and state officials, however, are not section 1983 "persons" for money damage lawsuits, the Supreme Court basing this decision on the statute's legislative history. State officials, therefore, must be sued in their individual capacities. Federal agents are not included in the language of section 1983, but the Court recognized that they can be sued in their individual capacities in a related lawsuit known as a *Bivens* action, titled after the case in which the Court recognized this right. Section 1983 litigation can result in money damages or injunctive relief. Prisoners' cases are more likely to raise claims that result in injunctions. Plaintiffs in section 1983 suits must allege and prove a violation of a federal right; claims involving state laws will not be considered under section 1983. The plaintiff must also show that the defendant was acting under "color of law." This means the defendant was acting under the cloak of state authority and within the scope of their employment. A defendant who violated clearly established policy is nonetheless acting under color of law if cloaked with government authority at the time of his actions. State officials can defend Civil Rights Act lawsuits by showing that they were protected by qualified immunity. This doctrine extends to officials who did not disregard constitutional rights about which a reasonable person would have known. With some exceptions, most state and local governments provide legal counsel to their employees who are sued under section 1983 and indemnify them if monetary damages are imposed. Concerned about the large number of civil rights lawsuits prisoners were filing, Congress enacted the Prison Litigation Reform Act in 1996 with provisions that make it more difficult for prisoners to file suit and for federal courts to intervene in the daily operations of penal institutions.

Inmates can also file state tort lawsuits against local and state officials by establishing that officials had a duty to them that they breached and which breach was the proximate cause of the prisoner's injury. Federal inmates can sue federal officials for personal injuries using the Federal Tort Claims Act. State and federal tort actions are not available for many of the types of constitutional violations that prisoners allege, such as violations of the First Amendment. Finally, there are federal and state level criminal sanctions that can be taken against officials who intentionally violate an individual's civil rights. They can be difficult cases to win because the burden of proof in a criminal case requires the government to prove that an intentional violation occurred beyond a reasonable doubt.

The fascinating study of the prisoners' rights litigation explosion is really a case study in how law evolves over time to reflect changes in society's attitudes, values, and beliefs. Individuals stepped into leadership roles at different points during the evolution. In the case of prisoner litigation, some of these individuals were prisoners who were willing to take the risk in the 1960s of voicing their complaints by taking them to court. Others were judges who understood the Constitution exists to protect everyone, even those persons incarcerated in penal institutions, and that the judiciary must make difficult and controversial decisions. Finally, there were lawyers who helped fashion new interpretations of the law that seriously challenged the status quo. The litigation explosion did not happen in a vacuum. Important to this case study is that the litigation explosion occurred during a time of immense social change and in a period during which Americans were reconsidering our basic values as a nation. To study the prisoner rights movement is to study how law contributes to social change, and, on the other hand, how it is also shaped by social change.

DISCUSSION QUESTIONS

1. What are the advantages for an inmate who files a section 1983 lawsuit versus a state tort lawsuit?

2. Describe qualified immunity and when it is available to a defendant in a civil rights lawsuit.

3. Examine your state's penal code for specific crimes that can be charged against state officials for violating the rights of prisoners.

4. Describe what elements a plaintiff must prove in order to prevail under section 1983.

5. Discuss the ramifications of the Prison Litigation Reform Act.

SUGGESTED READINGS AND REFERENCES

Bennett, Katherine and Del Carmen, Rolando V. (1997) 'A Review and Analysis of Prison Litigation Reform Court Decisions: Solution or Aggravation?' *Prison Journal* (77)4: 405.

Branham, L. (2002). *The Law of Sentencing, Corrections, and Prisoners' Rights* (6th ed.). West Publishing: St. Paul, MN.

Cheesman, Fred II., Hanson, Roger A., and Ostrom, Brian J. (2000) 'The Tale of Two Laws: The U.S. Congress Confronts Habeas Corpus Petitions and Section 1983 Lawsuits,' *Law and Policy* (22)2: 89.

Hanson, R. and H.W.K.Daley (1995). "Challenging the conditions of prisons and jails: A report on section 1983 litigation." Washington, D.C.: U.S. Bureau of Justice Statistics.

Harvard Law Review Association (2002) 'Developments in the Law: The Law of Prisons II: The Prison Litigation Reform Act and the Antiterrorism and Effective Death Penalty Act: Implications for Federal District Judges', *Harvard Law Review* (115): 1846.

Scalia, John (2002). "Prisoner Petitions Filed in U.S. District Courts, 2000, with Trends 1980-2000." Washington, D.C.: Bureau of Justice Statistics.

Schlanger, Margo (2003). "Inmate litigation." *Harvard Law Review*: 116, 1555. April 2003.

Smith, C. (2000). *Boundary changes in criminal justice organizations: The governance of corrections: Implications of the changing interface of courts and corrections.* Washington, DC: National Institute of Justice.

Key Terms

ADA: see Americans with Disabilities Act, below.

Access to courts: A constitutional right that courts have recognized although there is no specific provision in the Constitution providing for it. Based on the First Amendment and the due process clause, the right to access the court system is essential in order for prisoners to seek protection of their constitutional rights in general.

Administrative regulation: Legislatures give regulatory agencies the authority to adopt rules and regulations that are consistent with the statutes that created the agencies. Administrative rules and regulations are even more specific and detailed than statutory law. They address a myriad of circumstances with as much precision as possible.

Administrative segregation: A general term that refers to a classification where disruptive prisoners are assigned to a restrictive living environment. Different prison systems call it by different terms, including intensive management and special housing. Although inmates are assigned to this classification because they failed to abide by disciplinary rules, placement in segregation is an administrative classification decision and not punishment for a particular offense.

Americans with Disabilities Act: Passed by the U.S. Congress in 1990 to prevent government programs and services from discriminating or excluding individuals with disabilities.

Antipsychotic medication: Medication designed to treat certain types of serious mental illnesses that often have serious, adverse side-effects.

Attorney-client privilege: A privilege that dates back in English jurisprudence to the Sixteenth Century that states that whenever legal advice of any kind is sought from a professional legal advisor, the communications relating to that matter are made in confidence by the client and are permanently protected from disclosure by the legal advisor, unless the client waives the protection. The attorney-client privilege is also an ethical duty imposed on attorneys by the legal professions mandatory code of ethics.

Banishment: at common law, the permanent exclusion of a person from a country.

Bill of Rights: the first ten amendments to the U.S. Constitution, added in an effort to protect individual rights from infringement by the federal (and later state) government.

Body cavity search: a search of a nude inmate that includes a physical examination of

bodily openings that could contain contraband. The Supreme Court described the body cavity search in *Bell v. Wolfish* (1979) in footnote 39, "If the inmate is a male, he must lift his genitals and bend over to spread his buttocks for visual inspection. The vaginal and anal cavities of female inmates are also visually inspected. The inmate is not touched by security personnel at any time during the *visual* search procedure." Such searches are generally permitted upon reasonable suspicion and before and after a contact visit.

Case law: The rules that result from the legal precedents created in previously issued judicial decisions.

Cell restriction: Punishment for a disciplinary violation that requires a prisoner to remain in his or her cell for a certain number of days with access to personal items. Inmates are not permitted to work, attend programming activities, and recreate. Meals are served in the cell.

Civil disability: the loss of certain civil, or political, rights as a result of being convicted of a felony.

Civil Rights Act: A statute passed by the U.S. Congress in 1871 in response to the arbitrary and capricious enforcement of laws against the freed slaves by state and local officials in the South.

Class action lawsuit: A group of plaintiffs who share certain damages or types of legal claims and consolidate their arguments into a single lawsuit on behalf of the entire class. A court must approve a group of plaintiffs proceeding as a class action.

Classification: Classification assigns inmates to the appropriate institution and security level based on a system that evaluates each prisoner's security risk and programming needs. The system identifies the best housing placement and custody supervision for a prisoner along with medical, mental health, work, and educational assignments. Inmates are classified when they are first admitted into prison and re-classified at regular intervals during their incarceration.

Common law: law created by judges as they heard cases and settled disputes. Judges wrote down their decisions, and in doing so attempted to justify their decision by reference to custom, tradition, history, and prior judicial decisions.

Complaint: The name of the document filed by a plaintiff to initiate a lawsuit in federal court.

Conditions of confinement lawsuit: a lawsuit brought by an inmate alleging that the conditions of their confinement (as opposed to the fact of the confinement) are unconstitutional.

Consent decree: The parties to a lawsuit agree to the terms to settle the lawsuit. A judge must review and agree to the terms of a consent decree before it becomes binding. Consent decrees in prisoners' rights cases are often long and detailed and are the product of give and take on the part of the parties. The parties can also enter into a consent decree after the judge rules that one of the parties violated the law. In this case, the losing party decides to negotiate to reach an agreement about how the loser must remedy the situation.

Contraband: Items prisoners are not permitted to possess.

Contract leasing: A practice that was especially popular in the South in the last half of the 1900s. Prisoners were contracted to private businesses by the state. The private companies paid the state for the inmates' labor. Some businesses would transport the inmates to the work site during the day and return them to the institution at night. Other businesses would house and feed the inmates at the work site, essentially taking full responsibility for the prisoners' care.

Corporal punishment: the infliction of physical pain on an inmate.

Cross-gender search: a search of an inmate by a correctional officer of a different gender. Such searches are generally permitted if necessary to maintain institutional security.

Cruel and unusual punishment: punishment that, in the opinion of the courts, violates the 8th Amendment. It has been defined as the punishment that shocks the conscience of a civilized society or punishment that goes beyond legitimate penal aims.

Deadly force: the use of such force as could kill another person.

Determinate sentencing: Sentencing laws that set a definite or fixed term of incarceration for each individual offense. The offender is not released until he or she has completed the entire sentence. It can also be understood as an approach to sentencing that has resulted in jurisdictions enacting new sentencing statutes that significantly reduce a judge's discretion to sentence within a broad range of years and/or a parole board's discretion to release.

Double-celling: Assigning two inmates to one prison cell.

Double jeopardy: being tried twice for the same offense; a violation of the United States constitution and prohibited at common law.

Due process: A right created in the Fifth and Fourteenth Amendments to the U.S. Constitution that under certain circumstances requires officials to follow specific procedures before the government can take a person's life, liberty, or property.

Eighth Amendment: Constitutional amendment which bands "cruel and unusual" punishment.

Establishment Clause: the section of the First Amendment that prohibits the government from establishing, favoring, endorsing, or supporting religion.

***Ex post facto* law:** law enacted after an act and which retroactively impose punishment for that act.

Exclusionary rule: the rule created by the Supreme Court which requires that evidence obtained by the police in violation of the Fourth Amendment cannot be used at trial.

First Amendment: Constitutional amendment that includes individuals' rights to freedom of religion, freedom of speech, freedom of the press, the right to assemble peaceably and petition the Government to rectify grievances. This amendment has significant application in correctional facilities.

Fleeing felon rule: the rule which allowed law enforcement officers to use deadly force as a means of apprehending a suspect or offender who was about to escape.

Fourth Amendment: Constitutional amendment that limits when and where the government can search. Its protections apply when the subject of the search has a reasonable expectation of privacy; it is of very limited application in correctional facilities.

Free Exercise Clause: the section of the First Amendment that prohibits the government from prohibiting or in any way interfering with a person's right to practice the religion of their choice.

Fundamental rights: those freedoms essential to the concept of "ordered liberty," rights without which neither liberty nor justice would exist. These rights are determined by courts through reference to history, customs and tradition.

General conditions: probation/parole conditions that typically are applied to all probationers and parolees.

Good conduct time: Also called gain time, time off for good behavior, good credit time, earned good time. It allows inmates to be released before they have completed their entire sentence and is considered incentive for good behavior. States have different statutes that determine how much good time inmates receive for each day of time actually served.

"Hands off" doctrine: the unofficial legal doctrine that encouraged courts not to interfere in matters of prison operation, instead deferring to the specialized expertise and experience of correctional administrators.

Immunity: In the context of a civil rights lawsuit, the term refers to certain legal protections that the law provides to public officials who are named as defendants. There are several different types of immunity. Absolute immunity is extended to very few public officials who are defendants and protects them from all lawsuits for actions they take in the course of their employment. More common is qualified immunity. It protects certain defendants from being sued if there is evidence that the officials did not disregard clearly established statutory or constitutional rights of which a reasonable person would have known.

***In forma pauperis*:** A Latin phrase that means in the nature of a pauper. As used in the U.S. legal system, it is an application filed by indigent plaintiff to waive the fees to file a lawsuit or pay certain costs associated with filing a lawsuit.

Incidental contact: accidental contact between a parolee/probationer and someone they have been ordered not to associate with.

Incorporation: the process whereby the Supreme Court has determined that the various provisions of the Bill of Rights apply to the states via the Due Process Clause of the 14th Amendment.

Indemnification: When a governmental entity pays the legal damages on behalf of an employee who was found liable in a state tort or federal civil rights lawsuit.

Indeterminate sentencing: Sentencing laws that provide a broad range of years within which a judge sentence a convicted offender. The parole board decides on the actual length of incarceration.

Injunction: A court order that requires a party to a lawsuit to take a specific action or to stop engaging in a specific action.

Jailhouse lawyer: A prisoner who is self-trained in the law and provides legal assistance to other prisoners.

Judicial activism: A term used to describe judges who are aggressive in their interpretation of the law, especially the Constitution.

Judicial review: the power of a court to review legislation and determine whether it violates the Constitution.

***lex talionis*:** Latin phrase meaning an "eye for an eye."

Major disciplinary offense: Disciplinary rules are categorized as "major" or "minor." The terminology will differ from prison system to prison system but the concept is that a major offense is a violation of a serious or major rule, punished with more severe sanctions.

Mandatory minimum sentences: sentencing laws that specify a required minimum penalty for certain offenses.

Minor disciplinary offense: A violation of a less serious disciplinary rule and subject to less serious sanctions.

National Commission on Correctional Health Care (NCCHC): An independent, not-for-profit organization formed in the 1980s by the American Medical Association to develop policy and programs to improve the delivery of health care in correctional facilities. Today, the NCCHC sets standards (recommendations) that are widely recognized by experts in the health, legal, and corrections professions. The organization also offers accreditation, educational, and certification programs.

Natural rights: rights that humans are born with, that are inherent. Governments do not give these rights, they come with one's existence.

New judicial federalism: a tendency, developed in the last twenty years or so, in which state supreme courts look more frequently to their state constitution for guidance about the rights of their state residents, rather than relying on the federal constitution and Bill of Rights.

***Nolo contendere* plea:** Latin for "I will not contest it." A plea available in most jurisdictions that means the defendant is not contesting the government's case; however he or she is not admitting guilt. A *nolo contendere* plea is treated as a guilty plea for sentencing purposes.

Non-deadly force: use of force that is not calculated to kill someone. There are a number of rules and procedures that govern when and how correctional officers can use force.

PLRA: Prison Litigation Reform Act passed by the U.S. Congress in 1996 to limit the types and numbers of lawsuits inmates could file in federal court and to limit the type and scope of involvement that federal judges could engage in with respect to prisoner reform litigation.

Parole: a conditional release of a prisoner, generally under supervision of a parole officer, who has served part of the term for which he was sentenced to prison.

Pat down search: search of the outer clothing of a person. Such searches are permitted of all persons who enter a correctional facility.

Precedent: a prior decision by a court. This decision is used by future courts to guide them in their decision-making process.

Presentence investigation report: A report prepared by the probation department about the offender's crime and his or her background to help the judge decide on the offender's appropriate sentence.

Pretrial detainee: person detained in a correctional facility pending trial, during which time they are presumed innocent.

Prison legal assistance program: A program created by prison officials, in addition to or in place of a law library, to assist prisoners in researching legal issues and preparing legal documents.

Privatizing prison health care: States contract with private health care providers and managed care companies to provide some or all of the health care services to the prisoners as opposed to hiring the providers as state employees.

Pro se: when an inmate files a lawsuit without the assistance of legal counsel.

Probation: a sentence imposed for commission of crime whereby a convicted criminal offender is released into the community under the supervision of a probation officer in lieu of incarceration.

Procedural rights: rules the government must follow before depriving someone of their individual rights. Courts allow correctional administrators a great deal of leeway in how they discipline inmates, but do require some procedural safeguards.

Probable cause: the degree of suspicion that a police officer must have in order to obtain a search or arrest warrant. Probable cause to search is not required in a correctional facility, because the Fourth Amendment does not apply to the same extent as in the free world.

Proof beyond a reasonable doubt: The standard of proof in criminal cases applied by the judge or the jury in reaching the decision to convict. Although is it the highest standard of proof, it still does not require absolute certainty about the truth of the charges.

Proof by a preponderance of the evidence: The standard of proof used in civil trials which requires the plaintiff to show that the greater weight of the evidence supports his or her case. Although it is used primarily in civil cases, the law often requires it as the standard of proof for judges to use when making findings that are related to deciding sentences for convicted offenders.

Rational basis review: A test created by the courts for evaluating the constitutionality of laws and regulations that impact certain fundamental rights. Under the rational basis test, the government must show that the law or regulation acts in such a way that it reasonably advances a legitimate governmental goal or interest.

Reasonable expectation of privacy: the standard for determining when the Fourth Amendment applies. When the subject of a search or seizure has a reasonable expectation of privacy, he or she cannot be searched or seized unless the police have probable cause and/or a warrant. There is no reasonable expectation of privacy in prison.

Reasonable force: the appropriate degree of force to be used in a situation. The standard rule is that a correctional officer should use no more force than is necessary to protect themselves or to get an inmate to comply with a lawful order.

Regulation: Rules created by government agencies.

Remedy: In a prisoner rights lawsuit, the judge's order mandating the actions the government is to take to correct the problems that resulted in violating the Constitution or statute.

***Respondeat superior*:** A legal principle that allows supervisors or employers to be held liable for the torts committed by their subordinates/employees whether or not the supervisor or employer had actual knowledge of the actions at the time they occurred.

Scientific testing: a means of searching a person to determine whether their body contains contraband, such as drugs or alcohol. Examples include blood tests and urinalysis.

Search with equipment: a means of searching a person or container with a device, such as an X-ray machine or metal detector. The purpose of the search is to determine the presence of contraband.

Section 1983 lawsuit: a lawsuit brought by an individual alleging a government agent/actor has violated a federally protected right of the individual.

United States Sentencing Commission: A legislatively created commission charged with the responsibility of drafting sentences for criminal offenses.

Sentencing guidelines: Detailed and comprehensive sentencing laws created by sentencing commissions. The guidelines are intended to assist judges as they make sentencing decisions in individual cases. In some states that use guidelines, they are voluntary, meaning they are recommended sentences only and judges are free not to follow them. In states with presumptive guidelines, judges are required by law to sentence according to the guidelines. Any departure must be explained in writing and can be appealed by both the prosecution and the defense. Guidelines are periodically revised by sentencing commissions.

"Shocks the conscience" test: a test for the appropriate degree of force for correctional officers to use. Force was deemed excessive and violative of the constitutional rights of the inmate only if the conduct seemed so outrageous and inappropriate that it literally "shocked the conscience" of the court.

Solitary confinement: Sometimes called disciplinary confinement or punitive confinement to distinguish it from administrative confinement. It is punishment for a specific serious disciplinary infraction. Inmates assigned to solitary confinement cannot leave their cell for the length of the "punishment" and have limited or no access to personal items, television, and radio.

Specific conditions: probation and parole conditions that are specially tailored to the individual needs of a probationer or parolee.

***Stare decisis*:** a Latin phrase translated as "let the decision stand," it means courts will generally respect and follow the holdings of prior courts that have considered the same issue.

State-created liberty interest doctrine: Created through a series of U.S. Supreme Court decisions beginning with *Wolff v. McDonnell* (1974), it occurs when a state law or regulation creates a liberty interest that requires due process protections.

Statute: Laws created by popularly elected legislatures.

Statute of limitations: Laws that set the maximum period of time within which a lawsuit or claim must be filed.

Strip search: a visual examination of a nude inmate by a correctional officer, in an effort to determine whether the inmate has hidden contraband upon their person.

Three strikes sentencing laws: A generic term that describes a group of sentencing laws that some states have enacted to enhance (increase) the punishment of third-time repeat offenders. Three strikes laws vary from state to state with respect to their harshness and the types of offenses they address.

Tort: laws that provide the basis for civil lawsuits that seek damages for injury caused to a person or to property.

Totality of conditions lawsuit: Litigation filed by prisoners that challenges several, sometimes many, distinct conditions under which they live in the same lawsuit, which when considered together make for an living environment that violates the cruel and unusual punishment clause. Common conditions complained about in totality of conditions lawsuits include: lack of adequate cell space, inadequate plumbing/toilets/showers, poor ventilation, unsafe working conditions, lack of recreation areas or opportunities, unsanitary conditions, lack of nutritious meals, inadequate medical care.

Significant Supreme Court Cases

Alabama v. Smith, 490 U.S.794 (1989): When a greater penalty is imposed after trial than was imposed after a prior guilty plea, the relevant inquiry is whether there was a reasonable likelihood that the sentence imposed after trial was a product of judicial vindictiveness. As part of this inquiry, consideration must be given to the information that becomes available to a judge during a trial, such as additional facts about the offense and the demeanor of the accused.

Ali v. Federal Bureau of Prisons, 552 U.S. 214 (2008): The text of the Federal Tort Claims Act (FTCA) that exempts any claim arising from the assessment or collection of any tax or customs duty, or the detention of any property by an officer of customs or excise or any other law enforcement officer covers all law enforcement officers and is not limited to only officers engaged in enforcing customs or excise laws.

Apprendi v. New Jersey, 530 U.S. 466 (2000): The due process clause requires any fact that increases the penalty for a crime beyond what is the maximum provided by law be submitted to a jury and be proved beyond a reasonable doubt.

Arciniega v. Freeman, 404 U.S. 4 (1971): a parole condition which prohibits "association" with other ex-convicts does not apply to "incidental" contact.

Barron v. Baltimore, 32 U.S. 243 (1833): The Bill of Rights applies only to the federal government. This decision is later modified by the passage of the 14th Amendment.

Baxter v. Palmigiano, 425 U.S. 308 (1976): Prisoners do not have a right to counsel in an inmate disciplinary hearing, and an adverse inference can be drawn from a prisoner's decision to remain silent during a disciplinary hearing.

Bearden v. Georgia, 461 U.S. 660 (1985): Indigent persons on probation cannot have probation revoked solely because, through no fault of their own, they fail to pay fines or make restitution.

Bell v. Wolfish, 441 U.S. 520 (1979): To evaluate the constitutionality of conditions or restrictions on pretrial detainees, the proper inquiry under the due process clause is whether those conditions or restrictions amount to punishment of the detainees. Under that analysis, body cavity searches and a room search rule do not deprive pretrial detainees of their liberty without due process of law or any other constitutional guarantees.

Bivens v. Six Unknown Named Agents of the Federal Bureau of Narcotics, 403 U.S. 388 (1971): Although section 1983 does not apply to federal officers, individuals may seek damages for violations of their constitutional rights by federal officials.

Blakely v. Washington, 542 U.S. 961 (2004): Certain provisions of the Washington state sentencing guidelines violate the Sixth Amendment right to a trial by jury because they allow the imposition of sentences based on facts that have not been found by a jury beyond a reasonable doubt.

Block v. Rutherford, 468 U.S. 576 (1984): Based on the Court's holding in *Bell v. Wolfish* (1979), pretrial detainees do not have a constitutional right under the due process clause to contact visitation or the right to observe officials search their cells. Both prohibitions are reasonable, non-punitive responses to legitimate security concerns.

Booth v. Churner, 532 U.S. 731 (2001): The Prison Litigation Reform Act requires that prisoners who seek only monetary damages must exhaust all of available administrative remedies prior to filing a civil rights lawsuit, even in situation where the grievance process does not permit the award of monetary damages.

Bordenkircher v. Hayes, 434 U.S. 357 (1978): The government does not violate the due process rights of a defendant when a prosecutor threatens and then procures an additional indictment in order to induce a guilty plea.

Bounds v. Smith, 430 U.S. 817 (1977): The constitutional right of access to courts requires prison officials to assist prisoners in preparing and filing legal papers by providing prisoners with adequate law libraries or assistance from persons trained in the law.

Boykin v. Alabama, 395 U.S. 238 (1969): In order for a guilty plea to be accepted, the court's record must reflect that the defendant's plea was voluntary and that he or she understood the consequences of their plea.

Brady v. United States, 397 U.S. 742 (1970): A guilty plea that is otherwise voluntary and intelligent does not become involuntary because it is entered in hopes of avoiding the death penalty.

Burns v. Ohio, 360 U.S. 252 (1959): It is a constitutional violation to prohibit indigent criminal defendants from filing a leave to appeal because they are not able to pay the filing fee.

City of Boerne v. Flores, (1997): The Religious Freedom Restoration Act violates the Fourteenth Amendment.

City of Canton v. Harris, 489 U.S. 378 (1989): Under certain circumstances, a municipality may be held liable under section 1983 for violations of constitutional rights that result from a failure to train its employees. Inadequate training may serve as the basis for a section 1983 lawsuit only when the failure to train amounts to deliberate indifference to constitutional rights as evidenced by a municipal custom or policy.

Cleavinger v. Saxner, 474 U.S. 193 (1985): Members of a prison disciplinary committee are not entitled to absolute immunity as defendants in a section 1983 lawsuit. They are only entitled to qualified immunity.

Coker v. Georgia, 433 U.S. 584 (1977): The death penalty is grossly disproportionate for the crime of rape of a child and violates the Eighth Amendment.

Connecticut Board of Pardons v. Dumschat, 452 U.S. 458 (1981): It does not matter that clemency has been granted frequently, it is a discretionary decision and an inmate has no due process protections in the clemency system.

Connecticut Department of Public Safety v. Doe, 538 U.S.1 (2003): The Constitution's due process clause does not require that a hearing be conducted to determine whether a convicted sex offender can be subjected to the registration and notification requirements of Connecticut's Megan's Law.

Cooper v. Pate, 378 U.S. 546 (1964): Prisoners are entitled to file lawsuits against correctional officials under section 1983.

Correctional Services Corporation v. Malesko, 534 U.S. 61 (2001): The *Bivens* holding does not confer a right of action for damages in a civil right lawsuit against private entities acting under color of federal law.

Cruz v. Beto, 405 U. S. 319 (1972): Inmates who hold unconventional religious beliefs are still entitled to practice their beliefs in as comparable a situation as those who hold more conventional religious beliefs.

Cutter v. Wilkinson, 544 U.S. 709 (2005): Section 3 of the Religious Land Use and Institutionalized Persons Act (RLUIPA), which prohibits the government from imposing a substantial burden on the religious exercise of persons residing in or confined to an institution, does not violate the Establishment Clause of the First Amendment.

Daniels v. Williams, 474 U.S. 327 (1986): The due process clause does not protect a prisoner from a state official's negligent actions that cause unintended loss or injury to life, liberty, or property.

Employment Division of Oregon v. Smith, 494 U.S. 872 (1990): A state may deny unemployment benefits to a worker for using illegal drugs for religious purposes.

Estelle v. Gamble, 429 U.S. 97 (1976): Deliberate indifference by prison personnel to a prisoner's serious medical needs constitutes a violation of the cruel and unusual punishment clause of the Eighth Amendment.

Estelle v. Smith, 451 U.S. 454 (1981): The admission of a doctor's testimony at the penalty phase violates the Fifth Amendment privilege against self-incrimination if the defendant is not advised before the examination that he or she has the right to remain silent and that anything they say can be used against them. There is no basis for distinguishing between the guilt and penalty phase of a trial.

Ex parte Hull, 312 U.S. 546 (1941): Prison regulations that allow officials to screen prisoners' petitions for habeas corpus are unconstitutional.

Fare v. Michael C. 442 U.S. 707 (1979): The request by a juvenile probationer during police questioning to see his or her probation officer, after having received the Miranda warnings by the police, is not equivalent to asking for a lawyer and therefore is not considered an assertion of the right to remain silent.

Farmer v. Brennan, 511 U.S. 825 (1994): A prison officials' deliberate indifference to a serious risk of harm to an inmate violates the Eighth Amendment. Deliberate indifference requires a showing that officials were subjectively aware of the risk and failed to take reasonable steps to keep the inmate safe.

Gagnon v. Scarpelli, 411 U.S. 778 (1973): the requirements for a probation revocation hearing are identical to the requirements for a parole revocation hearing.

Greenholtz v. Inmates of Nebraska Penal and Correctional Complex, 442 U.S. 1 (1979): The Fourteenth Amendment's due process clause does not apply to the decision to release an inmate conditionally before the end of their prison term. If the language of a state's parole statute creates a liberty interest for prisoners in the parole decision, inmates may have constitutional due process protections as a result of the state law.

Gregg v. Georgia, 428 U.S. 153(1976): The death penalty for the crime of murder is not cruel and unusual punishment as long as the death penalty statute guides the judge's or jury's attention on an individual defendant and the circumstances of a specific crime.

Griffin v. Illinois, 351 U.S. 12 (1956): Indigent prisoners have a constitutional right to adequate and effective appellate review, including, at no cost, a certified copy of the proceedings of their trial.

Griffin v. Wisconsin, 483 U.S. 868 (1987): A law allowing warrantless searches of a probationer's residence by a probation officer and based on "reasonable grounds" is valid and does not violate the probationer's Fourth Amendment rights.

Griswold v. Connecticut, 381 U.S. 479 (1965): the various provisions of the Bill of Rights create a "penumbra" in which the whole was greater than the sum of the parts. In other words, the individual rights contained in the Bill of Rights, when examined together, implied the existence of other rights, including a general right to privacy.

Harlow v. Fitzgerald, 457 U. S. 800 (1982): A public official is not liable under section 1983 if his or her conduct does not violate a clearly established constitutional or statutory right about which a reasonable person would have known.

Harmelin v. Michigan, 501 U.S. 957 (1991): The Eighth Amendment does not require proportionality in sentencing unless the sentence is grossly disproportionate to the crime.

Helling v. McKinney, 509 U.S. 25 (1993): Prison officials who are deliberately indifferent to an inmate's future serious medical needs can violate the cruel and unusual punishment clause.

Hewitt v. Helms, 459 U.S. 460 (1983): Assignment of a prisoner to administrative segregation is not subject to protection from the Constitution's Due Process Clause. If, however, a state creates a liberty interest in its state laws or rules for inmates to remain in the general population, that interest is satisfied by an informal, nonadversarial review of the placement decision.

Hope v. Pelzer, 536 U.S. 730 (2002): handcuffing an inmate chain gang member to an iron rail for seven hours at a work site as punishment for being disruptive and disobeying an order violates the Eighth Amendment. The Supreme Court found no legitimate penological interest in the infliction of such unnecessary pain and suffering.

Houchins v. KQED, Inc., 438 U.S. 1 (1978): The press has no greater First Amendment rights of special access to information that is not available to the general public.

Hudson v. McMillan, 303 U. S. 1 (1992): the Supreme Court applied the *Whitley* standard to a situation involving only minor injuries to an inmate, and held that a "significant injury" to an inmate was not necessary for a use of force by correctional personnel to constitute "cruel and unusual punishment."

Hudson v. Palmer, 468 U. S. 517 (1984): The Fourth Amendment prohibition against unreasonable searches does not apply to prison cells. Further, destruction of inmate of property does not violate the Due Process Clause, so long as post-deprivation remedies are available.

Hughes v. Rowe, 449 U.S. 5 (1980): Placing a prisoner in administrative segregation without a hearing violates the due process requirements in the Constitution unless officials can demonstrate that segregation is necessitated by emergency circumstances.

Hutto v. Finney, 437 U.S. 638 (1978): Conditions in punitive segregation in the Arkansas prison system violated the cruel and unusual punishment clause of the Eighth Amendment.

Jaffee v. Redmond, 518 U.S. 1 (1996): there is a psychotherapist-patient privilege with respect to confidential communications.

Johnson v. Avery, 393 U.S. 483 (1969): In the absence of providing reasonable alternatives to assist illiterate or poorly educated prisoners, a state may not impose an absolute prohibition on prisoners furnishing legal assistance to other prisoners to help them prepare petitions for post-conviction relief.

Johnson v. California, 543 U.S. 499 (2005): Strict scrutiny is the proper standard for reviewing whether a department of corrections' policy segregating all prisoners on the basis of race in double cells for up to 60 days violates the Fourteenth Amendment's Equal Protection Clause.

Jones v. North Carolina Prisoners' Labor Union, Inc. 433 U. S. 119 (1977): Prison regulations prohibiting inmate solicitation of union membership, union meetings, and bulk mailings do not violate First Amendment rights of inmates nor the Equal Protection Clause of the Fourteenth Amendment.

Kansas v. Crane, 534 U.S. 407 (2002): The Kansas Sexually Violent Predator Act does not require a showing of that the offender lacks total or complete control of his or her conduct.

Kansas v. Hendricks, 521 U.S. 346 (1997): civil commitment of a sex offender who has completed a term of incarceration for a sex offense does not violate either the double jeopardy or ex post facto clauses because they restrict only punishment, and the commitment was civil, not punitive, in nature.

Kennedy v. Louisiana, 554 U.S. ____ (2008): The Eighth Amendment bars imposing the death penalty for the rape of a child.

Kentucky v. Thompson, 490 U.S. 454 (1989): State regulations that contain a nonexhaustive list of visitors who may be banned from visiting state inmates do not provide prisoners with a state created liberty interest for purposes of the due process clause of the Fourteenth Amendment.

Lewis v. Casey, 518 U.S. 343 (1996): To establish a violation under *Bounds v. Smith,* prisoners must demonstrate that they suffered actual injury as a result of deficiencies in the prison law library or legal assistance program which hindered or are hindering their efforts to pursue legal claims.

Lockyer v. Andrade, 538 U.S. 63 (2003) (and its' companion case, *Ewing v. California,* 538 U.S. 11 (2003)): California's three strikes and you're out law that sentences repeat felons to a prison term of 25-years to life does not violate the Eighth Amendment cruel and unusual punishment clause or any other clearly established federal law.

Marbury v. Madison, 5 Cranch 137 (1803): Congress violated the Constitution when it enacted a law that gave the Court authority to issue original writs of mandamus in cases not affecting Ambassadors, other public ministers and consuls or those in which a state is a party. This is the first case in which the Supreme Court asserted that a federal court has the power to declare an act of Congress unconstitutional.

McKune v. Lile, 536 U.S. 24 (2002): A prison based, mandatory sex offender treatment program that requires offenders to admit to sexual misconduct for which they have not been charged or convicted and which penalizes inmates who refuse to participate does not violate the Fifth Amendment's privilege against self-incrimination.

Meachum v. Fano, 427 U.S. 215 (1976): The Constitution does not require that a prisoner be afforded a due process hearing before transfer to a less favorable prison.

Mempa v. Rhay, 389 U.S. 128 (1967): Under the Sixth Amendment, a defendant has a right to the assistance of counsel at sentencing in a probation revocation hearing and imposition of a deferred sentence.

Miller v. French, 530 U.S. 327 (2000): The Prison Litigation Reform Act's automatic stay provision is mandatory and restricts federal judges from exercising their equitable powers to enjoin the stay. It does not violate the separation of powers doctrine created by the Constitution.

Mistretta v. United States, 488 U.S. 361 (1989): The United States Sentencing Commission Guidelines are constitutional.

Monell v. Department of Social Services, 436 U.S. 658 (1978): Municipalities, counties, and other local governmental agencies are "persons" under section 1983.

Monroe v. Pape, 365 U.S. 167 (1961): Actions of municipal police officers in conduct alleging illegal searches and seizures were performed under color of state law within the meaning of 42 U.S.C. section 1983.

Montanye v. Haymes, 427 U.S. 236 (1976): The Constitution does not require that a prisoner be afforded a hearing before transfer to another prison as a result of a prisoner's bad behavior.

Morrissey v. Brewer, 408 U.S. 471 (1972): due process requires that, at a minimum, parole revocation procedures include: (1) written notice of the claimed parole violation; (2) disclosure to the parolee of the evidence against him or her; (3) an opportunity for the parolee to present evidence and witnesses, and to be heard; (4) the right of the parolee to confront and examine witnesses; (5) a neutral and detached hearing committee; and (6) a written statement by the parole board of the evidence and reasons for revoking parole.

North Carolina v. Alford, 400 U.S. 25 (1979): An admission of guilt is not necessary for a guilty plea to be valid as long as it is voluntary and informed. Indeed the defendant can plead guilty and maintain his or her innocence and the plea be valid.

Olim v. Wakinekona, 461 U.S. 238 (1983): An interstate transfer does not violate an inmate's liberty interest because he or she has no justifiable expectation that they will be incarcerated in a particular state. Inmates, therefore, are not protected by the due process clause in interstate transfer situations.

O'Lone v. Estate of Shabazz, 482 U.S. 342 (1987): Prison policies that prohibit inmates from returning to the building in which religious services are held do not violate freedom of religion rights when those policies are reasonably related to legitimate penological interests.

Overton v. Bazzetta, 539 U.S. 126 (2003): The constitutionality of prison regulations that restrict visitation should be evaluated under the four-part *Turner v. Safley* (1987) test. If the regulations are rationally related to legitimate penological interests, they are valid and do not violate the First Amendment's right to association.

Palko v. Connecticut, 302 U.S. 319 (1937): Fundamental rights as those freedoms essential to the concept of ordered liberty, rights without which neither liberty nor justice would exist.

Parratt v. Taylor, 451 U.S. 527 (1981): A prisoner does not have a constitutional claim under section 1983 when the state provides procedures to address the loss of the inmate's property because of the actions of a correctional officer.

Pell v. Procunier, 417 U.S. 817 (1974): A prison regulation that prohibits face-to-face media interviews with prisoners does not violate the Constitution as long as alternative means of communication are available to both the media and to prisoners.

Pennsylvania Board of Probation and Parole v. Scott, 524 U.S. 327 (1998): The federal exclusionary rule, prohibiting the introduction of evidence seized in violation of the Fourth Amendment's protections against unreasonable search and seizure, does not apply to parole revocation hearings.

Pennsylvania Department of Corrections v. Yeskey, 524 U.S. 206 (1998): The Americans with Disabilities Act extends to prisons and prison inmates.

Ponte v. Real, 471 U.S. 491 (1985): The Constitution does not require that prison officials state their reasons for denying an inmate's request for a witness during a disciplinary hearing in the administrative record.

Porter v. Nussle, 534 U.S. 516 (2002): The exhaustion requirement in the Prison Litigation Reform Act applies to all prisoner lawsuits, whether they address general living conditions that impact many prisoners or specific events or episodes that impact one prisoner, and whether they allege excessive use of force or some other injury.

Procunier v. Martinez, 416 U.S. 396 (1974): Censorship of prisoner mail raises issues involving the First Amendment rights of the free world correspondents and is justified only if: 1) it furthers an important and substantial governmental interest in security, order, and the rehabilitation of prisoners, and 2) it is no greater than is necessary to further the legitimate governmental interest.

Procunier v. Navarette, 434 U.S. 555 (1978): Prison officials are entitled to immunity unless they knew or reasonably should have known that the actions they took violated a prisoner's constitutional rights.

Pulley v. Harris, 465 U.S. 37 (1984): The Eighth Amendment does not require a state appellate court, as part of a proportionality review, to compare the sentence in the death penalty case before it with the sentences imposed in similar capital cases.

Rhodes v. Chapman, 452 U.S. 337 (1981): Double-celling in and of itself does not constitute a violation of the cruel and unusual punishment clause.

Richardson v. McKnight, 521 U.S. 399 (1997): Correctional officers employed by a private prison management firm are not entitled to qualified immunity from suit by prisoners charging a section 1983 violation.

Ricketts v. Adamson, 483 U.S. 1(1987): In the event that a defendant breaches a plea agreement he or she has made with the prosecution, the parties return to the status quo.

Roberts v. United States,, 445 U.S. 552 (1980): The privilege against self-incrimination is not violated when a judge considers a defendant's refusal to cooperate with the government in determining an appropriate sentence.

Roberts v. United States 320 U.S. 263 (1943): the Supreme Court defined the purpose of probation as "to provide an individualized program offering a young or unhardened offender an opportunity to rehabilitate himself without institutional confinement under the tutelage of a probation officer and under the continuing power of the court to impose institutional punishment for his original offense in the event that he abuse the opportunity."

Robinson v. California, 370 U.S. 660 (1962): A state law that makes it a crime to be addicted to the use of narcotics, punishable by imprisonment for not less than 90 days to not more than one year, inflicts a cruel and unusual punishment in violation of the Eighth and Fourteenth Amendments.

Rummel v. Estelle, 445 U.S. 263 (1980): Mandatory life sentence for a third felony conviction involving theft of $120.75 does not violate the Eighth Amendment even though the prior felony convictions were for nonviolent offenses: theft for $80 and passing a forged check for $28.36.

Samson v. California, 547 U.S. 843 (2006): the Fourth Amendment does not prohibit a police officer from conducting a suspicionless, warrantless search of a parolee.

Sandin v. Connor, 515 U.S. 472 (1995): Under certain circumstances, states may create liberty interests that are protected by due process; however, these interests are generally limited to freedom from restraint which imposes atypical or significant hardship on the prisoner incident to the ordinary circumstances of being incarcerated.

Santabello v. New York, 404 U.S. 257 (1971): Once a plea bargain has been made and accepted, the defendant has the right to have the bargain enforced.

Saxbe v. Washington Post, 417 U.S. 843 (1974): A regulation that prohibits a person from entering a prison and designating a prisoner they would like to visit (unless that person is a lawyer, clergy, or friend/family member of the prisoner) does not violate the First Amendment because it does not deny the press access to sources of information available to the general public.

Selig v. Young, 531 U.S. 250 (2001): The civil, nonpunitive nature of a Washington state civil commitment statute for predatory sex offenders cannot be altered based on the way the statute is implemented, therefore, the Double Jeopardy and Ex Post Facto clauses do not apply.

Shaw v. Murphy, 532 U.S. 223 (2001): Prisoners do not have a First Amendment right to provide legal assistance to other prisoners.

Smith v. Doe, 538 U.S. 84 (2003): The retroactivity clause of the Alaska Sex Offender Registration Act does not violate the Ex Post Facto Clause because it in nonpunitive in nature.

Solem v. Helm, (1983): A life sentence for a felony conviction for writing a bad check, which would ordinarily involve a five year sentence, violates the Eighth Amendment, even though it was the defendant's seventh felony conviction.

Strickland v. Washington, 466 U.S. 668 (1984): The Sixth Amendment's right to effective assistance of counsel is violated when the defendant can establish: 1) counsel's performance was deficient; and 2) the reasonable probability that but for counsel's deficient performance the result in the proceedings would have been different.

Superintendent v. Hill (1985), 472 U.S. 445 (1985): Some evidence against the inmate is all that is constitutionally required to support a guilty finding at a disciplinary hearing on serious infraction.

Tennessee v. Garner, 471 U.S. 1 (1985): the case in which the Supreme Court limited police use of deadly force to instances involving the apprehension of a dangerous felon and set forth clear rules for its application.

Thornburgh v. Abbott, 490 U.S. 401 (1989): The proper standard of review for prison regulations that restrict prisoners' access to publications coming into the institution from the outside is the four-part test established in *Turner v. Safley* (1987), which evaluates whether the regulation is reasonably related to a legitimate penological interest. The standard of review established in *Procunier v. Martinez* (censorship of prisoner mail is justified only if it furthers an important and substantial governmental interest and is no greater than necessary to further that interest) is limited to evaluating regulations that address outgoing correspondence only.

Townsend v. Burke, 334 U.S. 736 (1948): Depriving a defendant of the assistance of counsel during sentencing violates the due process clause of the Fourteenth Amendment.

Trop v. Dulles, 356 U.S. 86 (1958): The Eighth Amendment, which draws its meaning from a maturing society's evolving standards of decency, does not permit Congress to enact legislation that allows a person's citizenship to be revoked as a punishment for a crime.

Turner v. Safley, 482 U.S. 78 (1987): A prison regulation that bans inmate-to-inmate correspondence is constitutional. Its constitutionality should not be evaluated under the standard established by *Procunier v. Martinez* (1974), but rather under a standard that determines whether the regulation is reasonably related to a legitimate governmental interest. This standard has four parts: 1) whether there is a valid rational connection between the prison regulation and the legitimate governmental interest that has been put forward to justify it; 2) whether there are alternative means of exercising rights that remain open to the prisoners; 3) the impact that accommodating the asserted constitutional rights will have on officers, other prisoners, and on the allocation of prison resources generally; and 4) the absence of alternatives to the challenged regulation as evidence of the reasonableness of the regulation.

Twining v. New Jersey, 211 U.S. 78 (1908): in this case the Supreme Court suggested that some of the individual rights in the Bill of Rights might be protected from state action, not because the Bill of Rights applied to the States, but because these rights "are of such a nature that they are included in the conception of due process of law." This became known as the "fundamental rights" or "ordered liberty" approach.

United States v. Booker, 543 U.S. 220 (2005): Certain provisions of the federal sentencing guidelines violate the Sixth Amendment right to a trial by jury because they mandate the imposition of sentences based on facts that have not been found by a jury beyond a reasonable doubt.

United States v. Brimah, 214 F.3d 854 (7th Cir. 2000): The exclusionary rule does not bar the introduction of illegally seized evidence in violation of the search and seizure clause, absent a showing that the government intentionally acted illegally in order to enhance the defendant's sentence.

United States v. Grayson, 438 U.S. 41 (1978): The Constitution does not prohibit a judge from considering a defendant's false testimony during the trial when determining the defendant's sentence.

United States v. Knights, 534 U.S. 112 (2001): when a police officer has reasonable suspicion that a probationer subject to a search condition is engaged in criminal activity, a warrantless search is constitutional based on the probationer's diminished expectations of privacy.

United States v. Watts, 519 U.S. 148 (1997): An acquittal does not prohibit a judge from considering the conduct underlying the acquitted charge when determining a sentence, as long as it has been proved by a preponderance of the evidence.

Vitek v. Jones, 445 U.S. 480 (1980): The involuntary transfer of a prisoner to a mental hospital triggers the protections afforded by the Due Process Clause of the Fourteenth Amendment, including written notice of a hearing, opportunity to present evidence, written reasons for the decision, and an impartial decision maker.

Washington v. Harper, 494 U.S. 210 (1990): The due process clause allows the state to treat a prisoner with serious mental illness with antipsychotic drugs against his will, if there is evidence that he is dangerous to himself or others and the treatment is in his medical interest. The due process clause does not require a judicial hearing before the state may involuntarily treat a prisoner with antipsychotic drugs, however, there must be some due process safeguards in place that assure the medication is not administered arbitrarily or capriciously.

West v. Atkins, 487 U.S. 42 (1988): A physician under contract with the state to provide health care to state prisoners is acting "under color of law" within the meaning of 42 U.S.C section 1983 when he or she is treating an inmate.

Whitley v. Albers, 475 U.S. 312 (1986): Use of deadly force during a prison riot constitutes cruel and unusual punishment only if it was the product of obduracy and wantonness. If the force was applied in good faith to maintain or restore discipline and not maliciously and sadistically for the purpose of causing harm, it does not violate the Eighth Amendment.

Wilkinson v. Austin, 544 U.S. 74 (2005): Assignment of a prisoner to a severely restrictive housing unit such as the Ohio State Penitentiary constitutes an atypical and significant hardship on an inmate in relation to the ordinary incident of prison life that gives rise to a liberty interest protected by the Due Process Clause. The due process protections provided by the state are sufficient to protect the prisoners' constitutional rights.

Will v. Michigan Department of State Police, 491 U.S. 58 (1989): A state is not a "person" under section 1983, and neither can state officials be held liable under section 1983 for actions they performed in their official capacities.

Williams v. New York, 337 U.S. 241 (1949): A judge does not violate the due process clause when he or she considers out-of-court information to assist him in making the sentencing decision.

Wilson v. Seiter, 501 U.S. 294 (1991): In order to establish a violation of the Constitution's cruel and unusual punishment clause, prisoners must establish that their conditions of confinement resulted from a culpable state of mind amounting to "deliberate indifference" on the part of prison officials.

Wolff v. McDonnell, 418 U.S. 539 (1974): The State may require that mail from an attorney to a prisoner be identified as such and that the attorney's name and address appear on the correspondence, and officials may open legal mail in the prisoner's presence in order to determine if it contains contraband. Officials may also require that an attorney who desires to correspond with a prisoner be required first to identify himself or herself and his client to prison officials to ensure that letters marked "privileged" are actually from a licensed attorney.

Also in *Wolff v. McDonnell*, the Supreme Court decided that prisoners have due process rights in prison disciplinary hearings that charge major offenses, including: 1) advance written notice of at least 24 hours before the hearing of the charges and the evidence relied on; 2) right to call witnesses and present documentary evidence unless security may be jeopardized; 3) illiterate inmates or inmates charged with serious infractions that will make it difficult for them to collect and present evidence have a right to assistance from a substitute counsel; 4) written statement of the findings upon which the decision is based; 5) decision by an impartial board or hearing officer.

Woodford v. Ngo, 548 U.S. 81 (2006): The Prison Litigation Reform Act's exhaustion requirement mandates the proper exhaustion of administrative grievance remedies. Failure to properly exhaust those remedies according to the administrative requirements requires that a prisoner's lawsuit be dismissed.

Woodson v. North Carolina, 428 U.S. 280 (1976): A statute that provides for the mandatory imposition of the death penalty violates the Eighth Amendment.

Index